Göttinger Wirtschaftsinformatik
Herausgeber: J. Biethahn[†] · L. M. Kolbe · M. Schumann

Band 102

Stephan Diederich

Designing Anthropomorphic Conversational Agents in Enterprises: A Nascent Theory and Conceptual Framework for Fostering a Human-Like interaction

CUVILLIER VERLAG

Herausgeber

Prof. Dr. J. Biethahn† Prof. Dr. L. M. Kolbe Prof. Dr. M. Schumann

Georg-August-Universität
Wirtschaftsinformatik
Platz der Göttinger Sieben 5
37073 Göttingen

Bibliografische Information der Deutschen Nationalbibliothek
Die Deutsche Nationalbibliothek verzeichnet diese Publikation in der Deutschen Nationalbibliografie; detaillierte bibliografische Daten sind im Internet über http://dnb.d-nb.de abrufbar.
1. Aufl. - Göttingen : Cuvillier, 2020
Zugl.: Göttingen, Univ., Diss., 2020

© CUVILLIER VERLAG, Göttingen 2020
Nonnenstieg 8, 37075 Göttingen
Telefon: 0551-54724-0
Telefax: 0551-54724-21

Alle Rechte vorbehalten. Ohne ausdrückliche Genehmigung des Verlages ist es nicht gestattet, das Buch oder Teile daraus auf fotomechanischem Weg (Fotokopie, Mikrokopie) zu vervielfältigen.
1. Auflage, 2020
Gedruckt auf umweltfreundlichem, säurefreiem Papier aus nachhaltiger Forstwirtschaft.

ISBN 978-3-7369-7216-2
eISBN 978-3-7369-6216-3

Designing Anthropomorphic Conversational Agents in Enterprises: A Nascent Theory and Conceptual Framework for Fostering a Human-Like Interaction

Dissertation

zur Erlangung des Doktorgrades
der Wirtschaftswissenschaftlichen Fakultät
der Georg-August-Universität Göttingen

vorgelegt von

Stephan Diederich

geboren in Dortmund

Göttingen, 2020

Betreuungsausschuss

Erstbetreuer: Prof. Dr. Lutz M. Kolbe
Zweitbetreuer: Prof. Dr. Jan Muntermann
Drittbetreuer: Prof. Dr. Michael Wolff

Tag der mündlichen Prüfung: 30. Juni 2020

Preface

We are experiencing a new wave of innovation and automation driven by technological progress, in particular in machine learning and natural language processing, that impacts manifold aspects in our lives. One phenomenon in this wave is the interaction with computers via natural language, which offers unprecedented opportunities to design technological artifacts with human characteristics and fundamentally changes the way we interact with technology.

To me, the idea of human-like machines is both fascinating and frightening. It gives rise to numerous questions ranging from the design and human perception of anthropomorphic artifacts to fundamental ethical concerns. While there is still some way to go until we can design interactive technology that completely emulates human appearance and behavior, I believe that the possibilities offered by current conversational technology already allow to investigate part of these questions and explore different application areas, in particular in organizations. With this in mind, I hope that my work contributes to a better understanding of human interaction with human-like natural language technology in an organizational context and helps to inform the design of anthropomorphic conversational agents in practice.

Reflecting on the last two years, I consider myself lucky. I enjoyed the support from various people during my Ph.D. studies, both from my private and professional life, and for this I am truly grateful.

First, I would like to thank my wife Ann Janine for her love and support throughout my academic journey as well as putting things back into perspective when I got worked up about smaller details in my research. I am infinitely grateful for our daughter, Lene Sofie, who brings so much joy in our life.

Furthermore, I thank my parents, Ria and Rainer, for their encouragement, support and ongoing trust during my Ph.D. studies. I am grateful for my sister, Christine, and her family Charlotte, Annelie, and Henning for enriching my life so much.

I would like to sincerely thank my first supervisor, Prof. Dr. Lutz Kolbe, for giving me the opportunity to pursue a research topic that fascinates me and for providing a pleasant and productive work atmosphere that, in my view, forms the basis for the success of the chair. Without your constant support, encouragement and commitment, this research project would not have been possible. I would also like to express my gratitude to my second supervisor, Prof. Dr. Jan Muntermann, and third supervisor, Prof. Dr. Michael Wolff, for their guidance and providing a fresh perspective on my work.

Additionally, I extend my gratitude to my colleagues at Roland Berger – Dirk Möbus, Carsten Rossbach and Frederik Hammermeister – for giving me the freedom to focus on this research project and their interest in my work. I further thank Dr. Christian Krys for his support and the fruitful exchanges during the Ph.D. meetings in Düsseldorf.

Furthermore, I would like to especially thank Prof. Dr. Gerrit Remané for sharing his knowledge and experience throughout the Ph.D. program.

I thank my all my current and former colleagues at the Chair of Information Management. My special thanks go to Dr. Alfred Benedikt Brendel for his continuous support, the enjoyable collaboration as well as his encouragement for my research. I am very grateful for my current colleagues at the chair – Tim, Maike, Christine, Sascha, Bernd, Christoph, Mathias, Kristin, Johannes, David, Lara, Daniel, Yachao, Fabian, and Hannes – for contributing so much to an enjoyable and successful research journey. I also extend my gratitude to my former colleagues, Prof. Dr. André Hanelt, Patryk Zapadka, Dr. Schahin Tofangchi, Dr. Daniel Leonhardt, and Dr. Sromona Chatterje for the great collaboration at the beginning of my Ph.D. studies.

Additionally, I would like to sincerely thank Prof. Dr. Stefan Morana and Prof. Dr. Simon Trang for their helpful feedback and substantial support for this research project.

Last but definitely not least, I thank my friends for their support, inspiration and the fun we have together throughout the years, especially Andre, Marcel, Denis, Peter, Asin, and Michael.

Hamburg, June 2020 *Stephan Diederich*

Abstract

Conversational agents (CAs), defined as software with which users interact through natural language, increasingly permeate our private and professional lives. They encompass different forms ranging from voice-based digital assistants like Siri or Alexa over physically embodied robots like SoftBank's "Pepper" to text-based agents like chatbots on company websites or social media. In particular text-based CAs in a company context attract interest both internally as well as at the customer interface to provide service or support sales due to their potential for automation while offering the feeling of a human-like interaction. However, many enterprise CAs in practice are not able to meet high user expectations and were sometimes even discontinued in the past. The agents' human-like appearance and behavior, fostered by so-called social cues like a human name and image, lead to high user expectations which are frequently out of line with the system's limited conversational capabilities or create feelings of uncanniness in the interaction. Thus, designing text-based CAs that offer a pleasant, human-like interaction experience while mitigating potential negative effects particularly due to limited conversational capabilities represents a substantial design problem.

To address this problem, six studies were conducted and compiled in this dissertation. These studies provide insights into the design of human-like, text-based CAs in a company context and show how different designs influence user perception of such technological artifacts. This work is grounded in two theories (Social Response Theory, Theory of Uncanny Valley) that hypothesize on the design and human perception of anthropomorphic artifacts. Through a set of experiments and a design science research project, this dissertation offers three key contributions: First, it proposes a nascent design theory to craft enterprise CAs that offer a human-like interaction experience despite the limited conversational capabilities given in present-day technology. Second, the conceptual framework derived from the synthesis of the studies' findings outlines how the perception of a CA and the outcomes from the interaction emerge from an interplay of context-, user-, and CA design-related characteristics. Third, the insights from the experimental studies show how aspects related to the design of a CA influence user perception both with regard to anthropomorphism as well as further outcome variables, such as service satisfaction or brand perception.

The findings presented in this dissertation have implications for researchers concerned with the design of CAs and human-like technological artifacts as well as for practitioners seeking to introduce natural language technology in their organizations. The limitations of this work as well as the results offer six promising opportunities for future research on the design of and human interaction with increasingly anthropomorphic conversational agents in a company context.

Zusammenfassung

Conversational agents (CAs), definiert als Software mit welcher Menschen über natürliche Sprache interagieren, finden zunehmend Verbreitung in Form von sprachbasierten, digitalen Assistenten wie Siri oder Alexa, Robotern wie SoftBanks' Pepper oder textbasierten Agenten wie Chatbots auf Webseiten oder in sozialen Medien. Für Unternehmen stellen insbesondere textbasierte CAs aufgrund ihres Potenzials für eine menschenähnliche Interaktion eine vielversprechende Technologie zur Innovation und Automatisierung verschiedener Tätigkeiten, sowohl intern als auch an der Kundenschnittstelle dar. In der Praxis bleiben CAs jedoch oftmals hinter den Benutzererwartungen zurück und wurden in verschiedenen Fällen sogar aus dem Betrieb genommen. Das menschenähnliche Erscheinungsbild und Verhalten von CAs, realisiert durch die Nutzung sozialer Signale wie einem menschlichen Namen und Avatar, führt zu hohen Benutzererwartungen, welche insbesondere über die begrenzte Systemfähigkeit hinausgehen oder ein befremdliches Gefühl bei Benutzern während der Interaktion erzeugen. Das Design textbasierter CAs im Unternehmenskontext, welche eine angenehme, menschenähnliche Interaktionserfahrung bieten und gleichzeitig potenzielle negative Effekte, insbesondere aufgrund eingeschränkter Dialogfähigkeit mitigieren, stellt somit ein wesentliches Designproblem dar.

Um dieses Problem zu adressieren wurden sechs Studien durchgeführt und in dieser Arbeit zusammengestellt. Die Studien liefern Erkenntnisse zum Design von menschenähnlichen, textbasierten CAs im Unternehmenskontext und zeigen wie Änderungen des Designs die Benutzerwahrnehmung dieser Systeme beinflussen. Hierzu stützt sich die Arbeit auf zwei Theorien (Social Response Theory, Theory of Uncanny Valley) zur menschlichen Wahrnehmung anthropomorpher, technologischer Artefakte. Auf Basis verschiedener Experimente und einem Design Science Research Projekt bietet diese Arbeit drei wesentliche Beiträge: Erstens wird eine aufkommende Designtheorie zur Gestaltung anthropomorpher CAs im Unternehmenskontext entwickelt, welche das Gefühl einer angenehmen, menschenähnlichen Interaktion bieten und negative Effekte aufgrund begrenzter Dialogfähigkeit mitigieren. Zweitens wird aus der Synthese der Studien ein konzeptionelles Framework hergeleitet, welches das Zusammenspiel von Kontext- und Benutzerfaktoren mit dem Design von CAs im Hinblick auf die Benutzerwahrnehmung und Ergebnisse der Interaktion beschreibt. Drittens geben die Studien Einblicke in die Wahrnehmung von menschenähnlichen CAs, sowohl im Hinblick auf Anthropomorphismus als auch auf weitere Aspekte wie Kundenservicezufriedenheit.

Die Erkenntnisse dieser Arbeit haben Implikationen sowohl für Forscher in den Bereichen CAs und anthropomorpher technologischer Artefakte als auch für Designer welche CAs in ihren Unternehmen einführen möchten. Die Limitationen dieser Arbeit als auch die Ergebnisse bieten sechs vielversprechende Richtungen für zukünftige Forschung zum Design und zur menschlichen Interaktion mit zunehmend anthropomorphen Agenten.

Table of Contents

List of Figures v
List of Tables vii
List of Abbreviations ix

A.   **Foundation** 1

    I.   **Introduction** 2
        I.1   Motivation 2
        I.2   Research Gaps and Research Questions 5
        I.3   Structure of the Thesis 9
        I.4   Research Positioning and Design 12
        I.5   Anticipated Contributions 15

    II.   **Research Background** 18
        II.1 Conversational Agents and their Application in Enterprises 18
        II.2 Social Response Theory: Computers Are Social Actors 22
        II.3 Theory of Uncanny Valley 25
        II.4 Anthropomorphic Design of Conversational Agents 27
        II.5 Synthesis: Pre-Understanding of Human-Like Enterprise CA Design 30

B.   **Studies on Anthropomorphic Design of Conversational Agents in Enterprises** 33

    I.   **Assessing the Status Quo** 34
        1.   **Study 1: On the Design of Enterprise Conversational Agents – A Synthesis of IS and HCI Research** 35
            1.1 Introduction 36
            1.2 Research Background 37
            1.3 Research Approach 40
            1.4 Results 42
            1.5 Discussion 51
            1.6 Concluding Remarks 57

II. Understanding Technological Limitations 58

1. Study 2: Not Human After All – Exploring the Impact of Response Failure on User Perception of Anthropomorphic Conversational Service Agents 59

1.1 Introduction 60
1.2 Related Work and Theoretical Background 61
1.3 Hypotheses and Research Model 65
1.4 Research Design 67
1.5 Results 71
1.6 Discussion 73
1.7 Concluding Remarks 76

2. Study 3: Design for Fast Request Fulfillment or Natural Interaction? Insights from an Online Experiment with a Conversational Agent 77

2.1 Introduction 78
2.2 Theoretical Background and Related Work 79
2.3 Hypotheses 82
2.4 Research Design and Method 84
2.5 Results 88
2.6 Discussion 90
2.7 Concluding Remarks 93

III. Exploring the Potential of Human-Like Design 94

1. Study 4: Emulating Empathetic Behavior in Online Service Encounters with Sentiment-Adaptive Responses – Insights from an Experiment with a Conversational Agent 95

1.1 Introduction 96
1.2 Related Work and Theoretical Background 97
1.3 Hypotheses 100
1.4 Method 102
1.5 Results 108
1.6 Discussion 111
1.7 Concluding Remarks 114

2. Study 5: Promoting Sustainable Mobility Beliefs with Persuasive and Anthropomorphic Design – Insights from an Experiment with a Conversational Agent 115

- 2.1 Introduction 116
- 2.2 Research Background and Related Work 117
- 2.3 Hypotheses Development 121
- 2.4 Research Design 124
- 2.5 Results 128
- 2.6 Discussion 130
- 2.7 Concluding Remarks 134

IV. Formulating a Nascent Design Theory 135

1. Study 6: Designing Anthropomorphic Enterprise Conversational Agents 136

- 1.1 Introduction 137
- 1.2 Related Work and Theoretical Background 139
- 1.3 Research Approach 143
- 1.4 Artifact Design and Implementation 145
- 1.5 Evaluation 149
- 1.6 Discussion 154
- 1.7 Limitations and Opportunities for Future Research 157
- 1.8 Concluding Remarks 158
- 1.9 Appendix 159

C. Contributions 163

I. Findings and Results 164

- I.1 Findings for the Status Quo of Conversational Agent Research 164
- I.2 Findings for Technological Limitations and their Impact 165
- I.3 Findings for the Potential of Anthropomorphic Design 168
- I.4 Findings for a Nascent Design Theory 170
- I.5 Synthesis of Findings: A Conceptual Framework for the Design of and Interaction with Anthropomorphic CAs in a Company Context 172

II.	**Implications**	**176**
II.1	Implications for Research	176
II.2	Implications for Practice	180
III.	**Limitations and Opportunities for Future Research**	**182**
III.1	Limitations	182
III.2	Opportunities for Future Research	185
IV.	**Concluding Remarks**	**188**
References		189
Appendix		x

List of Figures

Figure 1: Research Areas addressed in this Thesis 4
Figure 2: Research Framework 9
Figure 3: Structure of this Thesis 11
Figure 4: Classification of Conversational Agents 19
Figure 5: Enterprise CAs in Practice by KLM, Lidl and Mastercard 20
Figure 6: High-Level Architecture for Enterprise CAs 21
Figure 7: Social Response Theory 22
Figure 8: Conceptualization of the Theory of Uncanny Valley (Mori et al. 2012) 25
Figure 9: Empirical Evidence for the Uncanny Valley (Mathur and Reichling 2016) .. 26
Figure 10: Design Dimensions for Anthropomorphic CAs (Seeger et al. 2018) 28
Figure 11 (Study 1): Examples for Enterprise CAs 38
Figure 12 (Study 1): Literature Filtering Steps 42
Figure 13 (Study 1): Circle of Anthropomorphic CA Design 51
Figure 14 (Study 1): Constructs, Principles and Kernel Theories for CA Design 52
Figure 15 (Study 1): Proposed Research Framework 53
Figure 16 (Study 1): Contribution Types of the Reviewed Studies 54
Figure 17 (Study 2): The Uncanny Valley 64
Figure 18 (Study 2): Research Model 66
Figure 19 (Study 2): Experimental Conditions 68
Figure 20 (Study 2): Human-like CA without Response Failure (Condition 4) 68
Figure 21 (Study 2): PLS Structural Model (n = 165) 71
Figure 22 (Study 2): Mean Values differentiated by Cues (Dotted: Conditions 1 & 3) ... 73
Figure 23 (Study 3): Exemplary CAs with (left) and without Preset Answer Options 83
Figure 24 (Study 3): Interface with Control and Treatment Configurations 86
Figure 25 (Study 3): Differences between conditions for the three constructs 89
Figure 26 (Study 4): Research Model 102
Figure 27 (Study 4): Interface with Static (left) and Adaptive Configurations 104
Figure 28 (Study 4): Agent Architecture 105
Figure 29 (Study 4): Differences for the Constructs between the Groups 110
Figure 30 (Study 4): Mean Values by Gender (Dotted: Female Participants) 110
Figure 31 (Study 5): Research Model 123
Figure 32 (Study 5): Agent in Condition 4 (Material translated to English) 126

Figure 33 (Study 5): PLS Structural Model (n = 225) 129
Figure 34 (Study 6): Research Background 139
Figure 35 (Study 6): The Uncanny Valley (Mori et al. 2012) 142
Figure 36 (Study 6): Design Cycles and Research Activities 143
Figure 37 (Study 6): Meta-Requirements and Design Principles 146
Figure 38 (Study 6): Instantiated Design Principles (Material translated) 148
Figure 39 (Study 6): Evolution of Design Principles and Qualitative Feedback 162
Figure 40: Framework for the Design of and Interaction with Human-Like CAs 173

List of Tables

Table 1: Overview of Studies included in this Thesis 9
Table 2: Research Designs of the Studies in this Thesis 14
Table 3: Positioning of this Thesis in the Information Systems Discipline 15
Table 4: Summary of Anticipated Contributions 17
Table 5: Types and Examples of Social Cues and Social Responses 24
Table 6: Potential Positive and Negative Outcomes of Human-Like CA Design 30
Table 7: Fact Sheet of Study 1 35
Table 8 (Study 1): Components of a Design Theory (Gregor and Jones 2007) 39
Table 9 (Study 1): Research Approach Phases 40
Table 10 (Study 1): Results from the Literature Search 41
Table 11 (Study 1): Purpose and Scope of CAs 43
Table 12 (Study 1): Constructs 44
Table 13 (Study 1): Principles of Form and Function 45
Table 14 (Study 1): Statements of Artifact Mutability 46
Table 15 (Study 1): Testable Propositions 48
Table 16 (Study 1): Justificatory Knowledge Underlying the Studies 50
Table 17: Fact Sheet of Study 2 59
Table 18 (Study 2): Agent Statements with Response Failure (translated) 69
Table 19 (Study 2): Constructs, Items, and Factor Loadings 70
Table 20 (Study 2): Effect Sizes for Significant Paths according to Cohen (1988) 72
Table 21: Fact Sheet of Study 3 77
Table 22 (Study 3): Items, Measures, and Factor Loadings 87
Table 23 (Study 3): Descriptive Statistics and t-Test Results 88
Table 24 (Study 3): Results for Hypotheses 89
Table 25: Fact Sheet of Study 4 95
Table 26 (Study 4): Static and Sentiment-Adaptive Responses 106
Table 27 (Study 4): Constructs, Items, and Factor Loadings 107
Table 28 (Study 4): Descriptive Statistics and t-Test Results 108
Table 29: Fact Sheet of Study 5 115
Table 30 (Study 5): Dimensions for Anthropomorphic CA Design and Cues 121
Table 31 (Study 5): Conditions of the Experimental Design 125
Table 32 (Study 5): Constructs, Items, and Factor Loadings 127

Table 33 (Study 5): Results of Hypothesis Tests 130
Table 34: Fact Sheet of Study 6 136
Table 35 (Study 6): Overview of Exemplary Studies on CA Design 141
Table 36 (Study 6): Social Cues incorporated in the Artifact 149
Table 37 (Study 6): Constructs, Items, and Factor Loadings 152
Table 38 (Study 6): Descriptive Statistics and t-Test Results 153
Table 39 (Study 6): Evolution of Agent Responsiveness across Design Cycles 154
Table 40 (Study 6): Nascent Design Theory for Anthropomorphic Enterprise CAs 155
Table 41 (Study 6): Participants in qual. Requirements Elicitation and Evaluation 159
Table 42 (Study 6): Meta-Requirements and Quotes from Interviews (translated) 160
Table 43 (Study 6): Prototype Issues and Free-Form Feedback (translated) 161
Table 44: Findings of Study 1 164
Table 45: Findings of Study 2 166
Table 46: Findings of Study 3 167
Table 47: Findings of Study 4 168
Table 48: Findings of Study 5 169
Table 49: Findings of Study 6 170
Table 50: Main Findings for each Research Question 171
Table 51: Major Implications for Research 179
Table 52: Major Implications for Practice 182
Table 53: Opportunities for Future Research on Anthropomorphic CA Design 187

List of Abbreviations

API	Application Programming Interface
CA	Conversational Agent
CASA	Computers Are Social Actors
DSR	Design Science Research
HCI	Human-Computer Interaction
IS	Information System
IT	Information Technology
ML	Machine Learning
NLP	Natural Language Processing
PLS-SEM	Partial Least Squares Structural Equation Modeling

A. Foundation

The first part of this thesis is divided into two sections.

In the first section (A.I), the motivation for this work is presented, the research gaps and questions are described and the structure of the thesis outlined. Then, the section provides an overview of the research context and design followed by the anticipated contributions of this cumulative thesis.

The second section (A.II) introduces conversational agents (CAs) and their application in an enterprise context as the research background of this work as well Social Response Theory and the Theory of Uncanny Valley as the two main theories underlying this research. The section further provides an overview of anthropomorphic design of conversational agents.

I. Introduction

The first section (I.1) in this chapter highlights the motivation for and relevance of this research endeavour. Afterwards, the research gaps and questions addressed in this work are presented (I.2) followed be the thesis' structure (I.3), the research context and design (I.4), as well as an overview of anticipated contributions.

I.1 Motivation

> *"What I had not realized is that extremely short exposures to a relatively simple computer program could induce powerful delusional thinking in quite normal people."*
> (Weizenbaum, 1976, p. 371)

In the 1960s, German-American computer scientist Joseph Weizenbaum created ELIZA, the first well-known computer program with which users could interact in natural language. Named after Eliza Doolittle from George Bernard Shaw's play "Pygmalion", the program simulated a Rogerian psychotherapist by rephrasing the user's questions as responses. Originally designed to show the limitations of computers for understanding natural language, the story of ELIZA turned out differently as users developed emotional relationships with the program and interacted with it as if it was an actual human being. For example, the secretary of Joseph Weizenbaum once asked him to leave the room to be able to talk to ELIZA in private. These strong social responses to a computer program with very limited capabilities represent an early example of the emotional connections that humans form with technological artifacts exhibiting human-like characteristics, such as communication via natural language.

A few decades later, Nass and Moon (2000) conducted a series of experiments at Stanford University and found further evidence for what Weizenbaum had described. The researchers discovered that humans over-use social categories in their interaction with computers, such as gender or ethnicity, engage in social behaviors like politeness and reciprocity, and show premature cognitive commitments, for example when a medium is labeled as a "specialist". Nass and Moon formalized their findings in Social Response Theory and the related Computers Are Social Actors (CASA) paradigm, postulating that humans show social responses to computers even though they are aware that machines do not have feelings or intentions. These responses stem from the so-called social cues that computers provide, such as using words for output, interactivity (e.g. responding to human action) or performing human roles. Nass and Moon (2000, p. 7) conclude that "the more computers present characteristics that are associated with humans, the more likely they are to elicit social behavior". Viewing the experience described by Joseph Weizenbaum through the lens of Social Response Theory, it becomes apparent that communication via natural language, though in a very basic form at that time, represents a social cue leading to substantial social responses by humans.

Today, the interaction with technology via natural language attracts strong interest due to advances in natural language processing and machine learning (McTear 2017). CAs are now used in a variety of application domains both in private and professional life (Maedche et al. 2019). Organizations introduce CAs in application domains, such as customer service (Gnewuch et al. 2017; Wünderlich and Paluch 2017), marketing and sales (Baier et al. 2018; Vaccaro et al. 2018), or financial advisory (Dolata et al. 2019). For organizations, CAs represent a particularly interesting technology due to their potential for simulating human-like interaction experience fostered by the anthropomorphic design of such agents (Pfeuffer et al. 2019a).

Early success stories of anthropomorphic CAs in practice underline this potential: "Julie", the CA of the American railroad company Amtrak, answers more than 5 million service requests per year (NextIT 2018). H&M successfully introduced a virtual shopping assistant that provides individual clothing recommendations (Morana et al. 2017). A further example is "BlueBot" of the Dutch airline KLM, which provides information about flight connections (Vogel-Meijer 2018). In addition to these examples at the customer interface, companies are exploring internal use of CAs, such as for supporting new employees (Liao et al. 2018) or acting as an advisor to project teams (Paredes 2019). Similar to this popularity in practice, CAs are increasingly studied by (IS) researchers (Maedche et al. 2019), often with a focus on human-computer interaction (HCI). Different studies investigate the impact of specific social cues, such as dynamic response delays to simulate thinking and typing of a CA (Gnewuch et al. 2018b) or the representation of the agent with a name and gender (Cowell and Stanney 2005), on user perception in particular with regard to anthropomorphism and further outcome variables like service encounter satisfaction or brand perception.

While most studies place emphasis on the positive effects of anthropomorphic CA design, different researchers indicate the risks of potential negative effects, such as users experiencing feelings of strangeness due to being unsure whether they interact with a machine or a human being (Wünderlich and Paluch 2017). In this context, the Theory of Uncanny Valley (Mori 1970) hypothesizes on the relationship between the anthropomorphic design of an artifact and the emotional responses by humans to it. The theory in short postulates that increasing the degree of anthropomorphism increases the positive emotional responses of humans to the artifact. However, at a point close to achieving human-likeness, the artifact fails to maintain its lifelike appearance due to inhuman imperfections, and triggers strong negative emotional reactions by humans (Mori et al. 2012). In practice, these inhuman imperfections in particular comprise the limited conversational capabilities of CAs compared to humans. For example, IKEA's agent "Anna" was removed from the company's webpage in 2016 due to low customer satisfaction. While the CA was specifically designed to offer a human-like interaction, it lacked the necessary conversational capabilities to respond to the wide variety of user requests about prices, parts, opening hours, and Swedish meals, thus failing to maintain its purposefully designed human-like appearance (Rezvani 2020). Similarly, Ben Mimoun et al. (2012) argue that many CAs are not able to meet high user expectations, fostered by a human-like design, due to their inability to respond to a wide variety of user input and Luger and Sellen (2016) emphasize the gap between user expectations and system capabilities as one of the main reasons for CA failure.

In sum, anthropomorphic design of CAs can both lead to desirable social responses manifested in, for example, increased satisfaction with a company's service or better brand perception, but may also result in negative emotional responses when high expectations of users due to a human-like design are not fulfilled. Thus, from a designer's perspective, the problem arises of how to build anthropomorphic conversational agents that lead to positive social responses and at the same time mitigate the risk of negative emotional reactions particularly due to limited conversational capabilities.

This thesis seeks to address this problem through a set of experiments on specific aspects of a CA's design and a design science research (DSR) project that brings together findings from the experiments and existing prescriptive knowledge for CAs to propose a nascent design theory for anthropomorphic CAs in a company context. Addressing this design problem spans three different research areas (Figure 1). First, the phenomenon of interest are *Conversational Agents*, understood as software with which users interact through natural language. Second, the anthropomorphic design of CAs is investigated in this thesis due to its potential in a company context, drawing on existing theoretical knowledge on *Anthropomorphic Artifacts*. Third and finally, the focus of this thesis is on *Human-Computer Systems Design*, i.e. to provide actionable, prescriptive knowledge on how to build CAs.

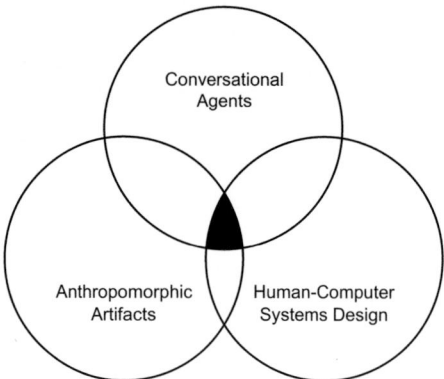

Figure 1: Research Areas addressed in this Thesis

I.2 Research Gaps and Research Questions

As outlined above, this thesis seeks to explore the anthropomorphic design of CAs in a company context. For this purpose, it focuses on four research questions that build on each other, and, together, address the overarching question of how to build human-like CAs. In the following, each question is derived by a specific gap in the knowledge base and afterwards the interaction of the questions is visualized in a research framework.

First, research on CAs – despite their emergence already several decades ago – has recently gained substantial interest in different disciplines, such as computer science (McTear 2017), social psychology (Krämer 2010), and also information systems (Schuetzler et al. 2014), covering topics prevalent in these disciplines, like architectural components of CAs in computer science (Sarikaya 2017) or resilience in social psychology (de Visser et al. 2016). In IS research, in particular scholars focusing on HCI, increasingly explore CAs for example with regard to agent authenticity (Wünderlich and Paluch 2017), privacy concerns (Saffarizadeh et al. 2017), or trust (Schuetzler et al. 2014). Similarly, recent HCI research in computer science studies topics like first impressions in human-CA encounters (Cafaro et al. 2016) or the effects of facial similarity on user responses to CAs (Vugt et al. 2010). In addition to these research foci, studies on the design of and interaction with CAs cover different forms of CAs, such as physically (Stock and Merkle 2018) or virtually (Araujo 2018) embodied CAs, and communication via speech (Purington et al. 2017) or text (Vaccaro et al. 2018). Furthermore, studies focus on CAs in different application domains from private life, such as health (Kim et al. 2013; Meier et al. 2019) or education (Hobert 2019; Winkler et al. 2019), as well as in professional contexts like customer service (Feine et al. 2019b; Wünderlich and Paluch 2017), collaboration (Seeber et al. 2019; Toxtli et al. 2018), or sales (Bertacchini et al. 2017; Vaccaro et al. 2018).

In short, the knowledge base on the design of and interaction with (anthropomorphic) CAs covers a wide variety of topics, forms of CAs, and application domains and, due to the recently increased research interest on natural language software and resulting number of studies, is dispersed. Hence, in order to accomplish the overarching research objective of this thesis, there is a need to first organize the existing body of knowledge, synthesize existing prescriptive knowledge in this area, and identify research gaps. Following the idea of "(re-)constructing the giant" as termed by vom Brocke et al. (2009), the first question aims to structure and assess existing knowledge on the design of CAs:

RQ 1: *What is the status quo of research on the design of and human interaction with conversational agents in a company context?*

Second, while CAs currently attract large interest in research (Diederich et al. 2019a; McTear 2017) and practice (Jacobs et al. 2017) alike, many CAs fell behind expectations (Luger and Sellen 2016) and disappeared in the past due to flaws related to their design (Ben Mimoun et al. 2012). In their assessment of 80 agents on French commercial websites, Ben Mimoun et al. (2012) investigated reasons for failure of CAs. The authors suggest that CAs in particular fall behind expectations due to limited conversational capabilities and argue that a mismatch between the human-like design of many CAs in practice and their actual capabilities results in negative user reactions (Ben Mimoun et al. 2012). Luger and Sellen (2016) similarly emphasize that user expectations are often substantially out of line with the systems' conversational capabilities and features.

In this context, Følstad and Brandtzæg (2017, p. 41) argue that the natural language interface in comparison to a graphical interface "is to a much greater degree a blank canvas where the content and features of the underlying service as mostly hidden from the user, and where the interaction is more dependent on the user's input". As a consequence of this wide variety of potentially unanticipated user input and the limited capabilities of present-day CAs, situations where the CA fails to provide a meaningful reply are likely to occur (Følstad and Brandtzæg 2017). Thus, in order to design CAs that are able to offer a human-like interaction in a professional context, there is a need to first understand the impact of limited conversational capabilities on user perception and to study how negative effects can be prevented or, at least, alleviated:

RQ 2: *What is the impact of limited conversational capabilities of CAs on user perception and how can negative effects be mitigated?*

The research question can be decomposed into two sub-questions. The first sub-question focuses on the (negative) impact of limited conversational capabilities of present-day CAs manifested in failure to provide a meaningful response in a professional service interaction:

RQ 2.1: *How does failure to provide a meaningful response influence user perception of anthropomorphic CAs in a professional encounter?*

The second sub-question aims to explore how to mitigate response failure. Specifically, CAs can be designed to provide preset answer options in the form of suggestions in the conversation to lead users to (conveniently) select one of the given options instead of thinking of and formulating a manual reply in natural language (Brandtzæg and Følstad 2018). However, as such answer options resemble elements from graphical interfaces and may be detrimental to the natural feeling in the interaction, the impact of such design elements on user perception needs to be investigated:

RQ 2.2: *How do preset answer options of text-based CAs influence user perception?*

Complementary to understanding the limited conversational capabilities of CAs, the potential of anthropomorphic CAs, as an emerging technology in a professional context, needs to be explored. Initial studies on anthropomorphic CA design investigate how to make CAs appear human-like by means of different social cues, such as dynamic response delays to indicate thinking and typing by the CA (Gnewuch et al. 2018b), a human name (Araujo 2018), or the use of self-references in a conversation (Schuetzler et al. 2018b). These studies find positive effects of the specific social cues incorporated in the agent's design on the perception of humanness of the CA. Furthermore, several studies indicate a positive impact on further outcome variables, such as service satisfaction (Gnewuch et al. 2018b), brand perception (Araujo 2018), trust (Cowell and Stanney 2005; de Visser et al. 2016), or information disclosure (Pickard et al. 2016). However, different authors indicate (potential) negative effects, for example regarding privacy concerns (Sohn 2019) or feelings of uncanniness when users are unsure whether they interact with a computer program or an actual human (Wünderlich and Paluch 2017). Against this background, the design and perception of an anthropomorphic CA requires careful evaluation (Seeger et al. 2018). In sum, recent research on anthropomorphic CAs provides valuable prescriptive knowledge on how to design human-like agents in a company context with a variety of social cues (Feine et al. 2019a) and how such designs influence user perception.

However, two aspects of human-like CAs, which are of particular relevance in a company context, are yet to be explored: the design of empathetic CAs and the design of persuasive CAs. While modeling empathy in CAs has been studied in HCI research for several years, in particular for physically embodied agents (Leite et al. 2013; Niewiadomski and Pelachaud 2010), it has not been investigated in a company context despite its relevance, for example in customer service (Larivière et al. 2017). Similarly, combining prescriptive knowledge from persuasive system design (Oinas-Kukkonen and Harjumaa 2009) with anthropomorphic CAs to craft persuasive agents can be useful for example in a marketing and sales context (Hanus and Fox 2015) yet has not been addressed in CA research so far. Hence, the third question is formulated as follows:

RQ 3: *How can empathetic and persuasive CAs be designed and how do such designs influence user perception?*

The third research question consists of two sub-questions related to the design of empathetic (1) and persuasive (2) anthropomorphic CAs in a professional context. First, while recent studies explore different social cues for anthropomorphic design of CAs in a company context, the main critique for CAs, in particular at the customer interface, remains that the technology dehumanizes the interaction as it "cannot provide the empathy a human agent can provide" (Yan et al. 2013, p. 7). According to Larivière et al. (2017), recognizing a conversation partners emotional state is considered one of the main factors that distinguishes service provision by humans and technology. Thus, there is a need to explore design approaches that serve to overcome such existing social limits of (conversational) technology, particularly in a company context (Frey and Osborne 2017). One approach to recognize emotional tonality in natural language communication is sentiment analysis, which automatically extracts information about the human's emotional state (Liu 2012). Combining sentiment analysis with adaptive responses in a CA's design has the potential to emulate empathy and thus contribute to the perception of humanness of an agent. Thus, the first sub question of RQ3 seeks to explore a sentiment-adaptive CA design and its impact on user perception:

RQ 3.1: *How does empathetic behavior of a CA based on sentiment-adaptive responses affect customer perception compared to a non-empathetic agent?*

Second, the design of CAs with effective persuasive capabilities can improve the potential of CAs in a company context, particularly in marketing and sales to influence customer beliefs, such as about products, and (purchase) behavior (Hanus and Fox 2015). While the importance of persuasion capabilities has long been recognized for human sales agents (Friestad and Wright 1999) and various design elements exist for persuasive system design (Oinas-Kukkonen and Harjumaa 2009), combining anthropomorphic design and persuasive system design remains to be explored. As many elements known from persuasive design rely on the system to behave like a human, such as praise, suggestions, or social roles (e.g. identifying the system as an expert for a specific topic area), bringing the two design approaches together seems to be promising endeavor. Hence, the second sub question of RQ3 focuses on the design of persuasive CAs to influence individual beliefs, exemplary in the context of sustainable, shared mobility:

RQ 3.2: *How can persuasive and human-like design of conversational agents positively shape individual beliefs?*

The formulated research questions aim to assess the status quo of CA research and organize existing prescriptive knowledge (RQ1), to better understand the impact of limited conversational capabilities and how to mitigate negative effects on user perception (RQ2), as well as to explore empathy and persuasive capabilities as two specific aspects of CA design with particular relevance in a company context (RQ3). After this improved understanding of the overarching design problem, the last step remains to build on findings from the previous research questions and existing know-how from the knowledge base for CA design to design, implement and introduce the artifact in the field as well as to formulate a nascent design theory (Gregor and Jones 2007). Thus, the fourth and final research question is formulated as follows:

RQ 4: *How can a CA in a professional context be designed to offer a human-like interaction while mitigating negative effects due to limited conversational capabilities?*

Figure 2 visualizes the four research questions and their interaction in the research framework for this thesis.

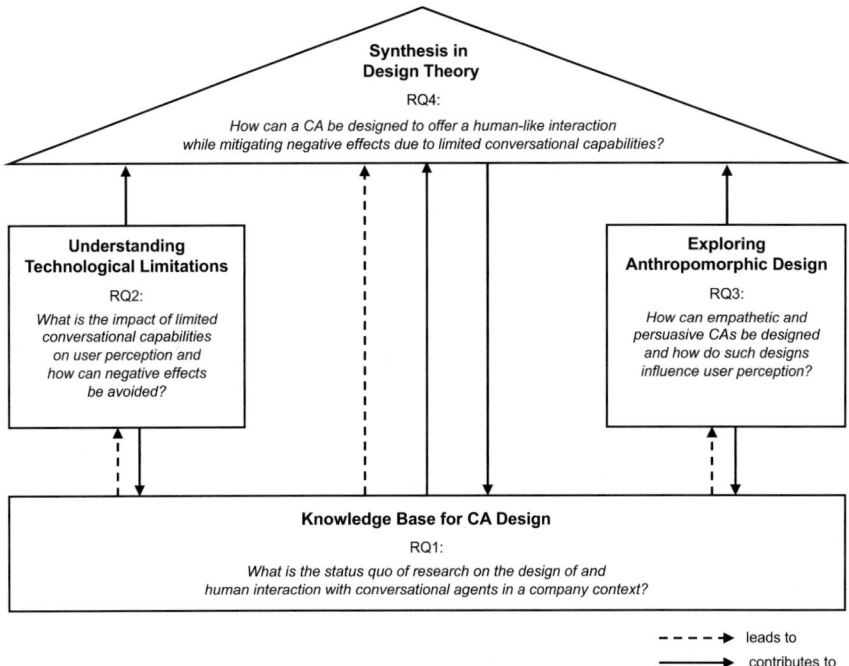

Figure 2: Research Framework

I.3 Structure of the Thesis

This dissertation is cumulative in nature and consists of three parts. Part A lays the foundation for this work by motivating the research endeavor (A.I.1) and highlighting the research gaps as well as research questions (A.I.2) followed by the thesis' structure (A.I.3). Afterwards, the research context and design (A.I.4) and anticipated contributions (A.I.5) are presented. The next chapter (A.II) provides an overview of CAs and their application in enterprises, introduces Social Response Theory and the Theory of Uncanny Valley as two key theories for the design of and interaction with anthropomorphic artifacts, as well as outlines existing conceptual and empirical studies on human-like design of conversational agents.

Part B represents the main body of this thesis, comprising six studies on the topic of CAs in a company context and their human-like design that address the formulated questions and contribute to closing the selected gaps in the knowledge base (Table 1).

Table 1: Overview of Studies included in this Thesis

No.	Outlet	Status	Ranking[1]	Section	RQ	Contribution
1	Journal of the Association for Information Systems	Revision (1st round)	A	B.I.	1	Overview of the status quo of CA research with a focus on IS and HCI as well as synthesis of existing prescriptive knowledge
2	European Conference on Information Systems (2020)	Accepted (conditionally)	B	B.II.	2	Understanding of the impact of response failure as a key technological limitation of CAs on user perception
3	European Conference on Information Systems (2019)	Published	B	B.II.	2	Assessment of the impact of preset answer options to mitigate response failure including changes in user perception
4	International Conference on Information Systems (2019)	Published	A	B.III.	3	Exploration of a design approach for empathetic CAs based on sentiment-adaptive responses and assessment of user perception
5	International Conference on Information Systems (2019)	Published	A	B.III.	3	Exploration of the combination of anthropomorphic and persuasive CA design and assessment of user perception
6	Business and Information Systems Engineering	Forthcoming	B	B.IV.	4	Nascent design theory for anthropomorphic CAs derived from the design and evaluation of a CA for a professional service firm

Part C summarizes and synthesizes the findings of this thesis. Afterwards, the implications for research and practice are presented followed by the limitations of this work and opportunities for future research.

Figure 3 visualizes the structure of this thesis.

---

1) According to VHB-JOURQUAL 3

A. Foundation

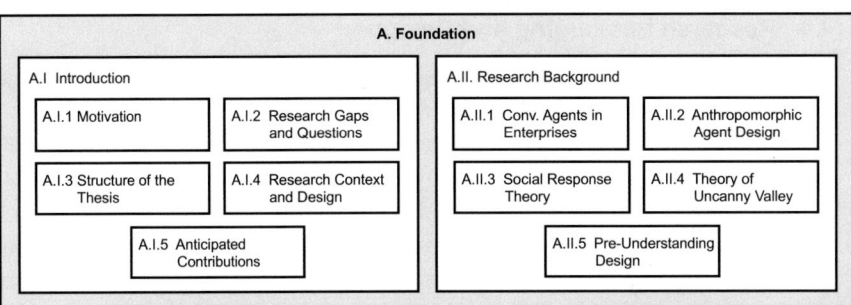

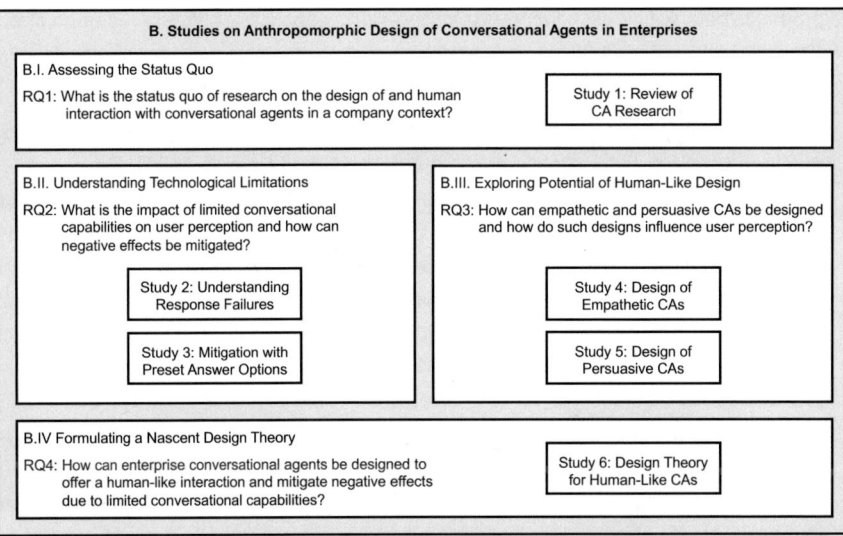

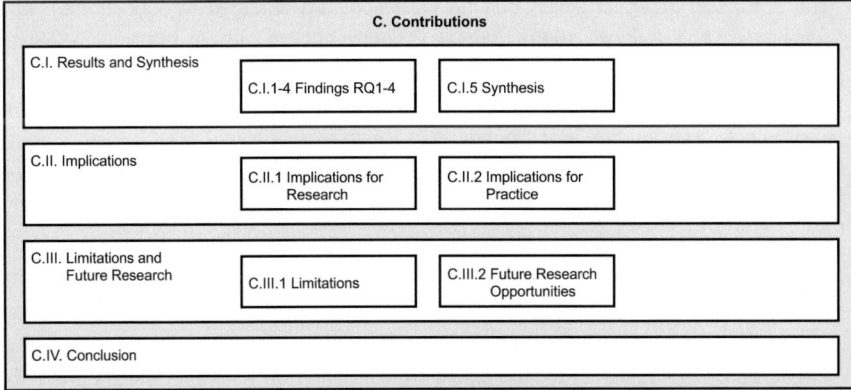

Figure 3: Structure of this Thesis

I.4 Research Positioning and Design

Information Systems (IS) research in general is concerned with generating knowledge to inform researchers and practitioners "how to understand, interpret, adapt to, and effectively manage technologies that have been and currently are in use, as well as emerging technologies whose impact are just being felt" (Banker and Kauffman 2004, p. 294). Due to its focus on the interaction of IT and humans (or human organizations), the IS discipline is part of the social sciences (Bhattacherjee 2012). Research in the IS discipline takes different epistemological stances (Goldkuhl 2012; Orlikowski and Baroudi 1991), follows different paradigms (Arnott and Pervan 2012; Hevner et al. 2004), produces different types of theories (Gregor 2006), consists of different research streams (Banker and Kauffman 2004), and employs various research methods. In the following, this thesis is positioned within the IS discipline with regard to these aspects.

Concerning the epistemological positioning, four different perspectives exist in IS research (Ågerfalk 2010; Goldkuhl 2012; Orlikowski and Baroudi 1991). First, *positivism*, is based on the assumption that an objective physical and social world exists independent of humans which can be theorized upon (Wynn and Williams 2012). Research following this epistemological perspective assumes that the world can be objectively apprehended, characterized, and measured (Orlikowski and Baroudi 1991) through systematic observation (Bhattacherjee 2012). Second, *interpretivism*, places emphasis on subjective meanings and social-political actions in which reality of humans is constituted. Instead of presuming the existence of an objective, observable world, it assumes that reality is socially constructed and attempts to understand "how and why individuals, through their socialization into, interaction with, and participation in, a social world, give it a certain status and meaning" (Orlikowski and Baroudi, 1991, p. 13). Third, *critical realism* assumes that social reality is historically constructed and not constrained to a particular state, but has unfulfilled potential which can be identified and changed through human action (Orlikowski and Baroudi 1991). Similar to interpretivism, critical realism understands social reality to be constructed by humans, but emphasizes objective properties which influence human experience in a continuous process. Fourth, *pragmatism*, is concerned with "action and change and the interplay between knowledge and action" (Goldkuhl 2012, p. 2) and emphasizes research that intervenes with the world instead of observing, for example through organizational change in action research (Baskerville 1999) or through the building of artifacts like in design science research (Gregor and Hevner 2013). In its essence, *pragmatism* exhibits a particular interest in change and how humans produce and continuously respond to it (Goldkuhl 2012). Concerning these epistemological stances, this thesis follows the perspective of *pragmatism* as it places emphasis on the design of technological artifacts and how different designs bring about changes in human perception.

Two distinct paradigms characterize research in the IS discipline: *behavior-oriented research* and *design-oriented research* (Arnott and Pervan 2012; Hevner et al. 2004). Behavior-oriented research aims to develop and verify theories that explain or predict behavior of humans or organizations in the context of the analysis, design, implementation, management, and use of IS to improve individual or organizational efficiency or effectiveness (Hevner et al. 2004). The behavioral paradigm is rooted in natural sciences research and aims for truth (Hevner et al. 2004). Design-oriented IS research is rooted in engineering and the sciences of the artificial (Simon 1996) and seeks to generate knowledge on how to design and implement IS artifacts (Gregor 2006) to address relevant problems of society, organizations, and individuals (Hevner 2007). IS research which follows a design-oriented paradigm ultimately values utility over truth (Iivari 2015). However, the designed artifacts are not exempt from theories derived in behavioral research, but rather draw on, apply, modify and extend existing kernel theories in an iterative, problem solving process (Markus et al. 2002; Walls et al. 1992). As Hevner et al. (2004) note, the two paradigms are fundamentally distinct yet complementary. According to Hevner et al. (2004, p. 76f), an opportunity to make significant contributions exists in "engaging the complementary research cycle between design science and behavioral science to address fundamental problems in the productive application of information technology". Following this idea, the research presented in this dissertation follows a design-oriented paradigm while advancing the understanding of the overarching design problem by engaging in behavior-oriented research. Thereby, this work acknowledges the complementarity of the two paradigms.

Furthermore, IS research can be distinguished by the generated type of theory. In her examination of the structural nature of theory in IS, Gregor (2006) proposes five types of theories: Analysis ("says what is"), Explanation ("say what is, how, why, when, and where"), Prediction ("says what is and what will be"), Explanation and Prediction ("says what is, how, why, when, where, and what will be"), and Design and Action ("says how to do something"). Against this background, the present thesis generates theoretical knowledge to explain and predict phenomena related to human interaction with anthropomorphic CAs (through behavior-oriented research) to better understand the design problem at hand, and, finally, contributes actionable, prescriptive knowledge (e.g. principles of form and function) to inform the design of these technological artifacts.

In addition to the type of produced theory, IS research can be differentiated by research streams. According to Banker and Kauffman (2004), five streams exist, each focusing on specific research phenomena, level of analysis, theories, and methodologies. The authors distinguish between the streams *Decision Support and Design Science* (concerned with the design of decision support systems in conjunction with human users and business processes), *Value of Information* (places emphasis on individual decision makers or technologies in a business process context, grounded for example in information economics), *Human-Computer Systems Design* (focuses on the design of and interaction of individual users with technological artifacts), *IS Organization and Strategy* (spans different levels of analysis from individuals to marketplaces, uses for example diffusion theory or transaction costs economics), and *Economics of IS and IT* (similarly focuses on multiple levels of analysis, draws on for example game theory or production economics). Due to the research focus on the design of a specific technology and the interaction of humans with it, this thesis belongs to the IS research stream of *Human-Computer Systems Design* (Banker and Kauffman 2004), using two prevalent research methods in this area (experiments, design science research) and aiming to produce prescriptive knowledge on how to build conversational agents.

The thesis contains six studies that investigate the design of CAs as an emerging technology for innovation and automation in enterprises by means of different research methodologies which are based on procedures established in seminal articles (Table 2).

Table 2: Research Designs of the Studies in this Thesis

No.	RQ	Methodology (Seminal Work)	Data Collection	Data Analysis
1	1	Systematic literature review (vom Brocke et al. 2009; Webster and Watson 2002)	Literature review	Coding
2	2	Online experiment with 2x2 design (Dennis and Valacich 2001)	Survey, conversation data	PLS-SEM
3	2	Online experiment with 2x1 design (Dennis and Valacich 2001)	Survey, conversation data	t-tests, regression
4	3	Online experiment with 2x1 design (Dennis and Valacich 2001)	Survey, conversation data	t-tests, regression
5	3	Online experiment with 2x2 design (Dennis and Valacich 2001)	Survey, conversation data	PLS-SEM
6	4	Design science research (Kuechler and Vaishnavi 2008)	Interviews, focus groups, survey, conversation data	Coding, t-tests, descriptive statistics

Specifically, Study 1 consists of a systematic literature review based on the guidelines by Webster and Watson (2002) and vom Brocke et al. (2009) to assess the status quo of IS and HCI research on CAs. Studies 2 to 5 contribute to closing part of the research gaps identified in Study 1 by means of experimental research (Dennis and Valacich 2001), each focusing on different design aspects of CAs and their impact on user perception. These experiments employ between-subject designs and vary either one specific design aspect (2x1, analysis primarily via t-tests) or two (2x2, analysis primarily via Partial Least Squares Structural Equation Modeling (PLS-SEM)). Finally, Study 6 employs a DSR approach (Kuechler and Vaishnavi 2008) to address the overarching design problem of how to build anthropomorphic CAs with the possibilities and limitations given in present-day technology. The study synthesizes prescriptive knowledge from the knowledge base and draws on two kernel theories to formulate design principles, instantiates them in an artifact in a specific context, and, after the evaluation with a combination of qualitative and quantitative methods, proposes a nascent design theory (Gregor and Jones 2007).

Table 3 summarizes the positioning of this thesis in the IS discipline with regard to the paradigm (Hevner et al. 2004), epistemological stance (Goldkuhl 2012; Orlikowski and Baroudi 1991), research stream (Banker and Kauffman 2004), research methods used in the studies included in this work (adapted from Palvia et al. 2004), and produced theory type (Gregor 2006).

Table 3: Positioning of this Thesis in the Information Systems Discipline

Epistemology	Positivism	Interpretivism	Critical Realism	Pragmatism	
Paradigm	Behavior-oriented			Design-oriented	
Theory Type	Analysis	Explanation	Prediction	Explanation and Prediction	Design and Action
Research Stream	Decision Support and Design Science	Value of Information	Human-Computer Systems Design	IS Organization and Strategy	Economics of IS and IT
Research Method	Case Study	Conceptual Model	Mathematical Model	Literature Analysis	Survey
	Secondary Data	Design Science	Experimental Research	Interview	Content Analysis

I.5 Anticipated Contributions

This thesis is intended to address the overarching problem of how to design anthropomorphic CA in a company context to foster a human-like interaction and cope with limited conversational capabilities existing in present-day natural language technology. Thus, the main contributions of this work are prescriptive in nature (Gregor 2006), particularly the resulting nascent design theory and the design principles contained in it (Gregor and Jones 2007). However, in the process of generating design-oriented knowledge, this work also produces descriptive knowledge through (1) the assessment of the status quo of CA research, including the identification of different research foci and gaps in the knowledge base, (2) the analysis of changes in user perception due to design-related aspects, such as the use of preset answer options or empathetic communication, and (3) contributing to a better understanding of the overarching problem class of crafting anthropomorphic technological artifacts with inhuman imperfections by iterating between designing and evaluating an artifact in a specific context as well as reflecting on the design problem at hand (Gregory and Muntermann 2014; Iivari 2015). These prescriptive and descriptive contributions are intended to add to three different research areas as described in the motivation for this research (Figure 1) and provide practical insights for building anthropomorphic CAs.

With regard to research on *Conversational Agents*, this thesis seeks to make three key contributions. First, the systematic review of CA research aims to organize the existing body of knowledge and provide an overview of research themes and the theoretical grounding (i.e. in the form of kernel theories) as well as identify research gaps and associated opportunities for future work in this area. Second, this research intends to synthesize existing knowledge on CA design in a professional context, thereby bringing together dispersed research from different organizational application domains like customer service (Gnewuch et al. 2018b; Wünderlich and Paluch 2017) or marketing and sales (Baier et al. 2018; Vaccaro et al. 2018) and with different research foci. Third, this research attempts to explore user-related characteristics influencing the perception of humanness in technological artifacts, such as age (e.g. Beer et al. 2015) or prior experience (e.g. Otoo and Salam 2018)) in a company context.

Concerning research on *Anthropomorphic Artifacts*, this work aims to contribute to a better understanding of the relationship between the human-like appearance of CAs as a specific type of technological artifact and its impact on user perception as postulated in Social Response Theory (Nass and Moon 2000) and the Theory of Uncanny Valley (Mori 1970). Furthermore, the studies presented in this thesis aim to provide insights into the use of social cues to offer a human-like interaction, such as empathetic communication, and how they contribute to the perception of anthropomorphism. In addition, this thesis is intended to allow for a better understanding of the transferability of knowledge from human-to-human communication to human-anthropomorphic CA interaction, for example by investigating the existence of gender-related differences in the perception of CA behavior in as service context as found in human service encounters (Chiu 2002).

Regarding the third research area, *Human-Computer Systems Design*, this thesis seeks to achieve a better understanding of the impact of limited conversational capabilities of present-day CAs on user perception as well as to propose and evaluate approaches to mitigate response failure (e.g. with preset answer options) as one of the key reasons for CA failure (Luger and Sellen 2016; Ben Mimoun et al. 2012). Complementary to investigating technological limitations, this thesis aims to contribute approaches for anthropomorphic CA design (e.g. with sentiment-adaptive responses or by combining elements from persuasive design (Oinas-Kukkonen and Harjumaa 2009) with social cues from anthropomorphic design) as well as to study relevant constructs (e.g. empathy, persuasiveness) in the context of designing human-like enterprise CAs.

Finally, this thesis is intended to provide contributions for *CA Designers* in practice concerned with building and introducing anthropomorphic CAs in their organizations. Specifically, it aims to produce actionable design principles that guide designers to craft human-like CAs and cope with limited conversational capabilities across organizational domains. Furthermore, this research seeks to shed light on the risks associated with a human-like design, particularly the ones related to users perceiving the artifact as uncanny or eerie (Strait et al. 2015), thus creating awareness for designers for potential unintended, negative effects of a human-like design. Finally, with regard to practical contributions, the studies attempt to contribute to a better understanding on the impact of specific design elements of CAs, such as preset answer options, on user perception. The anticipated contributions of this thesis are summarized in Table 4.

Table 4: Summary of Anticipated Contributions

Audience		Anticipated Contributions
Research	Conversational Agents	(1) Overview of the status quo of research CAs, including specific gaps in the knowledge base and theoretical grounding (2) Synthesis of (prescriptive) knowledge on the anthropomorphic design of CAs in a company context (3) Identification of user characteristics influencing the perception of CAs, such as age or prior experience with the technology
	Anthropomorphic Artifacts	(1) Improved understanding of Social Response Theory and Theory of Uncanny Valley in the context of human-like CAs (2) Insights into social cues and their impact on perception of the CA by individual users (3) Insights into the transferability of existing knowledge from human-to-human communication to human-anthropomorphic CA interaction
	Human-Computer Systems Design	(1) Insights into the impact of response failure on user perception and approaches how to mitigate them, particularly with answer options (2) Design approaches in the context of human-like CAs, e.g. sentiment-adaptive responses, and constructs for the evaluation (3) Exploration of combining design approaches, e.g. anthropomorphic and persuasive design
Practice	CA Designers	(1) Actionable design principles to craft anthropomorphic CAs and deal with limited conversational capabilities (2) Insights into the risks associated with a human-like design of CAs, such as uncanniness (3) Insights into the impact of specific design elements (e.g. preset answer options, sentiment-adaptive responses) on user perception

II. Research Background

The research focus of this thesis is on the anthropomorphic design of conversational agents in a company context as described in the previous chapter. Following the description of the motivation for this work, the research questions and design, as well as the anticipated contributions, this chapter presents the research background to provide the fundamentals and outline the theoretical grounding of this thesis. Thus, it places emphasis on seminal, mostly conceptual work and introducing the research field rather than on specific studies or single empirical observations, which are explained in more detail in the respective background sections of the studies included in this thesis.

This chapter presents the research background by providing an overview of CAs in enterprises (II.1), outlining Social Response Theory (section II.2) and the Theory of Uncanny Valley (II.3) as two theories for human perception of human-like artifacts with particular relevance for this work, and, introducing the topic of anthropomorphic CA design while contextualizing the theories (II.4). Finally, the research background is synthesized in a pre-understanding of human-like CA design (II.5).

II.1 Conversational Agents and their Application in Enterprises

The essential idea behind conversational agents is the interaction with technology through natural language as an alternative to graphical user interfaces (Dale 2016; McTear 2017). Instead of browsing through complex menus and manually entering input via a keyboard, CAs offer an intuitive way of interacting with complex applications using natural language similar to human-to-human interaction (Følstad and Brandtzæg 2017). While the idea of natural language interaction with technology already emerged several decades ago as outlined in the anecdote of ELIZA (Weizenbaum 1966), CAs just recently started to attract large interest in both research and practice. For example, the Gartner Hype Cycle for Artificial Intelligence (Goasduff 2019) shows chatbots and conversational user interfaces at its peak and Forrester Research highlights that voice and chat interactions with technology are quickly entering our daily lives (Koplowitz and Facemire 2018). Major technology companies, such as IBM, Google or Microsoft provide platforms, and small- to medium-sized organizations like IPSoft, Nuance, or pandorabots provide various platforms to design, build and integrate CAs in existing application landscapes (Diederich et al. 2019b). Similarly, mobile devices and computers are equipped out-of-the-box with virtual CAs, such as Apple's Siri, Google's Assistant or Microsoft's Cortana and speakers like Amazon's Alexa are making its way into private homes (Son and Wonseok 2018). Finally, text-based CAs in the form of chatbots gain strong attention as underlined by the example of Facebook where 100,000 bots were registered within one year after the Messenger platform was opened for external developers (Johnson 2018).

A. Foundation

A key reason for this increased popularity are the improved capabilities of present-day CAs driven in particular by advances in natural language processing and machine learning (Rzepka and Berger 2018). While early CAs consisted of primarily static, rule-based systems to detect user input based on a set of stored patterns and provided standardized responses, current CAs employ a wide range of approaches to interpret and respond to natural language input (Berg 2015; Knijnenburg and Willemsen 2016). In this context, Google CEO Sundar Pichai gave an outlook on future capabilities of CAs at its developer conference in 2018 when he showed Google Assistant calling a hairdresser and scheduling an appointment in a spoken dialogue with an actual human person without intervention from the user (Welch 2018).

As indicated by this plethora ranging from virtual assistants on mobile devices to text-based chatbots in specific domains, CAs as natural language software encompass different forms. According to Gnewuch et al. (2017), CAs can be distinguished according to their application domain (i.e. whether the CA focuses on a specific application domain, such as a customer service, or spans different areas like Siri or Alexa) and primary communication mode (i.e. whether users primarily communicate with the CA via written text or spoken word). Figure 4 visualizes the adapted classification of CAs proposed by Gnewuch et al. (2017) and presents exemplary CAs from practice. As indicated in the introduction, the focus of this thesis is on enterprise CAs as one form of text-based CAs in a specific application domain.

		Application Domain	
		Domain-Specific	General-Purpose
Primary Mode of Communication	Text-based	Enterprise CAs (e.g. Amtrak's Julie), health CAs, tutoring CAs, ...	Cleverbot, Eviebot, Mitsuku, ...
	Speech-based	In-car assistants (e.g. LINGUATRONIC), voice-based service agents, ...	Softbank's Pepper, Apple's Siri, Google's Assistant, Amazon's Alexa, ...

Figure 4: Classification of Conversational Agents

Text-based CAs, in practice often referred to as chatbots or chatterbots, in an enterprise context promise to innovate and automate business processes while offering the feeling of a natural, human-like interaction (Araujo 2018). Based on this promise, they are studied in research and introduced in practice for company-internal use, for example to support collaborative work (Elson et al. 2018; Toxtli et al. 2018), as well as at the customer interface to provide service (Hu et al. 2018; Quynh and Sidorova 2018) or contribute to the sales of products and services (Baier et al. 2018; Vaccaro et al. 2018). Examples for text-based enterprise CAs across different industries are "BlueBot" by the Dutch airline KLM that allows to search for and book flights as well as accompanies customers during their travel (Gutierrez and Khizniak 2018), "Margot" by Lidl which provides product recommendations (Dreyer 2018) or "KAI" by Mastercard (Sen 2016) which offers account and transaction information (Figure 5).

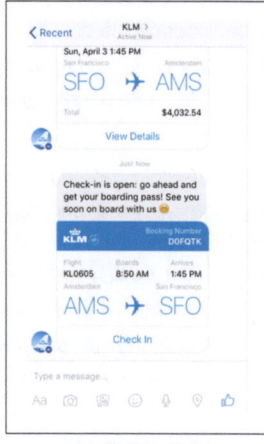

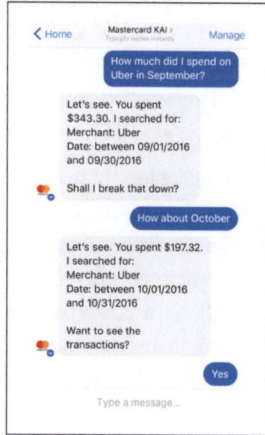

„BlueBot" by KLM   "Margot" by Lidl   "KAI" by Mastercard

Sources: Sen 2016, Dreyer 2018, Gutierrez and Khizniak 2018

Figure 5: Enterprise CAs in Practice by KLM, Lidl and Mastercard

While these and further practical examples emphasize the popularity of CAs for organizations, designing and implementing them remains a challenge as outlined in the motivation for this research endeavor. The interaction via natural language, together with other human-like characteristics of the design, such as the use of self-references (Sah and Peng 2015) like in the example of "KAI" ("I searched for...") or the expression of emotions (Wang et al. 2008) through emoticons as done by "BlueBot" lead to high user expectations regarding the system's conversational capabilities, similar to expectations for human-to-human communication (Go and Sundar 2019).

Users expect CAs to continuously provide context-dependent, meaningful responses across a sequence of conversational turns (Luger and Sellen 2016), contingent on what has already been communicated earlier in the dialogue (Go and Sundar 2019). Due to these high user expectations and the complexity of human communication through natural language, designing enterprise CAs represents "a transition from the design of visual layout and interaction mechanisms to the design of conversation" (Følstad and Brandtzæg 2017, p. 40).

A. Foundation

To better understand the complexity of conversation design and the technological capabilities of present-day enterprise CAs, a high-level and generic architecture of CAs is visualized in Figure 6. The wording to describe the components is based on Google Dialogflow (2019) as one of the most popular development platforms, however, the fundamental structure is similar across most of the platforms available on the market.

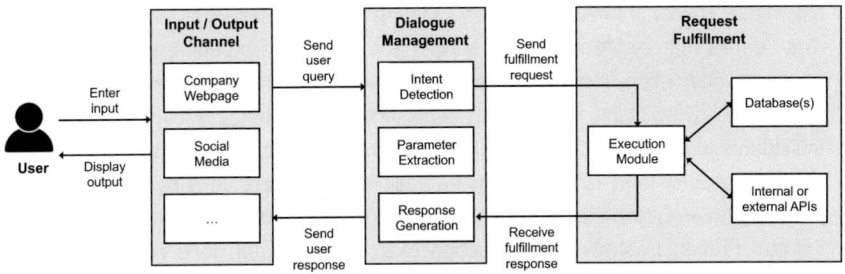

Figure 6: High-Level Architecture for Enterprise CAs

Typically, the design and implementation of a CA encompasses three components. First, the *Input / Output Channel* offers the user to enter input via natural language and displays the text output of the CA. The channel can for example be a chat window on the webpage of a company, social media (e.g. Facebook), or an application, such as Google Assistant or Skype. The second component, *Dialogue Management* processes the natural language input by detecting the user's intent (e.g. "book a flight from San Francisco on 2nd of April 2020") through matching the user input with a list of possible intents created by the developer. After successful detection of the intent, it extracts parameters (e.g. place of departure = San Francisco) as well as converts them into a machine-readable format. In case the intent detection fails, it sends a fallback response which is then displayed to the user and aims to repair the conversation, for example by asking the user to rephrase the request. The third component, *Request Fulfillment*, then executes the intent with the given parameters, potentially by search in databases (e.g. for flight information) or calling internal or external application programming interfaces (APIs). Afterwards, the fulfillment response is transmitted to the *Dialogue Management* component (e.g. list of flights), which converts it into natural language and forwards it to the *Input / Output* Channel that displays the response.

Against the background of this architectural approach to design CAs, their limited conversational capabilities, despite their current popularity, become apparent. Designers are required to manually create a list of various intents with which users might approach the agent, anticipate various formulations for the same intent and need to foresee conversational turns (e.g. customers switching between service requests).

II.2 Social Response Theory: Computers Are Social Actors

A key theory, particularly in the field of HCI research, to understand the interaction with technological artifacts with human-like traits and characteristics is the understanding of computers as social actors (Nass et al. 1994; Nass and Moon 2000; Reeves and Nass 1996). Referred to as the Computers Are Social Actors (CASA) paradigm or Social Response Theory, it postulates that humans respond mindlessly to technological artifacts to a degree that they apply social scripts from human-to-human interaction to human-computer interaction, meanwhile largely ignoring the artificial and mechanistic nature of a computer (Fogg and Nass 1997; Nass and Moon 2000). According to the theory, individuals turn their conscious attention to a subset of social cues (e.g. a female avatar of a digital assistant) leading them to classify the artifact as a social entity (e.g. the assistant having a female gender) while ignoring the obvious fact that it does not actually warrant human treatment or attribution (e.g. the assistant does not have an actual, biological gender).

Nass and Moon (2000) suggest that such social responses to technological artifacts occur mindlessly. Mindless behavior is characterized by focusing conscious attention to a subset of contextual cues (Langer 1992), which "trigger various scripts, labels, expectations, which in turn focus attention on certain information while diverting attention away from other information" (Nass and Moon 2000, p. 6). Thus, rather than considering all relevant features of a situation (e.g. viewing a digital assistant with a female avatar as a computer program) to consciously produce distinctions, humans mindlessly apply trivial scripts drawn from the past (Langer 1992). The researchers suggest that these mindless responses were developed early in the evolution of human life when primarily humans exhibited such social behavior (Nass and Moon 2000), thus people are hardwired to socially respond to things that seem to be alive (Fogg 2003). Figure 7 visualizes this core idea of Social Response Theory.

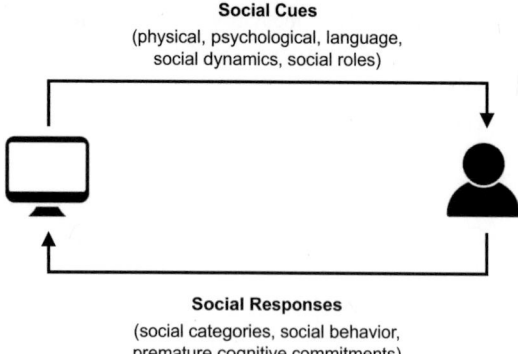

Figure 7: Social Response Theory

According to Fogg (2003), five primary types of *Social Cues* can be distinguished as shown in Figure 7. First, *physical cues* include features like a face, eyes, body, or movement of a technological artifact. For example, the humanoid robot "Pepper" by SoftBank Robotics exhibits a human-like face, including eyes that move in the direction where a sound occurs and blink from time to time (SoftBank 2020).

Second, *psychological cues*, include aspects like personality, preferences, empathy, or humor and can be conveyed for example by expressing simple emotions through words or using emoticons (Fogg 2003). More complex psychological cues, such as the ones related to personality, may require an interaction with an artifact for a longer period of time. Psychological cues and the social responses to them are in particular relevant in the context of persuasion. For example, the study on personality similarity by Fogg (2003) provided evidence that humans prefer a computer that matches their own personality with regard to dominant/submissive behavior during a task.

The third category, *language cues*, comprises cues, such as the use of natural language, both written and spoken, or language recognition (Fogg 2003). E-commerce websites, such as Amazon, extensively use language-related cues. For example, customers on Amazon are politely greeted by name and receive personalized recommendations (Fogg 2003). Thus, such websites foster substantial feelings of social presence in the interaction (Hassanein and Head 2007).

Fourth, cues in the category of *social dynamics*, encompasses features like turn-taking, cooperation or praise for good work. These cues stem from the unwritten rules of human interaction. For example, behavior-change support systems, such as running apps, praise the user after showing a desirable behavior (e.g. completing a run), using social responses to praise and to promote similar behavior by the user in the future (Oinas-Kukkonen and Harjumaa 2009).

Fifth, technological artifacts can assume *social roles*, such as teammates, doctors, teachers, or guides to trigger social responses by users (Fogg 2003). Examples for cues related to social roles are Joseph Weizenbaum's ELIZA with its role as a psychotherapist or applications like Norton Antivirus' "DiskDoctor" (Fogg 2003).

With regard to the social responses that these types of cues trigger, Nass and Moon (2000) found empirical evidence for three types of responses (Figure 7): In their experiments, the researchers observed that humans *over-use social categories*, exhibit *over-learned social behaviors*, and demonstrate *premature cognitive commitments*. Concerning the over-use of social categories, Nass and Moon (2000) found that humans mindlessly apply gender-stereotypes related to politeness and competence to voice output of a computer and that an agent's image matching the ethnicity of a participant yielded a higher attractiveness, trustworthiness, and intelligence in comparison to an ethnicity mismatch.

Furthermore, mindless behavior can result from over-learning habits and behaviors. Nass and Moon (2000, p. 12) describe that "individuals are so facile at performing some behaviors that once the script is initiated, they stop searching for additional context cues and simply respond according to the script". In this context, an experiment by Nass, Moon and Carney (1999) demonstrated that humans evaluated a computer's performance more positively when the computer asked about itself in comparison to evaluating its performance using pen and pencil or another computer, similar to positively biased evaluations in face-to-face settings with other, actual human persons.

The final type of social response is related to premature cognitive commitments humans show when interacting with technological artifacts. The early experiments in this area of Nass and Moon (2000) showed that the labeling of a simple TV in the sense of a "specialist" for the shown content led participants to perceive the content as significantly more interesting, informative and serious as well as of higher quality than the one of a "generalist"-labelled TV.

Table 5 summarizes types of social cues and social responses. In short, drawing on the seminal work by Nass and Moon (2000) and Fogg (2003) it can be concluded that technological artifacts with social cues trigger substantial mindless social responses by humans in their interaction with them. These studies emphasize substantial social responses by humans to artifacts that, from today's perspective, exhibit relatively simple and few social cues (e.g. television with a label). In their outlook, Clifford Nass and Youngme Moon (2000, p. 24) hypothesize that "the more computers present characteristics that are associated with humans, the more likely they are to elicit social behavior" and indicate the potential for social responses to emerging natural language software, agents with human-like features or computers expressing a wide range of different emotions.

Table 5: Types and Examples of Social Cues and Social Responses

Social Cues (based on Fogg 2003)	
Physical	Face, eyes, body, movement, ...
Psychological	Preferences, humor, personality, feelings, empathy, ...
Language	Interactive language use, spoken language, ...
Social Dynamics	Turn taking, cooperation, praise for good work, reciprocity, ...
Social Roles	Doctor, teammate, opponent, teacher, guide, ...
Social Responses (based on Nass and Moon 2000)	
Social Categories	Gender stereotypes, ethnicity match
Social Behaviors	Politeness, reciprocity
Premature Cognitive Commitments	Label as expert/specialist

II.3 Theory of Uncanny Valley

Around 50 years ago, the Japanese robotics professor Masahiro Mori published an essay in which he hypothesized on the human-like design of robots and the emotional responses of humans to them (Mori 1970). He suggested that the relationship between human affinity or familiarity with an anthropomorphic artifact does not follow a monotonically increasing function, but that there is a point where "a person's response to a human-like robot would abruptly shift from empathy to revulsion as it approached, but failed to attain, a lifelike appearance" (Mori et al. 2012, p. 98). This sharp drop in human affinity, where the attention shifts from the human-like qualities of a robot, or more abstractly of a (technological) artifact, to its inhuman imperfections, was termed by Mori (1970) as the "Uncanny Valley" (Figure 8).

In the English translation of the original Japanese essay, Mori et al. (2012) describe a prosthetic hand as an example for an Uncanny Valley-effect. A prosthetic hand resembles a human hand, such as false teeth are similar to real human teeth. However, once a person realizes that the hand, which seemed to be real at first sight, is actually artificial (e.g. when one recognizes a limp, boneless grip together with coldness during a handshake), she or he would experience a feeling of uncanniness or eeriness (Mori et al. 2012), thus losing sense of affinity. In this example, the prosthetic hand appears very human-like yet leads to a very low level of affinity or familiarity.

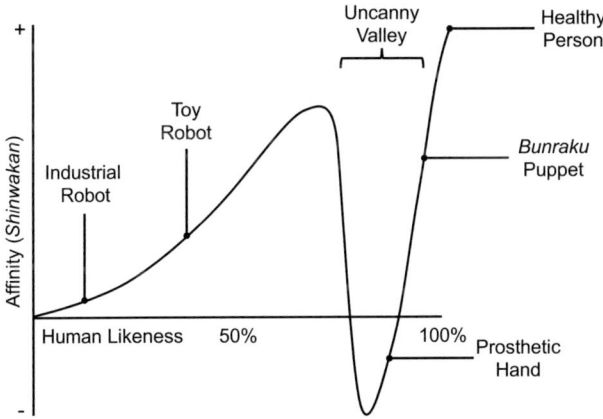

Figure 8: Conceptualization of the Theory of Uncanny Valley (Mori et al. 2012)

To explain the phenomenon of the Uncanny Valley and its underlying cognitive mechanisms, researchers, particularly from the field of psychology, suggest a number of theories, such as the violation of human norms, conflicting perceptual cues, or pathogen avoidance. For example, with regard to the violation of human norms, MacDorman and Ishiguro (2006) describe that the fall into the Uncanny Valley is caused by a change of standards by which an anthropomorphic artifact is measured, i.e. a cognitive shift from an artifact trying to appear human-like to a human failing to appear like a normal person. Following the alternative idea of conflicting perceptual cues (Ferrey et al. 2015), the cause for the Uncanny Valley lies in the cognitive dissonance individuals perceive when recognizing conflicting cues to mental category membership (e.g. humans, machines), leading to a strong feeling of discomfort (Devine and Elliot 1994). A further potential explanation, pathogen avoidance, suggests that uncanny stimuli trigger cognitive responses from human evolution to avoid potential sources of pathogens with a strong response of disgust (Moosa and Ud-Dean 2010).

As the theory by Mori (1970; 2012) was derived from conceptual deliberation instead of actual observations, different researchers conducted empirical studies. While these studies differed with regard to the used stimuli (e.g. morphed images, images of humans, robots, or virtual agents), they all tried to find empirical evidence for the Uncanny Valley. The results of most of these studies were in line with Mori's considerations or at least showed a significant related effect (e.g. Bartneck et al. 2009; Riek et al. 2009; Tinwell al. 2011; and Mathur and Reichling 2016). For example, Mathur and Reichling (2016) conducted an experiment with 80 different face stimuli of varying human likeness, asking 334 participants questions regarding the likeability and humanness of the faces. As shown in Figure 9, the findings of Mathur and Reichling (2016) were quite consistent with the graph postulated in the Theory of Uncanny Valley.

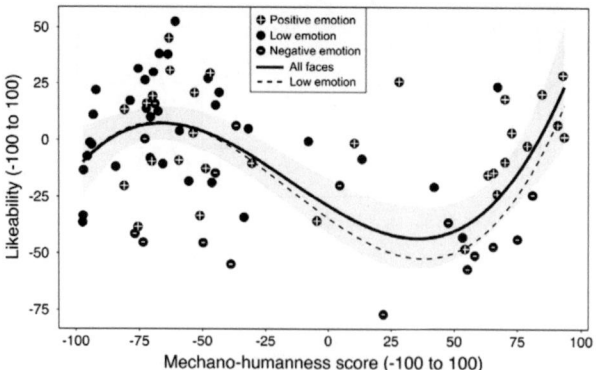

Figure 9: Empirical Evidence for the Uncanny Valley (Mathur and Reichling 2016)

The studies, however, by Hanson (2006) and Hanson et al. (2005) do not find empirical data supporting the existence of the Uncanny Valley. From their observations, the authors draw the conclusion that aesthetics in the design of an anthropomorphic artifact determine the emotional responses by humans instead of the degree of human likeness, suggesting that "if we remove these flaws to make them friendly, attractive, and seemingly alive, then the level of realism may not matter" (Hanson 2006, p. 4). Similar to the idea that additional aspects of an artifact's human-like design influence the emotional responses by humans, Rosenthal-Von Der Pütten and Krämer (2014) describe that individual human characteristics, such as age, gender, and personality traits, influence the perception of human-like artifacts.

To conclude, many empirical studies find evidence for the Uncanny Valley, or at least a related effect which might occur when designing anthropomorphic, but not perfectly human-like technological artifacts. At the same time, research in this area also indicates that further aspects in addition to a human-like design, such as aesthetics, as well as individual human characteristics influence the perception of such artifacts. Thus, the relationship between an artifact's human-like design, particularly of conversational agents, and its perception of humans is complex and contingent on factors that are yet not well understood, requiring careful evaluation of anthropomorphic artifact designs.

II.4 Anthropomorphic Design of Conversational Agents

Anthropomorphic design, understood as equipping inanimate objects with human-like traits and characteristics (Epley et al. 2007), seeks to elicit positive emotional responses by humans to (technological) artifacts and is widely used in today's life. Exemplary products with a human-like design include cars where the front resembles a human face with headlights as eyes and the air intake as the mouth (Windhager et al. 2008), leading customers to perceive the car as friendly, cute or even menacing (DiSalvo and Gemperle 2003), or autonomously-moving vacuum cleaner robots, such as iRobot's Roomba, which is often ascribed with a gender and personality by customers, viewing the machine as for example stubborn, crazy, or intelligent (Hendriks et al. 2011). In the IS discipline, anthropomorphic design is investigated for different types of technological artifacts and purposes, such as product recommendation agents (Qiu and Benbasat 2009) and their ability to induce trust and foster feelings of enjoyment or e-commerce websites in relation to consumers' willingness to pay (Yuan and Dennis 2019).

In the context of enterprise CAs, anthropomorphic design is of particular relevance due to the overarching goal of this technology to offering a human-like, positive interaction experience while automating specific tasks, such as the provision of customer service (Gnewuch et al. 2017). Following the idea of Social Response Theory (Nass and Moon 2000), the interaction with technology via natural language triggers substantial social responses by users (Gnewuch et al. 2018b; Gong 2008), which can be intensified through further social cues, such as equipping the CA with a name, gender, or a social role (Feine et al. 2019a). For crafting human-like CAs, Seeger et al. (2018) develop an anthropomorphic design framework (Figure 10) and propose three dimensions: A *human identity*, *nonverbal communication*, and *verbal communication*.

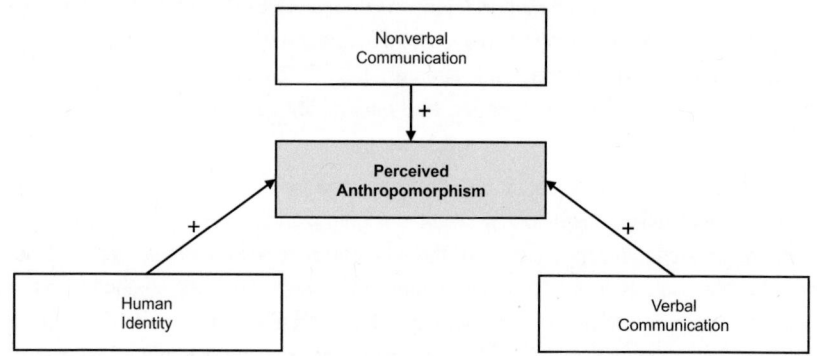

Figure 10: Design Dimensions for Anthropomorphic CAs (Seeger et al. 2018)

The first dimension, *human identity*, comprises social cues that support the identification of a human being in a technology-mediated interaction (Lampe et al. 2007). This design dimension includes equipping the CA with demographic information like a name, gender, ethnicity, or age (Cowell and Stanney 2005; Pfeuffer et al. 2019a), and a social role (e.g. the CA being a member of the customer service team). The demographic information can be complemented with a visual representation of the agent by means of a static image (Qiu and Benbasat 2009; Yuan and Dennis 2019) or interactive avatar (Seymour et al. 2017). The visual representation of the CA has a large impact on how users perceive an agent. For example, Gong (2008) conducted an experiment in which the anthropomorphic appearance of an agent was varied from humanoid robots to images of real human faces and found that higher perceived anthropomorphism in those representations lead to higher ratings of positive social judgment, trustworthiness and competency.

Verbal cues, as the second dimension, include the verbal communication of the CA, that is the choice of words and sentences as well as how the CA refers to itself and others in a conversation (Isbister and Nass 2000). Social cues in this dimension comprise for example the use of self-references in a dialogue (Sah and Peng 2015), greeting rituals like "Hello, how are you?" (Seeger et al. 2018), or telling anecdotes (Bickmore and Picard 2005). Furthermore, the use of emotionally-loaded statements like praise, congratulations, apologies, or concerns (Al-Natour et al. 2009; de Visser et al. 2016) represent social cues belonging to the dimension of verbal communication. In addition, the verbal communication of CAs can be varied with regard to the syntax and word choice to induce the perception of anthropomorphism, in particular by adjusting the agent's statements to the preceding user sentences or paraphrasing (Schuetzler et al. 2014).

The third dimension for anthropomorphic CA design, *non-verbal communication*, contains social cues conveying information without the actual use of words and sentences (Seeger et al. 2018). Examples for non-verbal cues include response delays to indicate thinking and typing in a dialogue (Gnewuch et al. 2018b), typing indicators (Gnewuch et al. 2018a) or the use of emoticons to express artificial feelings (Derks et al. 2008). CAs with interactive avatars (Seymour et al. 2018) or physical embodiment (Stock and Merkle 2018) can show non-verbal communication behavior with additional cues like facial expressions, hand gestures, or eye contact (Berry et al. 2005; Bickmore and Picard 2005; Pfeuffer et al. 2019b; Sakamoto et al. 2005).

In short, several social cues for CAs in the three design dimensions are available to make such agents appear human-like by design. Different studies in this research area have investigated the impact of these cues on user perception, in particular with regard to perceived anthropomorphism and other, partially context-specific outcome variables. For example, Araujo (2018) identified that the perception of anthropomorphism in a CA has a significant positive effect on the emotional connection that customers feel with a company. Similarly, Gnewuch al. (2018b) discover that dynamically delaying responses of a CA does not only increase perceived humanness of the agent but at the same times leads to a higher satisfaction in a customer service encounter. In the context of positive effects of anthropomorphic agent design, Qiu and Benbasat (2009) find empirical evidence that a human-like design for a product recommendation agent yields higher levels of social presence, trusting beliefs, perceived usefulness, and perceived enjoyment. Bickmore and Picard (2005) further discover that a human-like agent that uses social relationship building is trusted more, liked more, and respected more than an agent that does not use such social communication.

While these studies place emphasis on the desirable, positive impact of anthropomorphic CA design on user perception, several studies point out possible negative effects of a human-like agent design. In particular, scholars refer to potential effects related to the Theory of Uncanny Valley. For example, Seeger et al. (2018) highlight the need to find a matching set of social cues as non-verbal cues without the presence of cues from the other two design dimensions yield negative emotional reactions due to inconsistent perceptions of anthropomorphism. Similarly, Gnewuch et al. (2018b) argue that CAs, particularly chatbots, might reach a point of human likeness that is perceived as uncomfortable by users, thus anthropomorphic CA design needs to follow careful considerations to limit potential negative outcomes. Wagner and Schramm-Klein (2019) suggest that not fully adequate empathetic communication behavior by a CA can induce skepticism of users due to Uncanny Valley-effects. The results of Strait et al. (2015)

complement these studies on negative anthropomorphic CA perception by showing that feelings of uncanniness also lead humans to adjust their behavior by exhibiting greater avoidance for such encounters than with less human-like agents.

To conclude, anthropomorphic CA design and its associated social responses can lead to both positive and negative effects on user perception. Table 6 summarizes the effects of human-like CA design on user perception of such artifacts reported in these studies.

Table 6: Potential Positive and Negative Outcomes of Human-Like CA Design

Positive Outcomes of Anthropomorphic CA Design	
Araujo (2018)	Increased anthropomorphism, improved connection with brand
Gnewuch et al. (2018b)	Increased humanness, social presence, and service satisfaction
Qiu and Benbasat (2009)	Increased social presence, trust, usefulness, and enjoyment
Bickmore and Picard (2005)	Improved long-term relationship with the agent
Negative Outcomes of Anthropomorphic CA Design	
Seeger et al (2018)	Decreased anthropomorphism due to inconsistency of cues
Gnewuch et al. (2018b)	Decreased familiarity if human-likeness is too high
Wagner and Schramm-Klein (2019)	Skepticism towards human-like CA due to inadequate empathy
Strait et al. (2015)	Very human-like agents lead users to avoid them in encounters

II.5 Synthesis: Pre-Understanding of Human-Like Enterprise Conversational Agent Design

Drawing on the presented research background, it becomes apparent that the anthropomorphic design of CAs in a company context represents a relevant topic for practice as well as an interesting phenomenon to study grounded in theories on the interaction with anthropomorphic technological artifacts. Whiles CAs are introduced in various industries, organizations, and application domains to automate tasks and processes with a human-like interaction, particularly at the customer interface, crafting an appealing anthropomorphic design that copes with existing technological limitations represents a substantial design problem. In the best case, a human-like design exclusively affects user perception in a positive way (e.g. concerning the emotional connection with a brand or satisfaction with customer service). However, there is a substantial risk for fostering high user expectations through social responses to the CA's design which can, in case they are not fulfilled, lead to a very negative perception of the agent (Luger and Sellen 2016; Ben Mimoun et al. 2017).

The knowledge base for anthropomorphic CA design offers guidance to address this design problem by means of kernel theories, particularly Social Response Theory (Nass and Moon 2000) as well as the Theory of Uncanny Valley (Mori 1970; Mori et al. 2012) and emerging studies that provide conceptual frameworks (e.g. Seeger et al 2018) and insights on specific social cues (e.g. Araujo 2018; Gnewuch et al. 2018b). However, these studies focus on different aspects of a CA's (anthropomorphic) design, draw on different theories to derive design propositions, and use various research methods (Diederich et al. 2019a). Thus, as a first step towards addressing the overarching design problem, there is a need to organize and structure existing knowledge in this research area.

Furthermore, while practical examples, such as IKEA's Anna (Rezvani 2020), and empirical studies (Luger and Sellen 2016; Ben Mimoun et al. 2012) emphasize issues related to technological limitations of present-day CAs, there is a lack of research on how limited conversational capabilities of CAs influence user perception and, in particular, how a negative impact can be mitigated. These limited conversational capabilities in particular comprise the aspect of responsiveness of an agent in a conversation, i.e. its ability to provide a meaningful reply, which requires a better understanding in relation to user perception (Araujo 2018; Pfeuffer et al. 2019a). Complementing the research gap concerning technological limitations, the potential of anthropomorphic design in the context of CAs in a company context, based on the social responses to this technology, needs to be explored. In a professional context, in particular the design of human-like CAs with regard to the adequate display of emotions, for example empathy in a customer service encounter (Larivière et al. 2017; Yan et al. 2013) and persuasion, such as in a marketing and sales setting (Derrick and Ligon 2014) are relevant gaps that have not been addressed in the research community on CAs.

Finally, the presented studies on anthropomorphic CAs provide valuable insights into specific aspect of a CA's design, mostly derived through experimental research, however, they do not offer comprehensive guidance on how to craft human-like CAs in a company context. Thus, in order to contribute to solving the formulated overarching design problem, research is needed that synthesizes prescriptive knowledge in a constituent design theory (Gregor and Jones 2007) and presents an exemplary instantiation by means of an anthropomorphic CA in a real-life setting (Hevner et al. 2004; Nunamaker et al. 2015).

B. Studies on Anthropomorphic Design of Enterprise Conversational Agents

This cumulative thesis seeks to advance our understanding of how to design anthropomorphic conversational agents in a company context as described in Part A. To address the overarching design problem, four related research questions were derived that will be answered in the six studies included in the following Part B.

The first Chapter (B.I) contains the first study which organizes existing research on CAs through a literature review. In doing so, it answers RQ 1 regarding the status quo of research on the design of and human interaction with conversational agents.

Next, the second Chapter (B.II) comprises Studies 2 and 3 which focus on the technological limitations of CAs, particularly their limited conversational capabilities. Study 2 aims to better understand the impact of response failure on user perception of CAs. Study 3 then focuses on preset answer options as a mitigation approach for response failure during a conversation. Thus, Studies 2 and 3 together address RQ 2 concerning the impact of limited conversational capabilities as well as the mitigation of negative effects on user perception.

To complement this research on technological limitations, the third Chapter (B.III) includes Studies 4 and 5 that explore the potential of anthropomorphic CAs in an enterprise context with a focus on their sentiment-adaptive and persuasive design. Specifically, Study 4 investigates the emulation of empathetic communication behavior of a CA in a service encounter and Study 5 focuses on the combination of anthropomorphic and persuasive design elements to influence individual beliefs at the example of sustainable mobility. Collectively, these studies address RQ 3.

Finally, the fourth chapter (B.IV) consists of Study 6 that builds on results from the previous studies and existing prescriptive knowledge to iteratively design an anthropomorphic CA for a professional service company and formulate a nascent design theory. Thus, Study 6 answers RQ4 by providing comprehensive guidance on the design of human-like CAs in company settings.

The studies included in this cumulative dissertation were adapted to a small degree where required to ensure a consistent layout.

I. Assessing the Status Quo

In order to address the overarching design problem, there is a need to first structure and assess the existing, currently rather fragmented knowledge base on conversational agents. Thus, an organizing literature review (Leidner 2018) is required to support the effective and rigorous re-use of existing materials in the form of theories, frameworks, constructs, models, methods, and instantiations in future design-oriented research (Hevner et al. 2004). Study 1 therefore addresses this research gap based on established review methodologies in the IS discipline (vom Brocke et al. 2009; Webster and Watson 2002) and reports on the findings of a systematic in-depth review of 69 studies on from IS and HCI research.

1. Study 1: On the Design of Enterprise Conversational Agents – A Synthesis of IS and HCI Research

Table 7: Fact Sheet of Study 1

Title	On the Design of Enterprise Conversational Agents: A Synthesis of IS and HCI Research
Authors	Stephan Diederich*[1], Alfred Benedikt Brendel[1], Stefan Morana[2], Lutz M. Kolbe[1] 1) Chair of Information Management, University of Göttingen, Platz der Göttinger Sieben 5, 37073 Göttingen, Germany 2) Institute of Information Systems and Marketing, Karlsruhe Institute of Technology, Kaiserstraße 89-93, 76133 Karlsruhe, Germany *Corresponding author. Tel.: +49 551 3921170. E-Mail: stephan.diederich@stud.uni-goettingen.de
Outlet	Journal of the Association of Information Systems (JAIS)
Abstract	Conversational agents (CAs), defined as software that relies on natural language for user interaction, attract increasing interest in both academia and practice due to improved capabilities driven by advances in machine learning and natural language processing. CAs are increasingly used in private life and companies are exploring their capabilities for innovation and automation, such as in marketing and sales or customer service. Yet, they often fall behind expectations and are discontinued due to design related flaws. In this context, researchers in information systems and human-computer interaction have investigated diverse aspects regarding user interaction with CAs and have derived valuable insights on their design drawing on different kernel theories. However, these results remain distributed across a multitude of studies and are thus difficult to access for researchers concerned with CAs. In this article, we review 69 studies from IS and HCI research and apply a design theoretical lens to synthesize existing design knowledge. We contribute a consolidated set of constructs, design principles and kernel theories for anthropomorphic design, develop a framework to guide future research and reflect on the potentials and risks associated with the increasing human-likeness of CAs.
Keywords	Conversational Agent; Chatbot; Dialogue System; Design Science, Design Theory; Literature Review

1.1 Introduction

Technological advances continue to drive the digital transformation and have been changing the ways in which we live, work and interact with each other (McAfee and Brynjolfsson 2017). Machine learning and natural language processing are essential components in this development, making machines seemingly intelligent with the capability to converse in natural language (Brynjolfsson and McAfee 2016). A promising trend in this development is the increasing use of natural language to interact with software instead of traditional graphical user interfaces (McTear et al. 2016). These conversational agents (CAs) offer a variety of applications ranging from digital personal assistants in mobile devices, such as Siri or Google Assistant, to CAs for specific purposes, like in-car assistance or customer service. Recent examples of Facebook and Google underline the popularity and potential of CAs. After launching its new Messenger platform, more than 100.000 bots emerged on Facebook within the first year (Johnson 2018). Moreover, Google demonstrated the potential of CAs in the near future at its 2018 developer conference by having their assistant autonomously making an appointment with a hairdresser in a phone conversation with a real person (Welch 2018).

For organizations, CAs exhibit the potential to automate and innovate processes and tasks, both internally and at the customer interface (Manyika et al. 2017), and companies introduce them in areas like human resources (Liao et al. 2018), marketing and sales (Vaccaro et al. 2018) or customer service (Gnewuch et al. 2017). To design and implement a CA, companies can select from a multitude of platforms, such as IBM Watson Conversation or Dialogflow by Google, that support the design of CAs through rich natural language processing capabilities and different options for enterprise integration (Diederich et al. 2019b).

Despite this potential and availability of platforms, many enterprise CAs fall behind expectations and disappear due to flaws related to their design, such as inadequate appearance, lack of conversational abilities or unrealizable user expectations (Luger and Sellen 2016; Ben Mimoun et al. 2012). Thus, building a successful CAs remains a major challenge in practice. In research, user interaction and CA design has been explored in a multitude of studies, particularly in the field of human-computer interaction (HCI) through experimental research, and a renewed interest recently emerged in the information systems (IS) research community (Saffarizadeh et al. 2017). In general, CA research in IS is in strong conjunction with studies in the field of HCI, which is often the case for prevailing research phenomena (Lee et al. 2018).

Many studies investigate selected aspects regarding a user's interaction with a CA, such as perceived authenticity or empathy, and offer valuable insights into their design, however, these results remain distributed over a multitude of studies. Consequently, the knowledge base for CA design is highly fragmented and difficult to access for researchers seeking to study and investigate successful CA design and for practitioners searching for guidance during their implementation. In this study, we set out to bring together these insights by reviewing IS and HCI literature and drawing on the components of design theory as a structural element to organize and synthesize prior work (Gregor and Jones 2007). Thus, we aim to contribute by providing structure to the emerging prescriptive knowledge base (Gregor and Hevner 2013) on CA design.

The remainder of the paper is organized as follows. We first provide an overview of conversational agents and introduce our design theoretical lens based on the work by Gregor and Jones (2007). Then, we describe our research approach and present the insights on CA design from the studies structured according to the six essential design theory components. Building on our review, we discuss the results on CA design that we brought together, state limitations of our work and opportunities for future research, and close the paper with concluding remarks.

1.2 Research Background

1.2.1 Conversational Agents

CAs are based on the idea of interacting with users through natural language like in human- to-human conversation (Nunamaker et al. 2011; Schuetzler et al. 2018a). Terms such as virtual assistants, chatbots or natural language systems are often used synonymously (Gnewuch et al. 2017; Morana et al. 2017). CAs can be distinguished by their primary communication mode, representation, and context (Gnewuch et al. 2017):

- *Communication mode:* CAs can communicate via voice (Cowan et al. 2015), text (Schroeder and Schroeder 2018), or both
- *Representation:* CAs can be disembodied (Araujo 2018), virtually embodied (Hasler et al. 2013) or physically embodied (Nunamaker et al. 2011)
- *Context:* CAs can be used for general-purpose conversations or be domain-specific, e.g. for a specific task or business function (Nunamaker et al. 2011)

In this study, we focus on the design of CA that primarily communicate with their users via written text, are disembodied or have a virtual embodiment, for example by means of a static or interactive avatar, and are used in a company context. The basic idea to interact through natural language already existed in the 1960s when ELIZA, the first CA, was developed by Joseph Weizenbaum (1966). Since then, multiple studies were conducted addressing the interaction with CAs regarding aspects such as user trust (Elson et al. 2018; Seeger et al. 2017), authenticity (Wünderlich and Paluch 2017) or empathy (Leite et al. 2013; McQuiggan and Lester 2007). CAs were studied in different contexts, such as for tasks like legal research (Sugumaran and Davis 2001), lie detection (Nunamaker et al. 2011), or data analytics (Matsushita et al. 2004). With regard to their application in organizations, recent research has been conducted in different business functions, such as human resources (Liao et al. 2018) or marketing and sales (Qiu and Benbasat 2009; Vaccaro et al. 2018). In practice, different CAs emerged over the years (Figure 11), such as IKEA's Anna (Wakefield 2016), and often disappeared as they could not fulfill expectations (Knijnenburg and Willemsen 2016).

Most CAs in the past exhibited limitations regarding both understanding a user's intent and providing purposeful feedback due to their reliance on simple pattern-matching (Berg 2015; Knijnenburg and Willemsen 2016). However, with advances in natural language processing as well as machine learning, CA capabilities have strongly increased in the last years and led to a renewed interest in both research and practice (Gnewuch et al. 2017; Oracle 2016). For example, the Dutch airline KLM introduced a CA that helps users to find and book flights (Vogel-Meijer 2018), clothing brand H&M created an interactive bot for product recommendations (Morana et al. 2017), and railroad company Amtrak offers customer service through Julie, which answers five million requests per year (NextIT 2018).

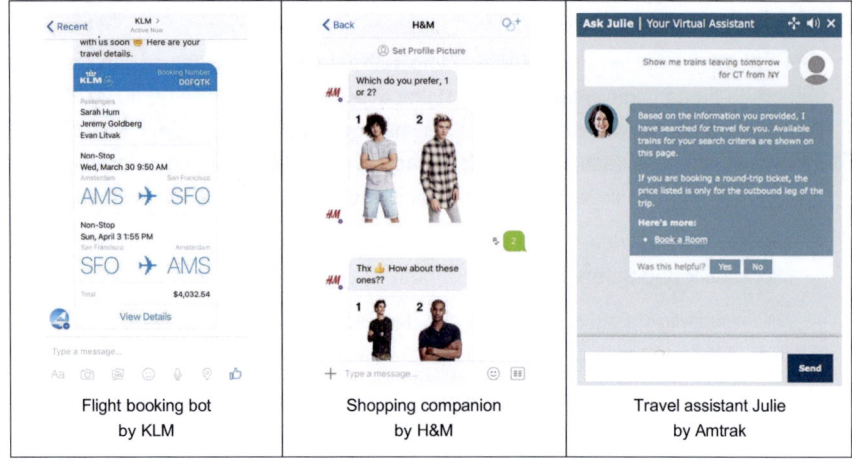

Figure 11 (Study 1): Examples for Enterprise CAs

1.2.2 Design Science and Design Theory

Theories that explicitly prescribe how to construct an artifact, for example, through methods or principles of form and function, called design theories (Gregor and Jones 2007), are an essential type of theory in IS research besides theories for analysis, explanation or prediction (Gregor 2006). A distinctive characteristic for design theories is the goal of maximizing utility, i.e. the use an artifact provides for a community of users and its consequently pragmatic nature (Hevner 2007; Iivari 2015). Various approaches exist to produce design theories (Mueller et al. 2014), for example, on the basis of heuristic theorizing (Gregory and Muntermann 2014) or through the iteration of different cycles regarding relevance, design and rigor as described by Hevner and colleagues (Hevner 2007; Hevner et al. 2004), which is one of the most commonly applied approaches (Mueller et al. 2014). The resulting artifact then contributes new solutions to known problems, applies existing solutions to new problems, or creates new solutions for new problems (Gregor and Hevner 2013). In this context, the contribution of design science research lies in the systematic formulation of design theories, such as how to solve certain problems (Gregor 2006). This knowledge can have different grades of maturity, ranging from a situated implementation to an abstract design theory (Gregor and Hevner 2013).

A design theory consists of six essential components according to Gregor and Jones (2007) as shown in Table 8. Two additional components of a design theory, principles of implementation and expository instantiation, refer to the actual implementation process and resulting artifact, which is not in the focus of this study as we seek to identify and bring together design knowledge regardless of the (technical) way in which the artifact is actually implemented. In this paper, we use the design theory components as a theoretical lens to structure and bring together knowledge on the design of CAs from existing studies. Thereby, researchers seeking to design CAs for organizations can more easily access the rather fragmented knowledge, use the components to guide their own research or identify gaps in the extant knowledge base.

Table 8 (Study 1): Components of a Design Theory (Gregor and Jones 2007)

Component	Description
Purpose and scope	What the system is for, the set of meta-requirements or goals that specifies the type of artifact to which the theory applies and in conjunction also defines the scope, or boundaries of the theory.
Constructs	Representations of the entities of interest in the theory.
Principles of form and function	The abstract "blueprint" or architecture that describes an IS artifact, either product or method/intervention.
Artifact mutability	The changes in state of the artifact anticipated in the theory, that is, what degree of artifact change is encompassed by the theory.

Component	Description
Testable propositions	Testable truth statements about the design theory.
Justificatory knowledge	The underlying knowledge or theory from the natural or social or design sciences that gives a basis and explanation for the design.

1.3 Research Approach

In order to gather existing studies on CAs and synthesize their results, we follow a process based on the combination of the guidelines for a systematic literature review by Webster and Watson (2002), vom Brocke et al. (2009) and Bandara et al. (2015). As our goal is to provide an organizing review of research on enterprise CA (Leidner 2018), we focus on the research outcomes of the studies in scope of this review and choose a conceptual organization (Cooper 1988) by means of design theory components (Gregor and Jones 2007). Our research approach consists of three phases, gathering the literature for the review, filtering studies on enterprise CAs, and coding the design theory components contained in the studies (Table 9).

Table 9 (Study 1): Research Approach Phases

	Phase 1: Gather literature	Phase 2: Filter studies	Phase 3: Extract components
Inputs	Search query	Literature database	Filtered literature database
Methods	Literature search	Closed coding	Closed coding
Steps	Conduct search and identify CA studies	Code CA characteristics and filter studies	Code design theory components
Results	Literature database	Filtered literature database	Design theory components

To initiate our literature review, we first identified the relevant outlets for our search process in phase 1. Extensive work on CAs was conducted in information systems (IS) and human-computer interaction (HCI) research (Gnewuch et al. 2017), thus we purposefully selected journals from these fields. For IS research, we focused on the Basket of Eight and for HCI we selected four well-regarded journals (Advances in Human-Computer Interaction, ACM Transactions on Computer-Human Interaction, Computers in Human Behavior and the International Journal of Human-Computer Studies) for our search. We extended these journals by high-quality conferences to take into account more recent work as CAs just gained a renewed interest in research a few years ago (Saffarizadeh et al. 2017; Wünderlich and Paluch 2017). Thus, we complemented our review with proceedings from major conferences in IS (ICIS, ECIS, HICSS, AMCIS, PACIS) and HCI (ACM CHI Conference on Human Factors in Computing Systems).

B. Studies on Anthropomorphic CAs

To gather studies, we used the Web of Science, AISeL, ACM Digital Library and the websites of the respective outlets. The search was conducted in August 2018 and has been updated in January 2019. The following search query was used:

((Conversational OR Interactive OR Virtual) AND Agent) OR Chatbot OR Digital Assistant)

The query returned 2.615 results in total for which we scanned titles and abstracts to identify studies with a focus on CAs. After this, 215 studies remained (Table 10, outlets in alphabetical order).

Table 10 (Study 1): Results from the Literature Search

Outlet	Search results	Focus on CA
ACM CHI Conference on Human Factors in Computing Systems	826	79
ACM Transactions on Computer-Human Interaction	33	5
Advances in Human-Computer Interaction	69	7
Americas Conference on Information Systems	349	5
Computers in Human Behavior	575	38
European Conference on Information Systems	97	2[1]
Hawaii International Conference on System Sciences	36	5
International Conference on Information Systems	103	13[1]
International Journal of Human-Computer Studies	403	52
Journal of Management Information Systems	3	3
Journal of the Association for Information Systems	-	2[1]
Pacific Asia Conference on Information Systems	99	4
Total	**2,593**	**215**

1) Identified through forward and backward search (partially)

In the second phase of our research, we subjected the 215 studies to a three-step filtering process. In the first step, we determined the primary mode of communication of the CA described in the studies. As enterprise CAs primarily communicate with users via written text (Gnewuch et al. 2017), we omitted studies that explicitly focus on the characteristics of speech-based communication. Second, we identified and omitted studies that deal with a physically embodied CAs, such as a robot that communicate with its users via natural language, as enterprise CAs are typically represented by virtual avatars (Wünderlich and Paluch 2017).

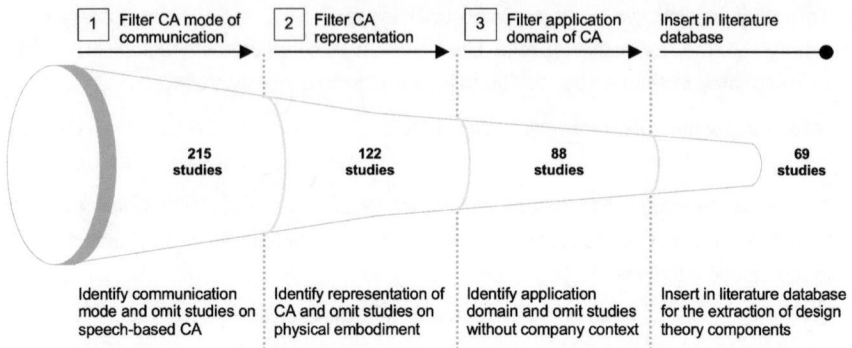

Figure 12 (Study 1): Literature Filtering Steps

In the last step, we considered the application domain of the studied CA in order to omit work that specifically deals with CAs in other contexts like education (e.g. Cheok et al. (2008)), or healthcare (e.g. Sundar et al. (2017)). After this coding and filtering process, our final literature database contained 69 studies. In the third phase, we coded the literature using the design theory components outlined in the research background, i.e. purpose and scope, constructs, principles of form and function, artifact mutability, testable propositions, and justificatory knowledge. Finally, we extracted and synthesized the design theory components.

1.4 Results

In the following sections, we present the results from our review structured along the six components of design theory (Gregor and Jones 2007). For every component, we summarize the results in a table and provide the corresponding references.

1.4.1 Purpose and Scope

The first design theory component, purpose and scope, essentially describes the intention behind the theory, its scope and boundaries (Gregor and Jones 2007). To structure the different purposes a CA can have, we follow the distinction of Chen et al. (2008), categorizing the purpose of IS into: informate, automate or transform. While two studies (Nguyen and Sidorova 2017; Saffarizadeh et al. 2017) see the purpose of CAs in information provision for individual tasks, most of the studies with explicitly stated purposes consider the scope of CAs as the automation of existing work (Table 11).

These studies consider collaborative settings (e.g. Balkanski and Hurault-Plantet 2000; Elson et al. 2018), handling customer service requests (e.g. Gnewuch et al. 2017; Wünderlich and Paluch 2017), providing information to new employees (Liao et al. 2018) or product recommendations in the context of marketing and sales (e.g. Qiu and Benbasat

2009; Wang and Benbasat 2005). Additionally, Fast et al. (2017) and Matsushita et al. (2004) investigate CAs that automate tasks related to data analytics. Finally, Abul et al. (2018) see the purpose of CAs in enhancing human cognition and intelligence, thus transforming how people conduct various tasks.

Table 11 (Study 1): Purpose and Scope of CAs

IS Role	Purpose	Reference
Informate	Information provision for individual tasks	Nguyen and Sidorova (2017), Saffarizadeh et al. (2017)
Automate	Automation in collaborative settings	Balkanski and Hurault-Plantet (2000), Elson et al. (2018), Le Bigot et al. (2007), Toxtli et al. (2018)
	Automation of customer service tasks	Araujo (2018), Gnewuch et al. (2018b, 2017), Hu et al. (2018), Quynh and Sidorova (2018), Wünderlich and Paluch (2017), Xu, Liu, Guo, Sinha, and Akkiraju (2017)
	Automation of marketing and sales tasks	Chattaraman et al. (2018), Chattaraman et al. (2012), Luger and Sellen (2016), Qiu and Benbasat (2009), Vaccaro, Agarwalla, Shivakumar, and Kumar (2018), Wang and Benbasat (2005)
	Automation of human resources tasks	Liao et al. (2018)
	Automation of data analytics tasks	Fast et al. (2017), Matsushita et al. (2004)
Transform	Transforming individual cognitive abilities	Abul et al. (2018)

1.4.2 Constructs

The reviewed studies exhibit different constructs or entities of interest for the researchers (Table 12). With regard to the first construct, authenticity, Wünderlich and Paluch (2017) investigate the effect of agent- and communication-related cues on authenticity perception by users of CAs. The second construct that we identified in our review, empathy, is used in three studies. For example, Xu et al. (2017) propose a design for a chatbot that utilizes sentiment analysis to provide empathetic responses to customer requests on social media, which in turn trigger positive emotional responses from users that might lead to a positive evaluation of the CA (Wakefield 2015). Furthermore, perceived human-likeness, or anthropomorphism, is used in multiple studies to measure how human-like a CA appears to its users while changing different CA characteristics, such as language style (Araujo 2018) or virtual representation (Gong 2008). Further studies focus on modality, i.e. the communication mode with which users interact with CAs, for example regarding a user's willingness to share personal information (Schroeder and Schroeder 2018) or the collaboration processes between humans and computer (Le Bigot et al. 2007). Another construct we found is persuasiveness, i.e. the ability of a CAs to persuade a user to do or believe a particular thing. For example, Adler, Iacobelli, and Gutstein (2016) explore the impact of different persuasive strategies on decision-making and their results indicate that an emotional positive approach might yield the best results regarding CAs persuasiveness. One of the most frequent constructs in user and CAs interaction is trust, for example in connection with judgments of agent expertise (Elson et al. 2018), communication mode (Schroeder and Schroeder 2018) and online product recommendations on retail websites (Vaccaro et al. 2018).

Table 12 (Study 1): Constructs

Construct	Reference	Description
Authenticity	Wünderlich and Paluch (2017)	Appearance of objects of art as what they are or what they claim to be
Empathy	Berry et al. (2005), Chiba and Ito (2012), Hu et al. (2018), Xu et al. (2017)	Being aware of and sensitive to feelings and thoughts of another without explicitly communicating them
Human likeness	Araujo (2018), Gnewuch et al. (2018b), Gong (2008), Schuetzler et al. (2018a), Tinwell and Sloan (2014)	Degree to which an being or artifact exhibits human-like characteristics
Modality	Le Bigot et al. (2007), Qiu and Benbasat (2009), Schroeder and Schroeder (2018)	Mode of communication via natural language (written or spoken)
Persuasiveness	Adler et al. (2016), Harjunen et al. (2018)	Quality of being able to make one want to do or believe a particular thing
Trust	Chattaraman et al. (2012, 2018), Elson et al. (2018), Saffarizadeh et al. (2017), Schroeder and Schroeder (2018), Vaccaro et al. (2018), Wang and Benbasat (2005)	Psychological state where one deliberately compromises the intention to accept vulnerability due to positive expectations of the intentions or behavior of another
Representation	Appel et al. (2012), Qiu and Benbasat (2009), Seymour et al. (2017), Wilson (2002)	Virtual representation of the CAs (e.g. by means of a static or interactive avatar)
Responsiveness	Chattaraman et al.(2018), Gnewuch et al. (2018b), Krämer et al. (2018), Schuetzler et al. (2018b)	Ability of the CAs to respond to the user's input in a responsive manner both in terms of content and timing
Self-disclosure	Saffarizadeh et al. (2017)	Voluntary sharing of any information about the self, e.g. thoughts, opinions, emotions or personal information
Social presence	Appel et al. (2012), Araujo (2018), Gnewuch et al. (2018b, 2017), Qiu and Benbasat (2009), Schuetzler et al. (2014, 2018b)	Feeling of personal, sociable and sensitive human contact conveyed through and within a medium
Social cues	Appel et al (2012), Gnewuch et al (2017), Mou, Xu, and Xia (2018), Seymour et al. (2017), Wünderlich and Paluch (2017)	Verbal or non-verbal hints, both positive and negative, such as (vocal) tone or facial expressions

Further studies place emphasis on the virtual representation of CA. For example, Qiu and Benbasat (2009) studied how an anthropomorphic interface affects a user's perceived social relationship with a CA and Seymour et al. (2017) explore interactive avatars in the context of user acceptance. Furthermore, responsiveness of a CA represents another construct used for example by Gnewuch et al. (2018b) with regard to CA response time and Schuetzler et al. (2018b) regarding follow-up questions asked by an agent. An additional construct used by Saffarizadeh et al. (2017) is self-disclosure by the CA. The authors study the effect of CA self-disclosure of the relationship between users' privacy concerns and their self-disclosure. Furthermore, many authors investigate social presence, for example in relation to user perception of the CA (Gnewuch et al. 2017), dynamically delayed responses (Gnewuch et al. 2018b), voice-communication (Qiu and Benbasat 2009), as well as adaptive responses depending on message content (Schuetzler et al. 2014). Finally, we find that social cues are of particular interest in the studies. For example, Gnewuch et al. (2017) state a fit between the cues produced by a CA and its context, as a key success factor for CA in customer service and Seymour et al. (2017) hypothesize that matching visual cues can contribute to a positive perception.

1.3.3 Principles of Form and Function

The authors of the studies at hand describe different principles of form, for example, regarding the representation of the CA, and function, such as the use of social cues (Table 13). A majority of these principles intend to make the CA seem more human-like, authentic and trustworthy through anthropomorphic interfaces (Qiu and Benbasat 2009; Schroeder and Schroeder 2018; Tinwell and Sloan 2014), social cues (Gnewuch et al. 2017; Wünderlich and Paluch 2017), and information self-disclosure.

Table 13 (Study 1): Principles of Form and Function

Principle	Reference
Increase the human-likeness of the CA through human features like a name, nationality, and gender, to improve trust and human-likeness.	Araujo (2018), Schroeder and Schroeder (2018), Tinwell and Sloan (2014)
Use social relationship building based on personalization to induce trust.	Wang and Benbasat (2005)
Equip the CA with conversational abilities to provide relevant responses to enhance social presence and increase perceived human-likeness.	Schuetzler et al. (2018b)
Provide the CA with agent-related social cues, such as an avatar and name, to increase perceived human-likeness and social presence.	Araujo (2018)
Let the CA use agent- and communication-related cues to make users infer authenticity and influence their attitude and behavior.	Wünderlich and Paluch (2017)
Increase the perceived human-likeness of the CA to enhance the user's willingness to repair misunderstandings in a dialogue.	Corti and Gillespie (2016)
Use adequate self-disclosure to increase the amount and depth of information a CA receives from the user.	Saffarizadeh et al. (2017)
Use anthropomorphic interface design, such as avatars, to enhance the social presence perceived by the user.	Qiu and Benbasat (2009)
Implement dynamic response times to facilitate a natural feeling in conversations and positively impact the CA perception by the user.	Gnewuch et al. (2018b)
Draw on positive emotional strategies to persuade users.	Adler et al. (2016)

Principle	Reference
Use natural language processing and enterprise system integration for natural communication and providing high-quality responses. Provide the CA with conversational abilities to deliver messages of situation-dependent length and segmentation for users. Let the CA make use of flexible conversation flows towards a specific goal with effective clarification, combination and error-handling. Use social cues that correspond to service agent characteristics, fit its context and manage user expectations toward CA capabilities.	Gnewuch et al. (2017)
Design the CA less responsive to avoid being too human-like and socially desirable responses when gathering sensitive information.	Schuetzler et al. (2018a)
Monitor response latency and pause times to detect deceptive user behavior.	Schuetzler et al. (2014)
Use automatic sentiment analysis of dialogue data to understand users' emotions and provide tailored responses	Hu et al. (2018), Xu et al. (2017)

1.4.4 Artifact Mutability

With regard to artifact mutability, or expected state changes of the CA over time, four aspects are described in the reviewed studies (Table 14). Elson et al. (2018) emphasize that CAs can learn about human behavior with regard to decision-making and adjust responses in order to mitigate bias in the user's analysis of problems and tasks. Saffarizadeh et al. (2017) describe that user and CA trust evolves through different states as they converse and share information via multiple interactions. Similarly, Wang and Benbasat (2005) highlight trust changes, both positive and negative, through interactions and their impact on how individuals use CAs. Furthermore, Schuetzler et al. (2018b) emphasize the need for continuous CA refinement over time in terms of responses, i.e. analyzing interaction logs to find areas where user input was not matched and extending CA responses accordingly.

Table 14 (Study 1): Statements of Artifact Mutability

Aspect	Reference	Description
Adjustment to individual user's tendency to defer recommendations	Elson et al. (2018)	CAs can be designed to consider human behavior in terms of decision-making and should be implemented in a way in which they mitigate bias in human decision-maker's analysis of problems
Enhancement of user self-disclosure over time	Saffarizadeh et al. (2017)	CAs can affect user self-disclosure by disclosing information about itself, thus going through different levels of user trust and information sharing
Trust in CA changes through multiple interactions	Wang and Benbasat (2005)	CA interactions shape initial trust beliefs positively or negatively over time, thus users will determine if and how they interact in the future
Continuous refinement of responses	Schuetzler et al. (2018b)	CA refinement can be conducted regularly by analyzing interaction logs to find areas where CAs failed to match user input and adjust responses

1.4.5 Testable Propositions

The authors of the reviewed studies formulated different hypotheses, which were often tested by means of laboratory experiments. These hypotheses cover the previously outlined constructs and make specific truth statements, which can inform the design of CAs. Table 15 summarizes the hypotheses that were verified, grouped by the main constructs they address. The formulation was standardized to improve readability.

Regarding the first construct, authenticity, Wünderlich and Paluch (2017) find a positive impact of CA authenticity on user's behavioral and attitudinal outcomes and emphasize the impact of social cues, both agent- and communication-related, on perceived authenticity. Concerning human-likeness, the results of Araujo (2018) indicate that a rather human-like CAs, implemented through design cues like name and language style, is associated with higher levels of mindful and mindless anthropomorphism compared to a CA that lacks these cues. Similarly, Gong (2008) finds that a more anthropomorphic representation leads to positive effects on social judgment and influence as well as perceived competency and trustworthiness. Concerning the communication mode of a CA, i.e. written or spoken natural language, the results of Schroeder and Schroeder (2018) show that voice-based communication positively impacts the willingness of a user to share personal information yet it does not affect anthropomorphism compared to reading the responses of a CA. Furthermore, one study (Adler et al. 2016) investigates the persuasive capabilities of a CA and finds that a strategy of positive, emotional persuasive statements works better than other, rational strategies. With regard to trust, four propositions can be found that emphasize the importance of this construct as it correlates with the perceived expertise of the CA, leads to relying on CA decisions when high uncertainty is involved, mitigates privacy concerns and contributes to a user's intentions to use and perceived usefulness of a CA (Elson et al. 2018; Saffarizadeh et al. 2017). Secondly, Qiu and Benbasat (2009) and Schuetzler et al. (2018b) highlight the positive effect of social presence on trusting beliefs, perceived enjoyment, perceived human-likeness and partner engagement. Concerning the virtual representation of CAs, Schuetzler et al. (2018a) showed that the visual embodiment of CAs increases socially desirable responding when posing sensitive questions and the experiment by Appel et al. (2012) indicates that a CA with a virtual representation leads to higher social effects than a CA with a simple text interface lacking an avatar. Additionally, different propositions are formulated in the studies regarding the responsiveness of a CA in terms of content, relevance as well as timing. Schuetzler et al. (2018a) find that increasing the responsiveness of a CA increases socially desirable responding, but only for sensitive topics, such as income or alcohol consumption. Schuetzler et al. (2018) propose that adaptive and relevant responses based on the content of a user's message increase the perceived human-likeness and social presence.

Table 15 (Study 1): Testable Propositions

	Proposition (P)	Reference
Authenticity	**P1:** Authenticity perception of the CA has a positive impact on users' behavioral and attitudinal outcomes. **P2:** Agent- and communication-related cues have an impact on users' authenticity perceptions.	Wünderlich and Paluch (2017)
Human-likeness	**P1:** A human-like CA is associated with higher levels of mindful and mindless anthropomorphism than a machine-like agent. **P2:** A more anthropomorphic CA representation receives more positive social judgment from users, exerts higher social influence, has a higher perceived competency and trustworthiness.	Araujo (2018) Gong (2008)
Modality	**P1:** Voice-based communication towards CA leads to higher willingness to share personal information than text-based communication. **P2:** Listening to a CA's voice does not affect anthropomorphism compared to reading.	Schroeder and Schroeder (2018)
Persuasiveness	**P1:** A CA that uses an emotional persuasive strategy is more successful than a rational one. **P2:** A CA that provides positive emotional statements is the most persuasive compared to other strategies.	(Adler et al. 2016)
Trust	**P1:** Judgement of CA expertise is highly correlated to the perceived trustworthiness. **P2:** In decision making tasks with high uncertainty, humans defer to the CA decision. **P3:** Trust mediates the relationship between privacy concerns and user self-disclosure. **P4:** Trusting beliefs in a CA positively affect perceived usefulness of the CA.	Elson et al. (2018) Saffarizadeh et al. (2017)
Representation	**P1:** Visual embodiment of a CA increases socially desirable responding. **P2:** A CA with a virtual representation leads to higher social effects than a CA without a virtual representation	Appel et al. (2012) Schuetzler et al. (2018a)
Responsiveness	**P1:** Increasing responsiveness of a CA increases user's socially desirable responding. **P2:** This influence on socially desirable responding exists only for sensitive questions. **P3:** Adapting responses based on message content results in higher perceived human-likeness. **P4:** Increased conversational relevance results in higher perceived partner human-likeness and higher perceived social presence. **P5:** Dynamically delayed responses yield higher perceived human-likeness, social presence and satisfaction than instant responses	Gnewuch et al. (2018b) Schuetzler et al. (2018a) Schuetzler et al. (2018b) Schuetzler et al. (2014)
Self-Disclosure	**P1:** CA self-disclosure positively affects user trust and user self-disclosure. **P2:** CA self-disclosure moderates the relationship between privacy concerns and user self-disclosure.	Saffarizadeh et al. (2017)
Social Presence	**P1:** Users' perceptions of social presence positively affect their trusting beliefs and perceived enjoyment. **P2:** Social presence leads to higher perceived human-likeness and partner engagement.	Qiu and Benbasat (2009) Schuetzler et al. (2018b)

Furthermore, Gnewuch et al. (2018b) test the impact of near-instant and dynamically delayed responses and suggest that dynamic delays lead to higher perceived human-likeness, social presence and user satisfaction than near-instant responses. With regard to self-disclosure, Saffarizadeh et al. (2017) confirm the hypothesis that self-disclosure by a CA positively affects user trust and self-disclosure apart from mitigating the effects of privacy concerns. Regarding the final construct, social presence, Qiu and Benbasat (2009) and Schuetzler et al. (2018b) propose that social presence positively affects users' trusting beliefs, perceived enjoyment, perceived human-likeness and engagement.

1.4.6 Justificatory Knowledge

Different justificatory knowledge underlies the studies reviewed in this analysis (Table 16). We find that the authors draw on six theories in their work: Social Response Theory and the Computers Are Social Actors (CASA) Paradigm (Nass and Moon 2000), the Cooperative Principle of Conversation (Grice 1975), the Theory of Uncanny Valley (Mori 1970; Mori et al. 2012), Self-Determination Theory (Ryan and Deci 2000), Social Penetration Theory (Altman et al. 1997), and the Theory of Collaborative Discourse (Grosz and Sidner 1986, 1990).

The main theory CA researchers refer to is Social Response Theory and the CASA paradigm (Nass and Moon 2000). Based on a review of three sets of experimental studies, Nass and Moon show that individuals mindlessly apply social rules and expectations to computers. CA researchers who draw on this theory and paradigm investigate human behavior toward CAs stemming from this paradigm, for example, by exploring how different genders of a CA (Qiu and Benbasat 2009) or different degrees of anthropomorphic CA representations (Gong 2008) are perceived. Design-oriented studies in this context argue to explicitly increase the human-likeness of CA, for example, by using anthropomorphic social cues (Araujo 2018; Gnewuch et al. 2017; Wünderlich and Paluch 2017) to increase social presence as well as induce further positive impacts, such as on user satisfaction.

A further theoretical concept underlying different CA studies is the Cooperative Principle of Conversation formulated by Grice (1975). The principle states that participants in a conversation are expected to observe a cooperative behavior regarding quantity (making a contribution that is informative), quality (making a contribution that is true), relation (making a contribution that is relevant) as well as manner (making a contribution that is socially adequate). The authors draw on these maxims in order to derive meta-requirements and initial design principles for CAs in a customer service context (Gnewuch et al. 2017) or to investigate whether popular CA follow these principles (Allwood et al. 2000). Additionally, Seymour et al. (2017), Gnewuch et al. (2017), and Tinwell and Sloan (2014) refer to the Theory of Uncanny Valley (Mori 1970) from robotics. The theory is concerned with the relation between user acceptance, or affinity, with regard to human-likeness of a robot (or software program). While increasing the human-likeness in general steadily increases affinity, there is one point with a sharp drop of affinity, the so-called Uncanny Valley, that takes place just before full anthropomorphism is reached, where robots and humans cannot be distinguished easily (Mori et al. 2012). For example, Seymour et al. (2017) suggest that interactivity, realized by means of an interactive 3D avatar that matches common human non-verbal cues, can contribute to overcoming the Uncanny Valley.

Table 16 (Study 1): Justificatory Knowledge Underlying the Studies

Theory	Reference	Description
Social Response Theory and Computers As Social Actors Paradigm	Appel et al. (2012), Araujo (2018), Chattaraman et al. (2018, 2012), Gnewuch et al. (2018b), Gnewuch et al. (2017), Gong (2008), Qiu and Benbasat (2009), Schuetzler et al. (2018a), Schuetzler et al. (2014)	Humans respond mindlessly socially to anything that shows human-like characteristics, incl. technology (Nass and Moon 2000)
Cooperative Principle of Conversation	Allwood, Traum, and Jokinen (2000), Danielescu and Christian (2018), Gnewuch et al. (2017)	Participants in a conversation are expected to follow a cooperative principle of conversation in terms of quantity, quality, relation, and manner (Grice 1975)
Theory of Uncanny Valley	Gnewuch et al. (2017), Seymour et al. (2017), Tinwell and Sloan (2014)	As realism of a robot increases, the human affinity increases as well, but only to a particular point where acceptance sharply drops before reaching the highest level of realism and human acceptance (Mori 1970; Mori et al. 2012)
Self-Determination Theory	Quynh and Sidorova (2018)	Macro theory for human motivation and personality that is concerned with the motivation behind choices people make without external influence (Ryan and Deci 2000)
Social Penetration Theory	Saffarizadeh et al. (2017)	Views personality as a multilayered element. As a relationship becomes stronger, more inner layers are unfolded and more information is shared (Altman et al. 1997)
Theory of Collaborative Discourse	Balkanski and Hurault-Plantet (2000)	Discourses, like other non-linguistic activities, involve different forms of collaborative behavior (Grosz and Sidner 1986, 1990)

Furthermore, Quynh and Sidorova (2018) draw on Social Determination Theory (SDT) in their laboratory experiment to investigate user satisfaction in comparison to traditional websites. SDT helps to examine the motivation choices people make (Ryan and Deci 2000) and has previously been applied in the context of e-learning (Roca and Gagné 2008). Social Penetration Theory (Altman et al. 1997) is applied by Saffarizadeh et al. (2017) in the context of user self-disclosure, trust and privacy with regard to CAs. Social Penetration theory is concerned with the development of relationships between individuals and regards personality as a multi-layered element where boundaries regarding breadth and depth of information disclosure relax over time as relationships between the individuals grow stronger. Based on a laboratory experiment, Saffarizadeh et al. (2017) find that active self-disclosure by the CA positively affects user trust and information disclosure. Finally, the Theory of Collaborative Discourse claims that discourses involve collaborative behavior (Grosz and Sidner 1986, 1990) which Balkanski and Hurault-Plantet (2000) use to build a model for cooperative human-machine communication in written dialogues.

1.5 Discussion

Our review brings together a rich body of research from IS and HCI journals as well as conferences on the design of conversational agents for enterprises. In the following, we discuss our results on the design of enterprise CAs, both with regard to their content as well as their contribution type, reflect on potential drawbacks from maximizing human-likeness of CAs, conceptualize areas for future research, and state practical implications for CA design.

1.5.1 Anthropomorphic Design of Conversational Agents

We observe that all studies emphasize the design of CAs as human-like as possible. As the traits and behavior of CAs include various social cues, such as a (human) name and virtual representation (Seeger et al. 2018) or delayed response times to simulate thinking of and typing a reply (Gnewuch et al. 2018b), they trigger social responses by their users (Moon 2003; Nass and Moon 2000), which in turn leads the user to form similar expectations towards the CA as to a human agent. These expectations need to be taken into consideration by designers that shape the traits and behavior of a CA in a conversation (Figure 13), which represents a fundamental challenge as user input varies strongly and simulating context-dependent, complex human behavior is a difficult endeavor (Følstad and Brandtzæg 2017).

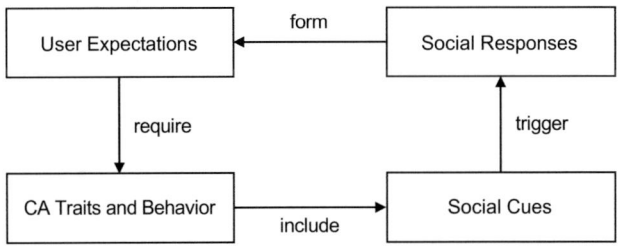

Figure 13 (Study 1): Circle of Anthropomorphic CA Design

In order to increase the degree of human-likeness of CAs in an enterprise context, different principles of form and function have been formulated in the reviewed studies (Table 13). These principles aim to increase the perceived authenticity, empathy, persuasiveness, and responsiveness of CAs, improve their human-like representation, induce user trust and facilitate a higher information disclosure by users, which ultimately increases the human-likeness of CAs (Figure 14). Six different kernel theories are used in the reviewed studies to inform the formulation of design principles and investigate human-CA interaction. In the context of CA research, we can consider Social Response Theory (Moon 2003; Nass and Moon 2000) as well as the Theory of Uncanny Valley (Mori et al. 2012) as grand theories which provide the fundamental basis for CA design. Furthermore, Social Penetration Theory (Altman et al. 1997), the Theory of Collaborative Discourse (Grosz and Sidner 1986, 1990), the Cooperative Principles of Conversation (Grice 1975), and Self-Determination Theory (Ryan and Deci 2000), all adapted from human-to-human communication, facilitate the formulation of principles that increase the responsiveness of CAs, thus representing mid-range theories in this context with a focus on a single construct.

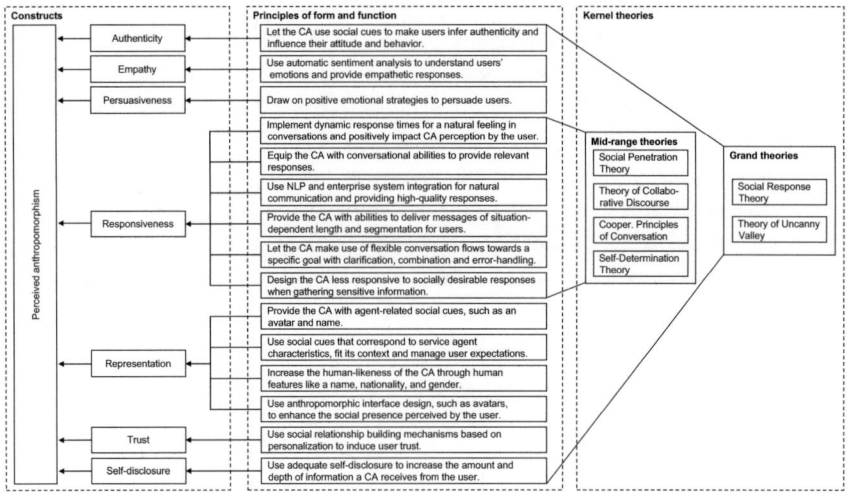

Figure 14 (Study 1): Constructs, Principles and Kernel Theories for CA Design

The constructs and principles of form and function reveal that the responsiveness of the CA as well as its representation are the main focus of current research, which appears to be obvious as one can expect human-like CA to be able to respond in a conversation like a real person would do and to share characteristics with humans regarding the representation, such as a name or avatar. Without the basic cues (human-like responsiveness and representation) users would not anthropomorphize the CA. The further constructs, such as authenticity and empathy are primarily relevant in specific contexts (e.g. empathy to handle frustrated customers) and therefore less often studied. Current research is primarily focused on either applying many different CA design principles to reach a certain outcome (design science) or understand the relation of a single design principle and its related construct on the perceived anthropomorphism (behavioral research). However, the relations between constructs and their collective impact on perceived anthropomorphism has yet to be investigated. Following this line of thought, we propose a research framework (Figure 15) that conceptualizes the relations among constructs. The group of first-order constructs include the primary features a CA has to have to function, that is a high level of responsiveness and an adequate representation. Complementary, second-order constructs are features that a CA can have, but they are not essential for general CA design and are context specific.

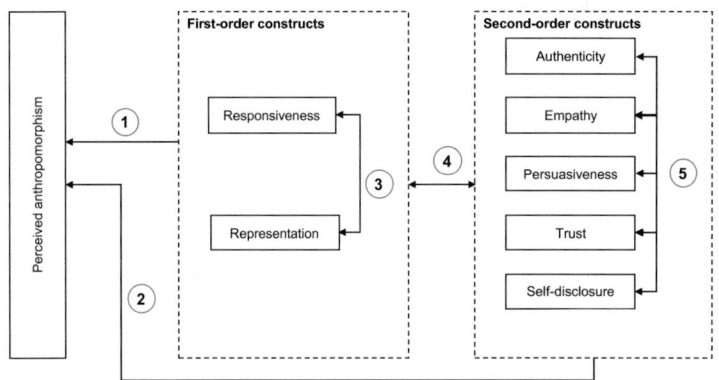

Figure 15 (Study 1): Proposed Research Framework

Based on our analysis, relations (1) and (2) are the most frequently researched ones, the other relations are yet to be addressed. Relation (3) addresses the interplay between responsiveness and representation. The main question for this relation is how to align a seemingly human representation of a CA with the responses that a CA provides in order to simulate human behavior that conforms to the user's perspective. Within the second-order constructs, relation (5) addresses the effects between the individual constructs. In this relation, one could investigate whether we can design a CA that is empathetic and trustworthy while at the same time having a high degree of persuasiveness. Lastly, we see great potential in investigating how first-order and second-order constructs influence each other (relation 4). An exemplary study to research this relation can be to alter the demeanor of the CA in order to increase its persuasiveness or empathy as done by Nunamaker et al. (2011) for physically embodied CA in the context of automated interviewing. We believe that addressing these relations can deepen our practical understanding of why some CAs fail to fulfill their intended purpose and provide the basis for incrementally increasing the degree of anthropomorphism of enterprise CAs.

1.5.2 Contribution Types of CA Design Research

The valuable contributions of the reviewed studies were generated with different research foci and approaches, such as the testing of relationships among constructs by means of laboratory experiments or design science research (Hevner et al. 2004) including an evaluation of the artifact in the field. The contributions thus vary with regard to the degree of abstraction, completeness and maturity of produced knowledge. Drawing on the idea of different levels of contribution types in design science research described by Gregor and Hevner (2013), we observe three main types of articles: First, 43 of the 69 studies investigate the relationship among selected constructs, such as the relationship between the relevance of CA statements in a conversation and human-likeness (Schuetzler et al. 2018b) or the availability of social cues on users' authenticity perceptions (Wünderlich and Paluch 2017). These studies do not specify a (narrow) context in which the supported hypotheses apply but emphasize a specific aspect of user-CA interaction in general, thus offering a higher degree of abstraction yet a lower level of completeness of knowledge. Second, six of the reviewed articles provide design principles or architecture descriptions, often with an expository instantiation, for CA design in a specific context, such as a tone-aware CA for customer service (Hu et al. 2018) or as a digital shopping assistant (Vaccaro et al. 2018). These prescriptive principles and architectures are rather complete descriptions of how to design a CA, however, exhibit a lower level of abstraction as they focus on a specific context. Thus, we consider both contribution types, context-specific operational principles/architecture and descriptions of context-independent relationships among constructs, to be on level 2 (Figure 16).

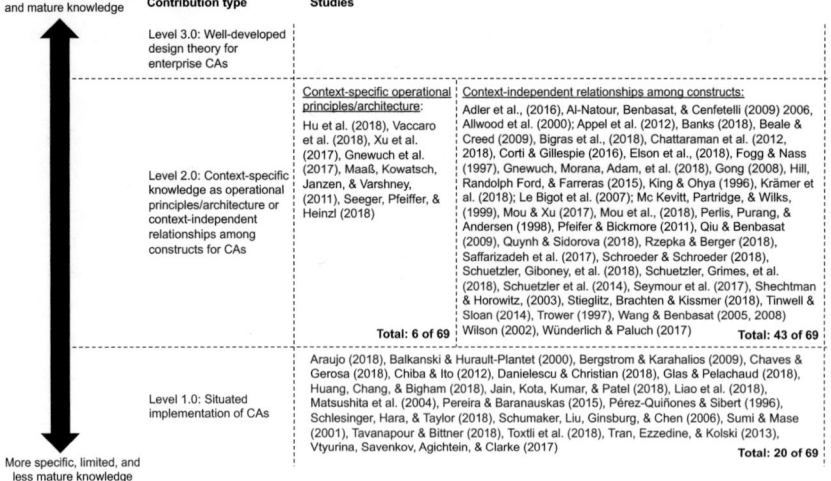

Figure 16 (Study 1): Contribution Types of the Reviewed Studies

Third, we consider 20 of the 69 studies to be situated implementations of CA, such as the crowd-powered conversational assistant Evorus (Huang et al. 2018) or the chatbot for idea platforms presented by Tavanapour and Bittner (2018). These studies contribute prototypical implementations in a specific, often innovative context, without the description detailed design principles or systematic evaluation of the designed artifact. Overall, those contribution types highlight that the design of and interaction with CA is an emerging research topic in the IS and HCI discipline (Morana et al. 2017; Seeger et al. 2018) where complete and mature prescriptive knowledge for design still needs to be developed, particularly through continuous synthesis of knowledge on specific aspects of CA design and the abstraction of design principles and architecture descriptions from specific contexts.

1.5.3 Going in (and hopefully out) the Uncanny Valley

As of now, researchers draw on Social Response theory (Moon 2003; Nass and Moon 2000) and suggest different features, such as social cues or human-like virtual embodiment, to enhance the human-likeness of CA as well as other aspects, such as user satisfaction. While we agree that this is certainly beneficial to increase user affinity and acceptance, we also recommend treating this tendency with caution. Different studies indicate potential risks of increasing human-likeness like users feeling insecure or even threatened and creating unrealistic expectations towards CA capabilities (Candello et al. 2017; Klopfenstein et al. 2017; Waytz and Norton 2014).

The theory of Uncanny Valley from robotics describes this aspect through a sharp drop in affinity and user acceptance before humans and robots, or CA, become indistinguishable (Mori et al. 2012). While few of the studies reviewed here refer to this theory (Gnewuch et al. 2017; Seymour et al. 2017; Tinwell and Sloan 2014), several authors indicate potential unintended outcomes of enhancing human-likeness (Gnewuch et al. 2018b; Schroeder and Schroeder 2018; Schuetzler et al. 2018b; Strait et al. 2015). For example, Schroeder and Schroeder (2018) describe that increasing human-likeness does not linearly increase with trust, but that users may feel threatened at one point. While most studies considered only one or few constructs, such as varying the virtual embodiment or the response time, future research can benefit from using several constructs to increase human-likeness of CAs as far as possible. This will allow an investigation of the interaction between constructs and better understand where the Uncanny Valley might come into play, as well as how this can be mitigated.

1.5.4 Building Enterprise Conversational Agents in Practice

For practice, our work offers three main insights for the design of CAs. First, the design theory components outlined in this study can be used to inform the design, particularly through the principles of form and function, by means of concrete features that can be implemented, such as sentiment detection to equip a CA with empathetic responses in customer service. Second, the constructs and testable propositions foster a better understanding of potentially reluctant user behavior in practice and provide recommendations for counter-measures, such as increase CA self-disclosure with artificial thoughts and emotions to improve the trust of users in CAs. Finally, our synthesis showed that practitioners should carefully consider the intended purpose of the CA and its context during the design process in order to avoid contributing to unintended user behavior, such as socially desirable responding when trying to elicit sensitive information.

1.5.5 Limitations and Opportunities for Future Research

Our work is not free of limitations and offers possibilities for future studies. The design theory components brought together in this paper exhibit various details and greater complexity that could not be discussed here. For example, the construct of trust in IT artifacts has long been investigated in IS research (Gefen et al. 2003; Lankton et al. 2015) and can be decomposed further into factors such as emotional and cognitive trust (Komiak and Benbasat 2006). Another example are social cues which can be decomposed into different types, such as physical, psychological, language, social dynamics and social roles (Fogg 2003). We suggest that future CA design research, for which different aspects exhibit particular relevance, such as user trust in a CA for sharing personal or sensitive information, places emphasis on these constructs and relevant insights in greater detail.

In addition to a more precise understanding of single constructs, we recommend to transfer existing design knowledge to new domains, for example to adapt existing design principles from customer service (Gnewuch et al. 2017; Hu et al. 2018) to further areas, such as human resources or marketing and sales in order to both identify commonalities and differences. Useful design features across contexts could then be abstracted, contributing to a better understanding of CA design for enterprises in general. Designing CA for specific contexts and abstracting the context-independent knowledge could potentially move CA design from individual implementations to a design that rather resembles the content management systems of websites where modules can be flexibly customized and added.

1.6 Concluding Remarks

The aim of this study was to systematically bring together prior work in IS and HCI research to inform the design of CA and thus add to the growing knowledge base on this interesting phenomenon. Using a design theoretical lens, we synthesize the results of 69 studies on CA design in an enterprise context and contribute a consolidated set of constructs, design principles and kernel theories for anthropomorphic CA design. While research on anthropomorphic CA design is still in its infancy, having lower levels of abstraction or a narrow focus either on specific design elements or application contexts, we observe a mix of studies that emphasize the groundwork of human communication, such as providing relevant and adequate responses, and studies exploring the intricacies of human-to-human dialogues like being empathetic or persuasive. Continuously synthesizing this emerging design knowledge can allow us to build CA that become better and better at simulating situation-dependent human-like communication behavior in different application domains.

We believe that CA in the context of our research, in particular due to the lack of a physical embodiment and communication via written text, represent a great and early opportunity to understand the potentials and risks associated with increasing the human-likeness of machines up to a point where they become indistinguishable from humans and understand where we might go in and out the Uncanny Valley.

II. Understanding Technological Limitations

The previous chapter provided the foundation for this research endeavor by increasing the accessibility of existing knowledge on CAs and their design. The following chapter adds to this knowledge base by focusing on the technological limitations of CAs, particularly with regard to limited conversational capabilities, and their impact on their perception by users.

Specifically, Study 2 investigates the impact of response failure by a CA in conversation (i.e. the inability to provide a meaningful, informative reply) on the judgment of the agent regarding the perception of anthropomorphism as well as the satisfaction with the overall service encounter. Building on the insights concerning the impact of response failure, Study 3 then investigates the use of preset answer options (i.e. suggestions in a conversation in the form of graphical buttons) as an approach to mitigate situations where a CA is not able to provide a meaningful response.

1. Study 2: Not Human After All – Exploring the Impact of Response Failure on User Perception of Anthropomorphic Conversational Service Agents

Table 17: Fact Sheet of Study 2

Title	Not Human After All: Exploring the Impact of Response Failure on User Perception of Anthropomorphic Conversational Service Agents
Authors	Stephan Diederich*, Tim-Benjamin Lembcke, Alfred Benedikt Brendel, Lutz M. Kolbe Chair of Information Management, University of Göttingen, Platz der Göttinger Sieben 5, 37073 Göttingen, Germany *Corresponding author. Tel.: +49 551 3921170. E-Mail: stephan.diederich@stud.uni-goettingen.de
Outlet	European Conference on Information Systems (ECIS), Marrakech, Morocco, 2020
Abstract	Conversational agents (CAs) have attracted the interest of organizations due to their potential for automated service provision combined with the feeling of a human-like interaction. Emerging studies on CAs indicate a positive impact of humanness on customer perceptions and explore approaches for their anthropomorphic design, comprising both appearance and behavior of the agent. While these studies provide valuable knowledge on how to design human-like CAs, we still lack an understanding of the limited conversational capabilities of this technology and their impact on user perception. Oftentimes, these limitations lead to frustrated users and discontinued CAs in practice. We address this gap by investigating the impact of response failure, understood as the inability of a CA to provide a meaningful reply, in a service context drawing on Social Response Theory and the Theory of Uncanny Valley. By means of an experiment with 169 participants, we find that (1) response failure is detrimental to the perception of humanness and increases feelings of uncanniness, (2) humanness (uncanniness) positively (negatively) influences familiarity and service satisfaction, and (3) the negative impact of response failure on user perception is significant yet it does not lead to a sharp drop as posited by the Theory of Uncanny Valley.
Keywords	Conversational Agent; Anthropomorphic Design; Social Response Theory; Theory of Uncanny Valley

1.1 Introduction

Conversational agents (CAs), defined as technological artifacts with which users interact through natural language (McTear et al. 2016), continue to gain interest in research (Maedche et al. 2019) and practice (Oracle 2016) alike. Praised for their potential to provide a human-like interaction experience, CAs are increasingly used in private as well as professional life. From a theoretical perspective, CAs are a particular interesting phenomenon as humans show social responses to these agents (Pfeuffer et al. 2019a). As posited by Social Response Theory (Nass and Moon 2000; Reeves and Nass 1996), the manifold social cues of CAs, such as the interaction via natural language, having a name and (human-like) avatar, or the expression of emotions through verbal and non-verbal communication, trigger social responses and lead users to anthropomorphize CAs (Seeger et al. 2018). Emerging design-oriented studies on human-like CAs provide valuable knowledge on the impact of social cues on user perception of humanness. Moreover, different research suggests further, mostly positive, effects, such as on service satisfaction (Diederich et al. 2019d; Gnewuch et al. 2018b), likability (Bickmore and Picard 2005), or trust (Cowell and Stanney 2005). To make these artifacts appear as human-like as possible, the growing knowledge base for anthropomorphic CA design offers a variety of social cues that can be incorporated in the design (Feine et al. 2019a).

While these studies provide valuable knowledge for crafting CAs with a human-like appearance and behavior, the current debate for anthropomorphic design neglects the practical problem of limited conversational capabilities. As these studies were primarily carried out by means of experimental research where users were given a specific set of tasks or interacted with a human in a Wizard-of-Oz setting (Diederich et al. 2019a), the CAs were able to provide relevant responses to the users' requests. In practice, however, designing agents that continuously offer meaningful responses in an evolving dialogue represents a major challenge (Følstad and Brandtzæg 2017). In fact, many CAs were discontinued particularly due to their inability to adequately respond to varying user input (Ben Mimoun et al. 2012). As anticipating user requests for natural language software is a challenging endeavor due to the unpredictability of such interactions, situations where a CA needs to provide some kind of fallback response are likely to occur and could remind users that they are still interacting with a machine that has limited capabilities (Ashktorab et al. 2019). Such failure to provide a meaningful reply might be detrimental to perceptions of humanness and further positive effects, thus diminishing the impact of social cues incorporated in the agent's design.

In our study, we seek to address this issue by investigating the impact of response failure on user perception with the following research question: *How does failure to provide a meaningful response influence user perception of anthropomorphic CAs in a service encounter?* Drawing on extant studies on anthropomorphic design of CAs, Social

Response Theory and Theory of Uncanny Valley, we develop a research model comprising eight hypotheses and test it in a 2x2 experiment with n = 169 participants and a between-subjects design. Our research makes three main contributions: First, it advances our understanding of the influence of response failure due to limited conversational capabilities on the perception of humanness and uncanniness of an agent. Second, the study demonstrates the positive (negative) impact of humanness (uncanniness) on familiarity and service satisfaction. Third, our experiment allows to better understand the magnitude of the effect of modest response failure on user perception of the CA, particularly depending on the agent's design.

We continue by outlining related work on anthropomorphic CA design and providing the theoretical background for our work. Afterwards, we derive eight hypotheses, introduce our research model, and describe the design of the experiment. We then present the results, discuss implications for the design of human-like CAs, and highlight limitations as well as directions for future research before closing with concluding remarks.

1.2 Related Work and Theoretical Background

The idea to interact with technology via natural language instead of graphical user interfaces emerged already in the 1960s (Weizenbaum 1966). However, it regained interest just a few years ago when advances in natural language processing and machine learning substantially increased the (conversational) capabilities of such technologies (McTear 2017). Today, conversational agents, defined as software with which users interact through natural language (McTear et al. 2016), are increasingly permeating our private and professional lives (Maedche et al. 2019) in various areas, such as customer service (Hu et al. 2018), marketing and sales (Vaccaro et al. 2018), human resources (Liao et al. 2018), financial advisory (Dolata et al. 2019), education (Crockett et al. 2017), healthcare (Meier et al. 2019), or individual task assistance (Son and Wonseok 2018).

In addition to these application areas, the different forms of CAs can be distinguished by their primary mode of communication and embodiment. In general, technology interaction through natural language can take place in spoken form, such as with Amazon's Alexa or Apple's Siri, or via written text like with chatbots on company websites or social media (Gnewuch et al. 2017). Furthermore, CAs can be physically embodied like service robots (Stock et al. 2019; Stock and Merkle 2018), have a virtual static avatar (Wünderlich and Paluch 2017), a virtual interactive avatar (Beer et al. 2015), or be disembodied, i.e. without any form of avatar at all (Araujo 2018). In this study, we focus on a CA with which users communicate via written text (chatbot) and a static virtual avatar (image) in a customer service context.

1.2.1 Conversational Service Agents and their Responsiveness

Customer service is currently one of the most popular application areas for CAs in enterprises where such agents can fulfill requests like handling complaints or providing product information (Gnewuch et al. 2017). While current CAs primarily cover rather simple, frequent, and repetitive service requests, they are expected to support or even fully assume increasingly complex tasks currently performed by human service personnel (Marinova et al. 2017; Verhagen et al. 2014). As technological components of service systems, CAs are positioned between current service technology that is always available but lacks the feeling of a human interaction, such as online portals for self-service, and human service provision, offering a personal contact but with limited availability. In practice, different examples for CAs in a service context can be found across industries (Oracle 2016). For example, the American railroad company Amtrak introduced the virtual agent "Julie" which now answers more than five million customer requests per year (NextIT 2018). Similarly, the clothing brand H&M offers an artificial sales agent that provides individual product recommendations which can be directly purchased from the company's online store (Morana et al. 2017). This popularity is further underlined by the example of Facebook where more than 100.000 agents were deployed in the first year after opening the Messenger platform (Johnson 2018).

Despite their popularity and success stories, many CAs fell behind high expectations in the past (Luger and Sellen 2016) and were often discontinued because of flaws related to their design (Ben Mimoun et al. 2012). In an assessment of 80 conversational agents on French commercial websites, Ben Mimoun et al. (2012) identified inadequate appearance and a lack of interactivity as well as intelligence as reasons for CA failure. The authors argue that a mismatch between the human-like appearance of CAs and their actual service possibilities as well as competence leads to negative customer reactions due to unfulfilled, high expectations. Likewise, Luger and Sellen (2016, p. 5286) find "user expectations dramatically out of step with the operation of the systems, particular in terms of known machine intelligence, system capabilities and goals". Hence, both studies suggest a gap between user expectations and technical capabilities as a main reason for negative perception of CAs and suggest different design approaches to manage user expectations more adequately.

Against this background, Følstad and Brandtzæg (2017) emphasize that a natural language interface resembles a blank canvas where the capabilities of the system are mostly hidden from the user and that designers need to anticipate a much larger variety of input compared to graphical user interfaces. Consequently, the authors argue that fallbacks in a conversation are likely to occur (Følstad and Brandtzæg 2017). Similarly, Go and Sundar (2019) highlight that equipping a CA with the ability to provide meaningful responses, contingent on what has already been communicated in a conversation, represents a substantial design issue.

Overall, we observe a growing popularity of CAs in a service context yet the implementation of sufficient conversational capabilities to respond to highly varying user input represents a major design challenge and leaves room for response failures in the interaction.

1.2.2 Social Response Theory and the Uncanny Valley in the Context of CAs

A key theory underlying the design of and interaction with CAs is Social Response Theory (Nass and Moon 2000; Reeves and Nass 1996). Social Response Theory posits that humans apply social rules as well as expectations to technology that exhibits traits or behavior usually associated with humans (Nass and Moon 2000). In a set of experiments, Nass and Moon (2000) discovered that humans overuse social categories, such as gender, and social behaviors, for example reciprocity, in an interaction with an anthropomorphic artifact. According to the researchers, the more human characteristics are present in a technological artifact, the stronger it leads to social responses (Nass and Moon 2000). As CAs typically exhibit a variety of social cues (Feine et al. 2019a), ranging from basic cues like the interaction via natural language and turn-taking in a conversation to more complex ones, such as understanding and expressing emotions, they trigger substantial social responses by humans. As suggested by Seeger et al. (2018), anthropomorphic design of CAs comprises social cues in three different dimensions: A human identity (e.g. age, gender, ethnicity), verbal cues (e.g. syntax and word variability or the use of self-references in a conversation), and non-verbal cues (e.g. response delays to indicate thinking or the use of emoticons to express emotions). In short, designers have various social cues at their disposal to make CAs seem as human-like as possible (Feine et al. 2019a).

Recent experiments on the perception of anthropomorphic CAs have mostly discovered positive effects of a human-like design, such as on social presence (Pereira et al. 2014), trustworthiness (Araujo 2018), persuasiveness (Gong 2008), enjoyment (Liao et al. 2018), or service satisfaction (Gnewuch et al. 2018b). However, some studies also indicate unintended potential negative effects. For example, Wünderlich and Paluch (2017) describe a risk of perceived uncertainty as to whether the user interacts with a machine or an actual human. Furthermore, Sohn (2019) discovers increased privacy concerns due to the mere presence of an anthropomorphic agent on an e-commerce website. In addition, Seeger et al. (2018) assume a negative effect on the perception of anthropomorphism in a CA when a CA includes social cues from all three aforementioned dimensions. Thus, the authors suggest to find an appealing combination of social cues instead of a "more is more" approach.

Against this background, Mori (1970) hypothesized on the relationship between human-like objects and affinity (or familiarity, as it is often translated from the original Japanese manuscript) decades ago in the Theory of Uncanny Valley. The theory, originally from the field of robotics, posits that there is no linear relationship between human-likeness of an object and positive emotional responses by humans to it, but that a sharp drop in affinity or familiarity exists before the object becomes fully human-like. MacDorman et al. (2009, p.2) describe this as a shift of human attention from the human-like qualities to the aspects that seem to be inhuman by stating that "as something looks more human it looks also more agreeable, until it comes to look so human that we start to find its nonhuman imperfections unsettling". This negative reaction termed as the Uncanny Valley comprises strong feelings of uncanniness due to the nonhuman imperfections of an object (MacDorman et al. 2009). Figure 17 depicts the Uncanny Valley as conceptualized by Mori (1970).

In the remainder of this study, we consider the ideas of Social Response Theory and the Theory of Uncanny Valley to explore the effects of practical response failures on the perception of human-like CAs in a service context.

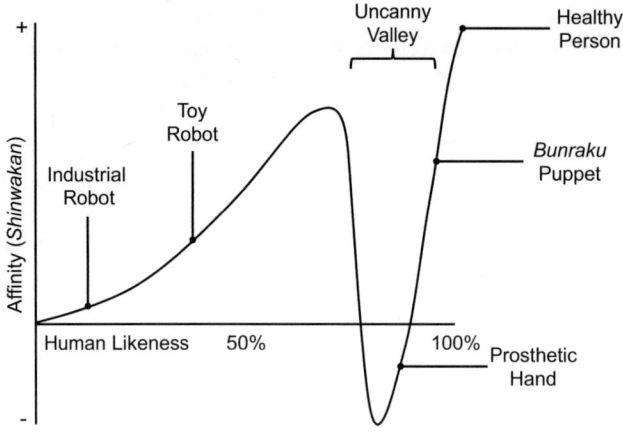

Figure 17 (Study 2): The Uncanny Valley

1.3 Hypotheses and Research Model

Our study aims for a better understanding of the impact of response failure by a human-like conversational agent in a natural language dialogue. For this purpose, we propose a research model comprising eight hypotheses. Drawing on Social Response Theory (Nass and Moon 2000; Reeves and Nass 1996), a human-like appearance and behavior by a technological artifact triggers social responses in humans. As Nass and Moon (2000) argue, the more technological artifacts, such as a computer, exhibit human-like characteristics, the more likely they trigger social reactions. In the context of CAs, emerging studies on anthropomorphic design indicate that social cues lead to perception of humanness in the interaction (Feine et al. 2019a; Wünderlich and Paluch 2017). In line with these studies and Social Response Theory, we first hypothesize:

H1:   Social cues have a positive impact on humanness of the agent.

Second, we propose that an appealing combination of social cues, comprising a human identity of the agent as well as verbal and non-verbal cues (Seeger et al. 2018), reduces feelings of uncanniness when interacting with the agent. Different studies on anthropomorphic design indicate positive effects of social cues, such as on likability (Bickmore and Picard 2005; Cowell and Stanney 2005), trust (Nunamaker et al. 2011; de Visser et al. 2016) or enjoyment (Qiu and Benbasat 2010). Thus, we suggest that social cues reduce feelings of uncanniness when interacting with a CA.

H2:   Social cues have a negative impact on uncanniness of the agent.

Against the background of the Theory of Uncanny Valley, Mori et al. (2012, p. 98) hypothesize that a "person's response to a humanlike robot would abruptly shift from empathy to revulsion as it approached, but failed to attain, a lifelike appearance". While there can be many reasons why a CA may not be able to sustain a human-like appearance in a dialogue, we argue that one of the most likely reasons is the inability to provide a meaningful response due to the complexity and unpredictability of user input in a natural language interaction (Følstad and Brandtzæg 2017). As a result, this failure to respond would shift a user's attention to the fact that she or he is not interacting with an actual human, decreasing the perception of humanness in the conversation:

H3:   Response failure has a negative impact on humanness of the agent.

We additionally expect an agent's inability to provide a meaningful response to induce feelings of uncanniness (Tinwell and Sloan 2014) as it constitutes a strange situation that does not conform with the users expectations towards a human-like conversation (Luger and Sellen 2016). Thus, we formulate our fourth hypothesis as follows:

H4:   Response failure has a positive impact on uncanniness of the agent.

Furthermore, anthropomorphized artifacts have been known for their ability to induce feelings of familiarity (Epley et al. 2007) because anthropomorphic cues make it easier for the user to connect with the technology, potentially even on a personal level (Burgoon et al. 2000). Hence, we suggest that perception of humanness in an artifact positively impacts familiarity:

H5: Humanness has a positive effect on familiarity of the agent.

Next, we consider the relation between uncanniness and familiarity. Based on a similar reasoning as for the fifth hypothesis, we argue that feelings of uncanniness in the interaction are detrimental to familiarity in line with the Theory of Uncanny Valley (Mori 1970; Mori et al. 2012):

H6: Uncanniness has a negative impact on familiarity of the agent.

Finally, different studies on CAs in a service context argue for a positive relation between social cues, such as dynamic response delays to indicate thinking and typing of an agent response (Gnewuch et al. 2018b) or sentiment-adaptive responses to emulate empathy (Hu et al. 2018) and associated perceptions of humanness on service satisfaction. Similarly, we expect negative feelings of uncanniness to be detrimental to service satisfaction. Thus, we hypothesize:

H7: Humanness has a positive impact on service satisfaction.

H8: Uncanniness has a negative impact on service satisfaction.

Figure 18 summarizes our eight hypotheses and visualizes the research model.

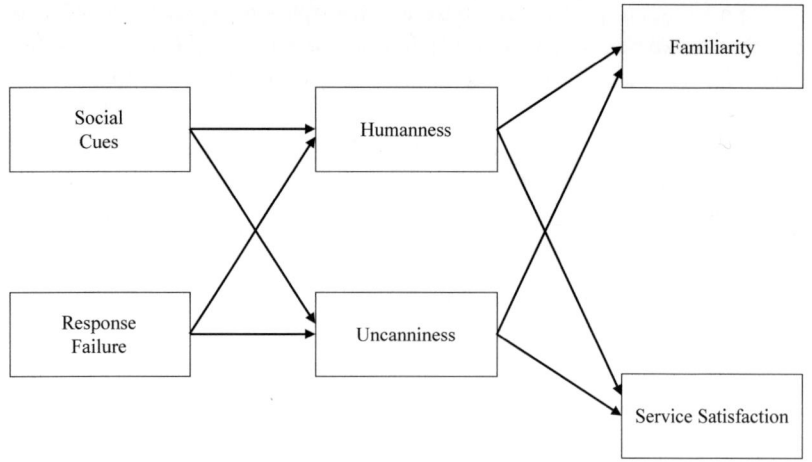

Figure 18 (Study 2): Research Model

1.4 Research Design

We tested our hypotheses regarding anthropomorphic design and response failure in an online experiment with a text-based CA. To provide a familiar and understandable context and task, we selected a customer service setting with an online retailer. In the following, we describe the data collection procedure and sample, the four experimental conditions, the manipulation check, as well as the measures used in the post-experimental survey.

1.4.1 Data Collection Procedure and Sample

The participants of our experiment were asked to interact with a virtual service agent of a fictitious online retailer to track and cancel an existing order as well as to ask for a confirmation. Every participant received a link to a briefing website in which we described the context of the experiment (online retailer), the structure (interaction with a virtual customer service agent followed by a questionnaire) as well as the participant's tasks. The tasks comprised contacting the service agent and finding out the current order status for a given identification number, authenticating with the agent, asking for order cancellation as well requesting a confirmation via e-mail. Similar to recent studies on CAs (e.g. Gnewuch et al. 2018b; Diederich et al. 2019d), we selected a rather specific set of tasks to enable a structured, comparable dialogue across the conditions and contribute to the responsiveness of the agent in the interaction. After successful completion of the last task, the CA provided a link to the questionnaire. Overall, participation in the experiment took around nine minutes.

Our sample has a size of n = 169 with the participants' ages ranging from 19 to 59 years (mean: 27.8 years) and a share of 40.6% female persons. Four participants provided straight-line answers and were thus removed from the sample, decreasing the final sample size to n = 165. A monetary compensation was not provided for participation in the experiment. The participants were recruited from personal networks and comprised mainly students from a German university.

1.4.2 Experimental Conditions

For the experimental conditions, we designed four instances of a conversational agent using the natural language platform Dialogflow by Google (2019). Dialogflow provides the technical capabilities to detect a user's intent from a written natural language statement and formulate a response. All agent instances received the same set of training phrases. We varied anthropomorphic design and responsiveness of the agents as visualized in Figure 19.

		Social Cues	
		Few	Many
Response Failure	With	**Condition 1** Agent with few social cues and with response failure	**Condition 2** Agent with many social cues and with response failure
	Without	**Condition 3** Agent with few social cues and without response failure	**Condition 4** Agent with many social cues and without response failure

Figure 19 (Study 2): Experimental Conditions

The two instances with a human-like design received a set of social cues to make the agents appear human-like. Against the background of the three anthropomorphic design dimensions proposed by Seeger et al. (2018), we provided the agent with a comic-like avatar of a female customer service employee (Gong 2008), gave it a human name (Cowell and Stanney 2005) and a gender (Nunamaker et al. 2011) to establish a human identity. We further integrated self-references (Sah and Peng 2015), self-disclosure (Schuetzler et al. 2018b), a personal introduction and greeting (Cafaro et al. 2016), and variability in syntax as well as word choice for the agent's responses (Seeger et al. 2018) in terms of verbal cues. With regard to non-verbal cues, we added dynamic response delays to indicate thinking and typing of replies (Gnewuch et al. 2018b) in combination with blinking dots (de Visser et al. 2016) as well as the use of emoticons to express emotions (Wang et al. 2008). Figure 20 visualizes the human-like design with exemplary social cues.

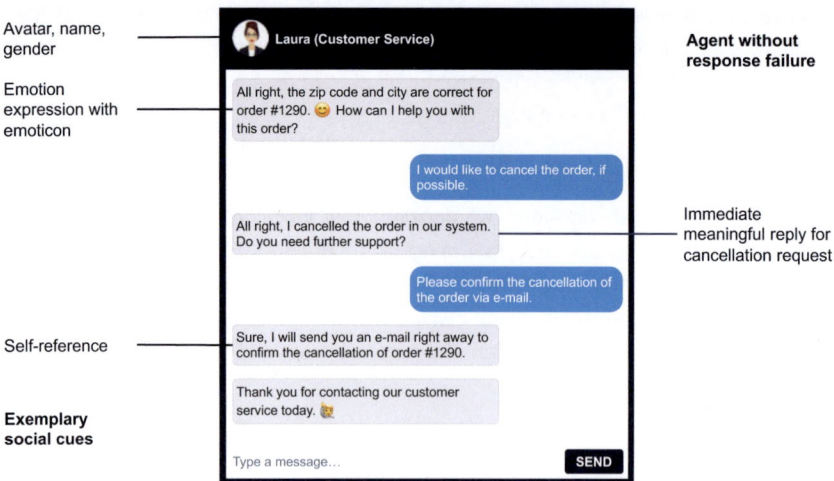

Figure 20 (Study 2): Human-like CA without Response Failure (Condition 4)

With regard to the second dimension, response failure, we designed the agent in conditions 1 and 2 to indicate a lack of understanding at one point in the interaction. When the participants in those conditions requested to cancel the given order, the agent politely responded that it did not understand the user's input and asked for reformulation of the request for two times. After the participant entered the request a third time, the agent provided a meaningful response and confirmed the cancellation. Table 18 shows CA's responses in the two conditions with low responsiveness.

Table 18 (Study 2): Agent Statements with Response Failure (translated)

Iteration	Condition 1 (few social cues)	Condition 2 (many social cues)
1	"Unfortunately, I do not understand your request."	"Unfortunately, I do not understand your request. Can you please reformulate it?"
2	"Unfortunately, I do not understand your request."	"I am so sorry, but I do not understand what you are saying. Can you please formulate it differently?
3	"Your order is now cancelled."	"All right, I cancelled the order in our system. Do you need further support?"

1.4.3 Manipulation Check

To check whether the manipulation of the responsiveness dimension was successful in the sense that participants only received meaningless responses as intended without a multitude of further fallback replies, we analyzed the conversation data provided by Google Dialogflow. Reviewing the interactions with the agents in the four conditions showed that in most cases the agents demonstrated the communication behavior as intended with an overall average of additional conversational fallbacks of around 1.5 responses per interaction. All conditions showed similar average fallbacks between 1.7 and 1.4 messages, comprising situations in a dialogue where the agent did not understand a user's intent. Thus, only a minimal number of fallbacks, similar across all groups, existed in the interactions.

1.4.4 Measures

Every participant was asked to complete a survey to measure perceptions of humanness, uncanniness, familiarity, and service satisfaction. We used established measurement instruments for the four constructs. Humanness and familiarity were both measured on a 9-point semantic differential scale with items from Holtgraves and Han (2007) and MacDorman (2006) respectively. To measure feelings of uncanniness, we adapted a 7-point Likert scale based on the studies by MacDorman, Green, Ho and Koch (2009) and Tinwell and Sloan (2014). Similarly, service satisfaction was measured on a 7-point Likert scale using items from Verhagen et al. (2014).

Furthermore, we collected demographic information (age, gender) and information on the frequency of digital assistant use (e.g. Siri, Alexa, and chatbots). Finally, we asked for free form feedback on the perception of the agent. We added attention checks by inverting two items in the survey.

Table 19 (Study 2): Constructs, Items, and Factor Loadings

Constructs and items	Loadings	Scale and source
Humanness (α = .904, CR = .927, AVE = .680)		
Extremely inhuman-like - extremely human-like	.887	9-point semantic differential scale (Holtgraves and Han 2007)
Extremely unskilled - extremely skilled	.882	
Extremely unthoughtful - extremely thoughtful	.853	
Extremely impolite - extremely polite	.671	
Extremely unresponsive - extremely responsive	.821	
Extremely unengaging - extremely engaging	.816	
Uncanniness (α = .911, CR = .932, AVE = .698)		
I perceived the agent as eerie.	.665	7-point Likert scale (MacDorman et al. 2009; Tinwell and Sloan 2014)
I perceived the agent as inhuman-like.	.784	
I perceived the agent as strange.	.880	
I perceived the agent as unappealing.	.909	
I perceived the agent as inclement.	.853	
I perceived the agent as unpleasant.	.895	
Familiarity		9-point semantic differential scale (MacDorman 2006)
Extremely strange - extremely familiar	n/a	
Service Satisfaction (α = .888, CR = .931, AVE = .819)		
How satisfied are you with the agent's advice?	.914	7-point Likert scale (Verhagen et al. 2014)
...the way the agent treated you?	.854	
...the overall interaction with the agent?	.944	

Table 19 shows the constructs, items, and factor loadings as well as Cronbach's α, composite reliability (CR) and average variance extracted (AVE). Following the suggestions by Gefen and Straub (2005), items with loadings larger than .60 were used in the analysis. Humanness, uncanniness, and service satisfaction showed sufficient values for CR (larger than .80), Cronbach's α (larger than .80) as well as AVE (larger than .50) considering the levels proposed by Urbach and Ahlemann (2010).

1.5 Results

We tested our hypotheses on the impact of response failure in combination with human-like CA design in a service context using partial least squares (PLS). Following the suggestions by Chin (1998), we calculated the significance of path coefficients with a bootstrapping resampling approach with 5,000 samples. The resulting path coefficients, R^2 values for the dependent variables as well as significance levels are shown in Figure 21. All analyses were carried out using SmartPLS 3.

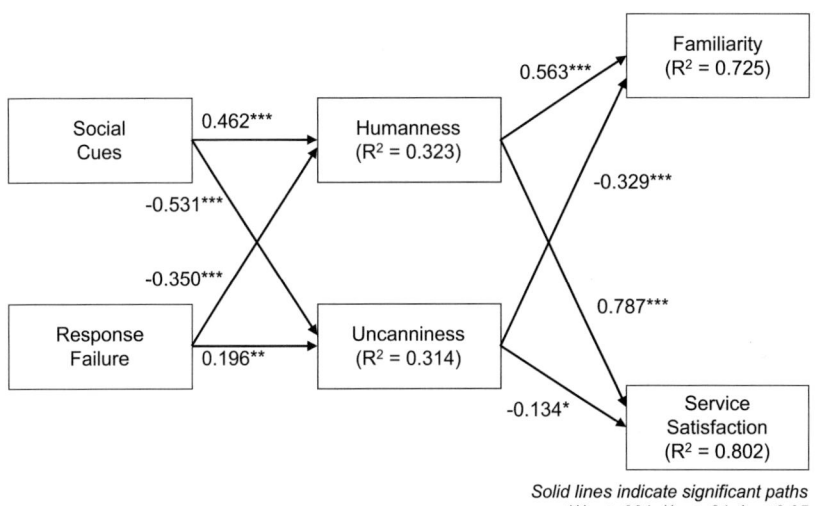

Solid lines indicate significant paths
***$p \le .001$, **$p \le .01$, *$p \le 0.05$

Figure 21 (Study 2): PLS Structural Model (n = 165)

The paths between social cues and humanness as well as uncanniness show significant relationships. In line with Social Response Theory, we find empirical evidence that social cues positively impact humanness of an agent (Social Cues → Humanness, β = 0.462, $p \le .001$), thus confirming our first hypothesis. Furthermore, a human-like design with social cues has a negative impact on uncanniness, providing support for the second hypothesis (Social Cues → Uncanniness, β = -0.531, $p \le .001$). With regard to response failure, we observe a negative impact on humanness (Response Failure → Humanness, β = -0.350, $p \le .001$) and a positive impact on uncanniness (Response Failure → Uncanniness, β = 0.196, $p = .004$), as stated by hypotheses three and four. Our data further indicates a positive impact of humanness on familiarity with the agent (Humanness → Familiarity, β = 0.563, $p \le .001$) and a negative impact of uncanniness (Uncanniness → Familiarity, β = -0.329, $p \le .001$) as proposed in hypotheses five and six. Finally, we find empirical support for the impact of humanness and uncanniness on service satisfaction: Humanness positively contributes to service satisfaction (Humanness → Service Satisfaction, β = 0.787, $p ≤ .001$) while uncanniness has a detrimental influence on user satisfaction with the service encounter (Uncanniness → Service Satisfaction, β = -0.134, $p = .017$).

To complement the results for our research model, we also analyzed the effect of the control variables that comprised demographic information of the participants (age, gender) as well as prior experience with digital assistants and chatbots. However, the variables did not exhibit significant paths to the latent variables.

Furthermore, we assessed the size of direct effects with the f^2 values. Using the levels proposed by Cohen (1988), we interpreted values of 0.02, 0.15, and 0.35 as small, medium, and large sizes respectively. All significant relationships had direct effect sizes that exceeded the small effect threshold (Table 20). Direct effects with a small size comprise the paths between response failure and uncanniness (f^2 = 0.054) as well as uncanniness and service satisfaction (f^2 = 0.036). Medium-sized direct effects include social cues (f^2 = 0.0313) and response failure (f^2 = 0.175) to humanness as well as uncanniness to familiarity (f^2 = 0.155). Large effect sizes can be observed from social cues to uncanniness (f^2 = 0.407) and from humanness to familiarity (f^2 = 0.453) as well as to service satisfaction (f^2 = 1.24).

Table 20 (Study 2): Effect Sizes for Significant Paths according to Cohen (1988)

Small effect ($f^2 ≥ 0.02$)	Medium effect ($f^2 ≥ 0.15$)	Large effect ($f^2 ≥ 0.35$)
Response Failure → Uncanniness	Response Failure → Humanness	Humanness → Familiarity
Uncanniness → Service Satisfaction	Uncanniness → Familiarity	Humanness → Service Satisfaction
	Social Cues → Humanness	Social Cues → Uncanniness

Finally, we indicatively compared the differences of the means for the latent variables to investigate whether a strong negative emotional response as postulated in the Uncanny Valley Theory can be observed (Figure 22). Our dataset indicates that participants who received a design with many social cues showed substantially stronger negative reactions (Δ = 1.59) to response failure with regard to familiarity than participants that interacted with a machine-like CA with few social cues (Δ = 0.42) while the differences between the means for humanness (Δ = 1.44, Δ = 1.15), uncanniness (Δ = -0.66, Δ = -0.28) service satisfaction (Δ = 1.11, Δ = 1.97) were comparatively smaller.

B. Studies on Anthropomorphic CAs

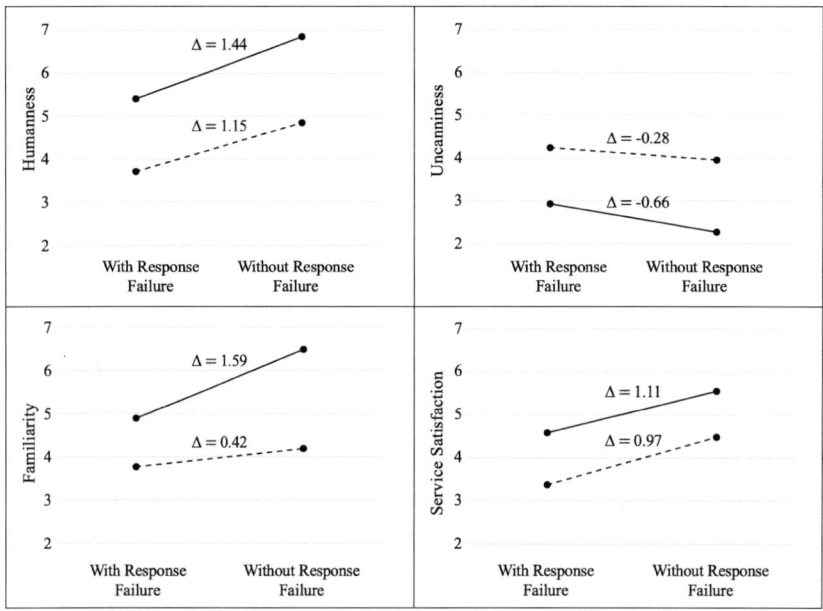

Figure 22 (Study 2): Mean Values differentiated by Cues (Dotted: Conditions 1 & 3)

1.6 Discussion

Our study provides empirical evidence for the negative impact of response failure of CAs in a service context on the perception of humanness as well as a positive influence on unintended uncanniness of an agent. Furthermore, the results show a positive impact of humanness in a service encounter on familiarity and satisfaction as well as a detrimental impact of uncanniness on these variables. In the following, we discuss implications of our results for service provision with CAs as well as their anthropomorphic design, indicate limitations, and suggest opportunities for future research.

1.6.1 Implications for Designing Anthropomorphic Conversational Agents

The results of our experiment emphasize a negative impact of response failure of a CA on user perception in the context of a service encounter. Participants that interacted with a CA that exhibited response failure indicated a lower perception of humanness, familiarity, and service satisfaction as well as increased uncanniness of the agent. Even if the response failure in conditions 1 and 2 can be considered rather modest and the CA in all cases was ultimately able to complete the user's service request, the negative impact on user perception was substantial. The qualitative, free-form feedback on the CA's design underlines this effect. For example, participants that interacted with a CA with response failure stated that they perceived the agent as "incomplete" or criticized that they had to "ask for order cancellation a thousand times". Furthermore, one participant commented that "What is the purpose of the nice design if the computer does not understand me?". Thus, the CA's failure to respond was immediately recognized by the participants in the respective experimental conditions. With regard to anthropomorphic design of conversational (service) agents, our data therefore emphasizes the importance of sufficient conversational capabilities in line with other recent studies, such as Luger and Sellen (2016) or Schuetzler et al. (2018b).

Considering the results from our analysis of direct effect sizes (Table 20), even a rather modest failure to respond in the conversation led to a medium-sized detrimental effect on the perception of humanness of the agent. Interestingly, the large variety of social cues incorporated in the design of the human-like agent (conditions 2 and 4) exhibited a comparable effect size on humanness. Thus, our experimental data indicates that even small response failure leads to a substantial negative effect on humanness with an effect size comparable to impact of the rich social cues on humanness of the agent.

With regard to a potential Uncanny Valley-effect (Figure 17), our data does not exhibit a sharp drop in familiarity or increase in uncanniness of the magnitude posited by the original theory. While a substantial negative impact on user perception of response failure can be observed in our data, the mean values for familiarity (uncanniness) are still higher (lower) in the conditions with a human-like design with many social cues than in those with a machine like design with few social cues (Figure 22). Interestingly, however, the difference in familiarity depending on response failure seems to be larger for the human-like CAs ($\Delta = 1.59$) than the difference for the CAs with a machine-like design ($\Delta = 0.42$). This could be in line with a small decrease in familiarity at the beginning of the Valley's sharp drop. Drawing on the, admittedly conceptual, idea of Mori's (1970) theory, our data could indicate that current anthropomorphic designs of CAs may achieve a level of human-likeness close to the beginning of the Uncanny Valley yet not reaching it. Alternatively, there could be a differently structured curve that describes the relationship between familiarity and human-likeness for CAs as MacDorman (2006), for example, report in their analysis of human reactions to robot video clips.

Three main implications for the design of anthropomorphic design of CAs, particularly in a service context, can be drawn from these results: First, the perception of humanness of a conversational service agent, enabled by a rich combination of social cues, positively contributes to familiarity and, in particular, service satisfaction. These results are in line with the findings of for example Gnewuch et al. (2018b) or Diederich et al. (2019d). According to our data, crafting CAs with an appealing human-like representation and behavior is thus generally desirable in a service context according to our data. Second, equipping the CA with sufficient conversational capabilities to mitigate and adequately handle response failures should be a key consideration when designing an agent due to the substantial negative impact of even modest response failures. While the designer's task of anticipating a wide variety of user input is admittedly a challenging one (Følstad and Brandtzæg 2017), treating conversations as the core object of a CA's design is essential to build agents that fulfill user expectations and are able to maintain a human-like behavior (Clark et al. 2019). Furthermore, designers should carefully reflect on and select coping strategies to handle unanticipated situations in a conversation (see for example Ashktorab et al. (2019) for an overview and initial evaluation). Third, due to the absence of very strong negative effects as posited by the Theory of the Uncanny Valley, a human-like design is favorable even if small response failure may take place. Accordingly, with response failures still occurring in practice, equipping the CA with various social cues seems to be nonetheless advantageous, at least for a modest number of conversational fallbacks.

1.6.2 Limitations and Opportunities for Future Research

Our research exhibits different limitations and indicates opportunities for future research on anthropomorphic CA design. The experimental setting offered the benefit of control yet lacked realism (Dennis and Valacich 2001). Similar to other studies on CA design, we provided the participants with a set of rather specific tasks. Hence, we were able to create a setting in which the agent consistently failed to provide a meaningful response for around two times, which allowed us to better understand the impact on user perception of the agent by comparing the experimental groups. However, in a practical interaction with a CA, response failures are likely to occur with different frequency depending on the agent's design. In addition, our experiment was conducted in a specific context (customer service of an online retailer) with users expecting the agent to be able to fulfill their rather trivial service request (order cancellation). Therefore, we suggest that future studies explore the impact of response failure in different, potentially more complex (service) contexts and, in particular, in situations where the agent is not able to ultimately fulfill a customer's request.

Furthermore, our findings concerning the rather strong detrimental impact of agent response failures in a conversation offer two directions for future studies. First, design-oriented research can be conducted to investigate how response failure can be mitigated, such as by providing a more transparent structure with the agent or having the CA suggest answers in the interaction as frequently done in practice by means of quick reply buttons, thereby leading the conversation in a direction where the agent is able to provide relevant responses again. Second, different approaches in a service context to react to unexpected input can be conceptualized and empirically tested, such as polite and personal context-specific fallback responses or offering the possibility to contact a human service employee.

1.7 Concluding Remarks

CAs in organizational contexts promise to provide automated service that is always available and resembles the feeling of a human interaction. However, the limited conversational capabilities of current agents often lead to situations in which agents fail to provide meaningful replies in a service encounter. As such response failures may negatively impact the perception of anthropomorphic CAs and are neglected in current research, we conducted an online experiment to better understand the relationship between response failure and user perception human-like of CAs.

Our findings provide evidence for the detrimental impact of even small response failures on the perception of humanness and uncanniness and highlight the positive (negative) impact of humanness (uncanniness) on familiarity and service satisfaction. Furthermore, our data does not indicate a very strong negative emotional reaction to response failure of human-like CAs as proposed by the Uncanny Valley, but highlights a substantial, yet comparatively moderate negative effect. The findings from our experiment have implications for research, especially regarding the Uncanny Valley-effect in the context of anthropomorphic conversational service agents. Our results further provide practical insights for designers by confirming the positive impact of anthropomorphic CA design for innovative service provision and by emphasizing the need to mitigate response failures in natural language interactions.

2. Study 3: Design for Fast Request Fulfillment or Natural Interaction? Insights from an Online Experiment with a Conversational Agent

Table 21: Fact Sheet of Study 3

Title	Design for Fast Request Fulfillment or Natural Interaction? Insights from an Online Experiment with a Conversational Agent
Authors	Stephan Diederich*, Alfred Benedikt Brendel, Sascha Lichtenberg, Lutz M. Kolbe Chair of Information Management, University of Göttingen, Platz der Göttinger Sieben 5, 37073 Göttingen, Germany *Corresponding author. Tel.: +49 551 3921170. E-Mail: stephan.diederich@stud.uni-goettingen.de
Outlet	European Conference on Information Systems (ECIS), Stockholm, Sweden, 2019
Abstract	Conversational agents continue to permeate our lives in different forms, such as virtual assistants on mobile devices or chatbots on websites and social media. The interaction with users through natural language offers various aspects for researchers to study as well as application domains for practitioners to explore. In particular their design represents an interesting phenomenon to investigate as humans show social responses to these agents and successful design remains a challenge in practice. Compared to digital human-to-human communication, text-based conversational agents can provide complementary, preset answer options with which users can conveniently and quickly respond in the interaction. However, their use might also decrease the perceived humanness and social presence of the agent as the user does not respond naturally by thinking of and formulating a reply. In this study, we conducted an experiment with N=80 participants in a customer service context to explore the impact of such elements on agent anthropomorphism and user satisfaction. The results show that their use reduces perceived humanness and social presence yet does not significantly increase service satisfaction. On the contrary, our findings indicate that preset answer options might even be detrimental to service satisfaction as they diminish the natural feel of human-CA interaction.
Keywords	Conversational Agent; Chatbot; Dialogue Design; Online Experiment

2.1 Introduction

Conversational agents (CAs), i.e. software that interacts and exchanges information with its users through natural language, currently attract strong interest in both research and practice (McTear 2017; Oracle 2016). While the idea of natural language interaction with computers dates back several decades (Shawar and Atwell 2007) and has been studied under various terms, such as product recommendation agents (Qiu and Benbasat 2010; Wang and Benbasat 2005), virtual agents (Baylor 2009; Bickmore et al. 2009), or dialogue systems (McKevitt et al. 1999; Zadrozny et al. 2000), present CAs exhibit improved capabilities, in particular driven by advances in natural language processing and machine learning (Berg 2014; Knijnenburg and Willemsen 2016). With these improved capabilities researchers now explore the design of and interaction with CAs in a variety of domains (Diederich et al. 2019a) ranging from customer service (Gnewuch et al. 2017; Hu et al. 2018; Stock and Merkle 2018) to rather specific application areas, such as idea platforms (Tavanapour and Bittner 2018) or data analytics (Fast et al. 2017; Matsushita et al. 2004). Due to the natural interaction with CAs and variety of social cues provided by these agents, humans show social responses (Appel et al. 2012; Gong 2008) that need to be considered in the design process (Gnewuch et al. 2017; Seeger et al. 2017). As increasing the perceived humanness of CAs by adjusting its representation and communicative behavior is associated with other positive effects (Araujo 2018; Gong 2008), such as on perceived usefulness, different design elements have been studied to make CAs seem as human-like as possible. These aspects include for example the representation of a CA (Araujo 2018; Seeger et al. 2018), the delay of responses to display pauses for thinking and typing (Gnewuch et al. 2018b), personalized communication with users (Holtgraves et al. 2007), or designing a CA similar to its user (Al-Natour et al. 2006).

For CAs that interact with users via written text, often described as chatbots, different elements are available to design its representation, for example with a name or avatar (Hanus and Fox 2015; Wünderlich and Paluch 2017) and communicative behavior, for example the use of emoticons or self-references (Seeger et al. 2018). Thus, these elements influence the degree of perceived humanness and social presence. In particular, text-based CAs can suggest responses to its users in the form of preset answer options. These design elements allow the user to quickly and conveniently respond to a chatbot's statement without the need for manually formulating and typing a reply. While the use of such elements reduces the required effort for a user to reply in a conversation, it could also diminish the natural feeling in the interaction and the sense of human contact as those elements rather resemble traditional graphical user interfaces (Brandtzæg and Følstad 2018), such as simple buttons that can be clicked or touched.

In this study, we investigate the specific effect of these design elements to better understand how they impact user perceptions of and user satisfaction with text-based conversational agents with the following research question: *How do preset answer options of text-based CAs influence perceived humanness, social presence, and service satisfaction?*

We address this research question by means of an online experiment with a text-based CA in a customer service context, thus contributing to the growing knowledge base on (anthropomorphic) CA design. The remainder of this article is structured as follows: We continue by providing the research background for our work, in particular with regard to the design of CAs and underlying theories, and develop our hypotheses on the impact of preset answer options in human interaction with CAs. We then present our research design, an online experiment with a focus on perceived humanness, social presence, and service encounter satisfaction, as well as our results. Finally, we discuss the implications for the design of CAs, indicate limitations of our work, and outline opportunities for future research.

2.2 Theoretical Background and Related Work

The fundamental idea of CAs is to use natural language to converse on a common topic and exchange information like in a human-to-human interaction instead of traditional graphical interfaces (Berg 2014; McTear et al. 2016). CAs can exist in a variety of forms with regard to the communication mode (Lee et al. 2009), their embodiment (Lee et al. 2006), and application context (Nunamaker et al. 2011). The communication can take place both via spoken language, often referred to as virtual personal assistants, or through written text, often called chatbots or dialogue systems (Gnewuch et al. 2017; Morana et al. 2017). Conversational agents can be physically embodied (e.g. Featherman et al. 2011; Nunamaker et al. 2011), have an interactive digital embodiment (e.g. Groom et al. 2009; Von Der Pütten et al. 2010; Seymour et al. 2017) or a static digital embodiment (e.g. Hu et al. 2018; Seeger et al. 2018). CAs can be used for general-purpose or in specific domains (Nunamaker et al. 2011), both in private and professional life. These domains include for example customer service (Araujo 2018; Gnewuch et al. 2017; Hu et al. 2018; Stock and Merkle 2018), marketing and sales (Chattaraman et al. 2012; Hanus and Fox 2015; Qiu and Benbasat 2009; Vaccaro et al. 2018; Wang and Benbasat 2005), human resources (Liao et al. 2018), data analytics (Fast et al. 2017; Matsushita et al. 2004), and collaborative team settings (Elson et al. 2018; Strohmann et al. 2018). In this study, we focus on text-based CAs with a static virtual embodiment in customer service as an exemplary domain.

The idea of human-computer interaction through natural language emerged already several decades ago when Joseph Weizenbaum presented the first CA, called ELIZA

(Weizenbaum 1966). Since then, a variety of CAs emerged and often disappeared (Ben Mimoun et al. 2012) due to the reliance on simple pattern matching approaches and the provision of a limited set of responses (Knijnenburg and Willemsen 2016). However, with significant developments in the fields of natural language processing and machine learning, present CAs exhibit strongly increased capabilities (Berg 2014). The example of Google Assistant, who made an appointment with a hairdresser in a spoken conversation at the last I/O developer conference (Welch 2018) underlines this potential of today's CAs. With these capabilities, CAs gained momentum in research and practice alike (Oracle 2016; Saffarizadeh et al. 2017; Wünderlich and Paluch 2017). Companies from different industries, such as Amtrak (NextIT 2018), Starbucks (Perez 2016), H&M (Morana et al. 2017) or KLM (Vogel-Meijer 2018), introduce CAs to innovate and automate tasks in customer service or sales and begin to realize its potential. For example, the American railroad company Amtrak introduced "Julie" to provide customers with an easy-to-use possibility to find and book tickets online, which answers more than 5 million questions annually and generated more than 1 million USD in savings for customer service within a single year (NextIT 2018).

2.2.1 Design of Conversational Agents

Despite the capabilities of modern CAs, successful design represents a major challenge, in particular due to high user expectations that often cannot be fulfilled by the system (Luger and Sellen 2016). As CAs provide different types of social cues (Von Der Pütten et al. 2010; Seeger et al. 2018), such as in the agent's human-like representation or in the language itself, users apply social rules and form expectations to them as posited in social response theory (Nass and Moon 2000). These social responses to CAs offer potential and are associated with risks at the same time: On the one hand, we can transfer existing theories and concepts from human-to-human communication to understand and design digital communication with CAs. For example, Danielescu and Christian (2018) and Gnewuch et al. (2017) draw on Grice's Maxims as universal mechanisms for cooperative conversations (Grice 1975), Saffarizadeh et al. (2017) use social penetration theory (Altman et al. 1997) to study self-disclosure in human-CA communication, and Burgoon et al. (2016) apply expectancy violations theory (Burgoon and Jones 1976) in the context of CAs. On the other hand, social responses to CAs form high user expectations towards these systems, which are often not in line with their capabilities (Brandtzæg and Følstad 2018; Luger and Sellen 2016). A case study by Ben Mimoun et al. (2012) on the disappearance of agents on 80 French commercial websites indicated that many CAs fail due to appearance inadequacy as well as lack of interactivity and intelligence. Ben Mimoun et al. (2012, p. 607) describe that "[…] when implementing the agent, the company might fail to define and present its limits to consumers. Users thus cannot understand limits of the agent's capacities and become frustrated with its inability to answer their questions".

Researchers have investigated a variety of social cues to account for the social responses and resulting user expectations. Such cues can be categorized along three dimensions of anthropomorphic CA design: human identity, non-verbal cues, and verbal cues (Seeger et al. 2018). These cues range from the representation of the CA (Cowell and Stanney 2005; Hanus and Fox 2015; Shamekhi et al. 2018) in the category of human identity over non-verbal cues like smiling (Biancardi et al. 2017; Harjunen et al. 2018; Krämer et al. 2013) or showing empathetic demeanor (Beale and Creed 2009; Leite et al. 2013; De Rosis et al. 2003; Shi et al. 2018) to verbal cues, such as self-references (Seeger et al. 2018). For their design, scholars use the technical possibilities of CAs to deliberately mimic human behavior, such as dynamically delayed response times for thinking and typing a response (Gnewuch et al. 2018b) or automatic sentiment detection of user statements to provide adequate and empathetic answers (Bertacchini et al. 2017; Hu et al. 2018). However, using the available technical possibilities to successfully design a CA that is able to fulfill user expectations in terms of adequate representation and communication behavior in a specific domain remains a challenging endeavor (Brandtzæg and Følstad 2018).

2.2.2 Social Response Theory and Social Presence in the Context of CAs

The social cues provided by CAs, both verbal and non-verbal as well as with regard to the agent representation, elicit social responses in humans and can convey a sense of human contact in the interaction. These phenomena are explained by social response theory and the concept of social presence.

Social response theory (Nass and Moon 2000; Reeves and Nass 1996) and the paradigm of Computers As Social Actors (Nass et al. 1994) is the main theoretical foundation underlying CA research, particularly the work by scholars from Information Systems and Human-Computer Interaction disciplines (Gnewuch 2018b). Through a review of three sets of experimental studies, Nass and Moon (2000) posit that individuals mindlessly apply social rules and expectations to computers once they receive cues associated with human traits or behavior. The researchers showed that humans overuse human social categories, such as gender stereotypes, show and expect social behaviors, such as reciprocity, and exhibit social responses with respect to the "personality" of a computer program. Furthermore, Nass and Moon (2000, p. 97) hypothesize that "the more computers present characteristics that are associated with humans, the more likely they are to elicit social behavior".

Social presence represents another theoretical concept that is often used in CA research. It encompasses "the sense of human contact embodied in a medium" (Gefen and Straub,

1997, p. 390), which is often related to the richness of the communication. For example, a video conference makes the conversation partner more salient than a chat message (Schuetzler et al. 2014). Studies on social presence have shown that even small adjustments, such as adding personalized greetings (Gefen and Straub 2003) or human images (Cyr et al. 2009) to websites, positively influence perceived social presence for an artifact. In turn, social presence has been shown to improve trust (Gefen and Straub 2004), self-efficacy beliefs (Baylor 2009), and enjoyment as well as perceived usefulness (Hassanein and Head 2007).

As CAs can provide rich characteristics that are associated with humans and can use a variety of social cues, in particular through natural language itself, they trigger considerable social responses by users (Gong 2008) and have the potential to convey a substantial feeling of human contact in human-computer interaction (Appel et al. 2012; Chattaraman et al. 2012; Nunamaker et al. 2011).

2.3 Hypotheses

The main distinctive characteristic of CAs is the use of natural language in the interaction with users (Berg 2014; McTear et al. 2016), which allows to intuitively interact with such programs (Shawar and Atwell 2007). CAs that provide relevant information in natural language and a responsive manner, e.g. with follow-up questions or reciprocity, are shown to contribute to different positive aspects, such as user engagement (Schuetzler et al. 2018b) or satisfaction (Chattaraman et al. 2012). When interacting with users through natural language, text-based CAs, or chatbots, can use elements known from digital human-to-human communication, such as emoticons (Park and Sundar 2015) to indicate emotions or images (Yu et al. 2017) to increase the richness of the conversation and elicit associated positive effects (Dennis et al. 2014). However, designers of CAs have an additional element at their disposal: To provide a set of predefined answer options in a conversation (Brandtzæg and Følstad 2018). These allow users to swiftly and easily respond in a conversation. Both approaches can be found in present CAs. For example, the CA by Starbucks (Figure 23) suggests different replies for placing orders, adding items, or customizing drinks (Bishop 2016). In contrast to the design of Starbucks, the agent by Staples (Topbots 2016) exclusively relies on manual formulation and typing of replies like in a human-to-human text-based communication.

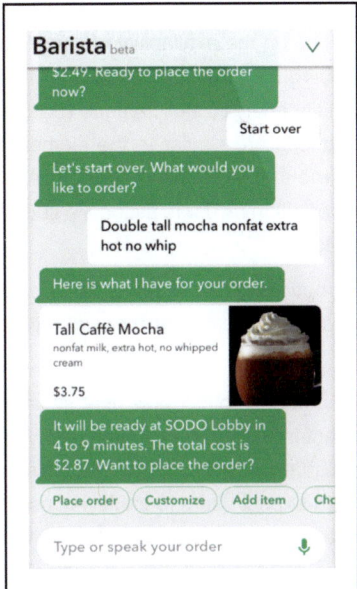 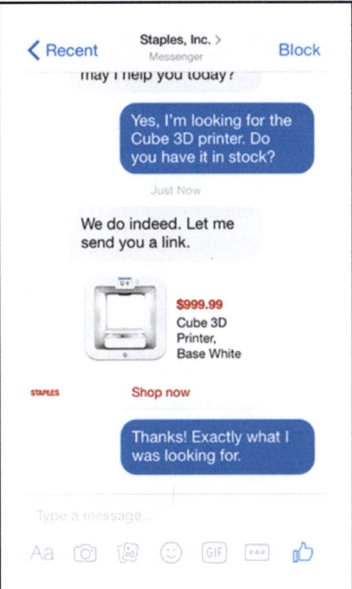

Figure 23 (Study 3): Exemplary CAs with (left) and without Preset Answer Options

While such elements can have positive effects, for example that users do not need to manually type their response and thus can reach their goals in the conversation faster, or make it easier to guide conversations towards a specific goal for the designer, they can also negatively impact the interaction by reducing the natural feeling and sense of human contact in the conversation (Brandtzæg and Følstad 2018). While being aware of the potentially divergent impact of such elements is certainly beneficial for designers of CAs, it has not been investigated in the past to the best of our knowledge. To address this gap, we formulate three hypotheses.

First, based on social response theory (Nass and Moon 2000; Reeves and Nass 1996), we hypothesize that the use of preset answer options in a conversation is detrimental to the perceived humanness of a chatbot as it represents a cue known from traditional, graphical user interfaces. It diminishes the natural feeling in a conversation, well-known from human-to-human communication, concerning the thinking of and formulating (e.g. typing) a response to the previous statement in the dialogue. Thus, we formulate our first hypothesis as follows:

H1: A chatbot that provides preset answer options yields a lower level of perceived humanness than a chatbot that exclusively relies on manually typed natural language responses by the user.

Similarly, the perceived social presence, defined as the sense of human contact in a mediated interaction (Short et al. 1976), depends on the availability of cues known from human-to-human communication, such as seeing the conversation partner in an image (Kahai and Cooper 2003) the use of emotionally charged descriptions (Hassanein and Head 2007). As preset buttons for answer options are similar to the elements used in traditional graphical user interfaces, we presume that their use in human-CA interaction reduces the sense of human contact in a conversation as users associate such elements with graphical instead of conversational interfaces:

H2: *A chatbot that provides preset answer options yields a lower level of perceived social presence than a chatbot that exclusively relies on manually typed natural language responses by the user.*

Furthermore, preset answer options have the potential to increase user satisfaction with the CA and service provision by providing a faster and more convenient way to achieve a goal in a conversation. As most users are acquainted with the use of such suggestions from text messaging on mobile phones, we can expect users to intuitively use them in a conversation with a CA. Such elements can reduce the time needed for formulating and typing a reply, thus decreasing the overall time needed for solving a customer request. As customers require as few waiting time as possible for the fulfillment of a service request (Taylor 1994), in particular in a technology-mediated service setting (Elmorshidy 2013; Larivière et al. 2017), the use of preset answer options represents a promising approach to immediately attend to customer needs and thus increase a user's satisfaction with the service. Hence, we formulate our third hypothesis as follows:

H3: *A chatbot that provides preset answer options leads to a higher user satisfaction than a chatbot that exclusively relies on manually typed natural language responses by the user.*

2.4 Research Design and Method

In order to test our hypotheses, we conducted an online experiment with a between-subjects design to avoid carryover effects (Boudreau et al. 2001). For the experiment, we chose a customer service context as it is one of the main application domains of conversational agents in enterprises (Stock and Merkle 2018; Verhagen et al. 2014; Xu et al. 2017) and is intuitively understandable for the participants. The experiment took place in November 2018 over a span of several days.

2.4.1 Data Collection Procedure and Sample

The participants received a briefing document, in which we explained the context (chatbots in a company context at the example of customer service) and structure of the experiment (interaction with the bot with subsequent survey) as well as described the participants' tasks. Every participant received the same document to make sure that the participants have exactly the same information for the experiment (Dennis and Valacich 2001). The document further contained a link to the chatbot, which randomly assigned the participant to the control or treatment configuration. Each participant was supposed to complete three tasks:

1. Find out the order status for order number 480219
2. Change the delivery address for the order to Any Street 45, Any City, Any State 12345
3. Request e-mail confirmation of the changes to johndoe@mail.com

After completing the third task, the chatbot provided a link to the online survey. Overall, the participation in the experiment took around 10 minutes per participant. Our study has a sample size of N = 80 participants ranging from 18 to 47 years old (mean: 33 years) and a share of 50.6% female and 49.4% male persons. Similar to the CA experiment by Seeger et al. (2018), we recruited native speakers through the panel company clickworker (2018) and participants received a small compensation for their effort.

2.4.2 Control and Treatment Configurations

To conduct the experiment, we implemented two instances of the same chatbot using Dialogflow by Google. Both instances were prepared with the same training phrases and modeled dialogue corresponding to the experimental tasks. The chatbot could understand and process different wording of the same statements and was able to extract, validate and repeat different parameters, such as the order number or e-mail address to indicate that it understood a user's request. We further created a straightforward web interface (Figure 24) to provide direct access to the chatbot and minimize distraction during the experiment as alternative platforms for deployment, such as Facebook, could provide deflective information during the interaction.

In the implementation, we considered three types of anthropomorphic design dimensions (human identity, verbal cues, and non-verbal cues (Seeger et al. 2018)) to establish a common baseline for both instances with regard to perceived anthropomorphism and associated positive effects (e.g. on social presence (Araujo 2018) and social judgment (Gong 2008). With regard to the human identity, the chatbot received a name, Linda, and a static comic avatar which represented a female customer service agent. Regarding verbal cues, the chatbot used self-references, e.g. "I will do my best to assist you" and emotional expressions, e.g. "Great, I changed the delivery address". We further equipped the chatbot with non-verbal cues, i.e. the use of emojis (e.g. for greeting a user) and dynamic response delays (Gnewuch et al. 2018b) with a visual indicator that the chatbot is typing. In addition, we let the chatbot self-disclose itself as a software program ("Even though I am not human, I will do my best to assist you") and use the extracted parameters (e.g. order number) in its response to contribute to the perceived responsiveness (Al-Natour et al. 2009; Saffarizadeh et al. 2017).

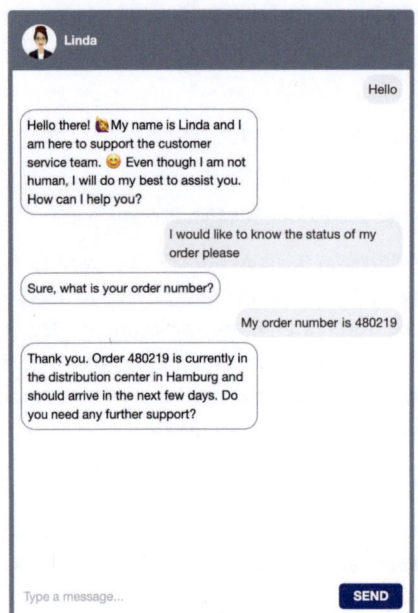 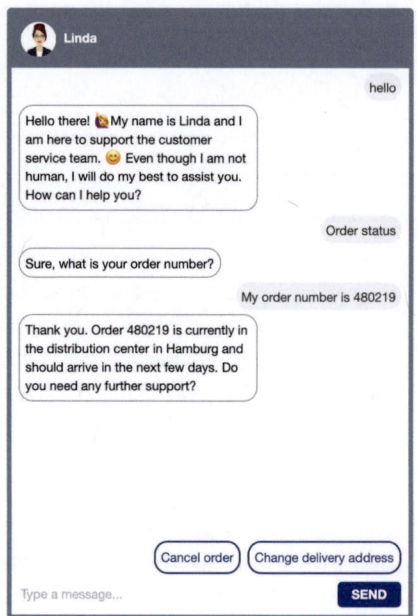

Figure 24 (Study 3): Interface with Control and Treatment Configurations

Overall, both chatbot instances were identical except for the provision of preset answer options in the treatment configuration. The treatment chatbot showed pre-defined buttons that provided the users with different options for their response (see Figure 24, interface on the right). For example, the chatbot provided the options "Product information", "Order status", and "Complaint" after greeting the user. These buttons could be clicked by the user to directly send a reply to the chatbot and thus avoid the need of typing a (potentially) whole sentence as a response. In contrast, participants in the control group had to manually type their request. For all of the three tasks (retrieve order status, change delivery address, and request e-mail confirmation) the treatment configuration provided a set of buttons of which one corresponded to the user's respective task.

2.4.3 Measures

Following the interaction with the chatbot, the participants completed a survey in which we measured how human-like and socially present the users perceived their conversation partner as well as how satisfied they were with the service encounter. For our survey design, we adapted measurement instruments established in previous studies and applied in the context of CAs (Gnewuch et al. 2018b), namely perceived humanness (Holtgraves et al. 2007), social presence (Gefen and Straub 1997), and service encounter satisfaction (Verhagen et al. 2014). We measured perceived humanness on a 9-point semantic differential scale and social presence as well as service encounter satisfaction on a 7-point Likert scale. We further added two control questions by inverting two items, skill for perceived humanness and personalness for social presence. Table 22 summarizes the three constructs including their composite reliability (CR) and average variance (AVE) extracted, as well as the items and measured factor loadings.

Table 22 (Study 3): Items, Measures, and Factor Loadings

Constructs and Items	Factor Loading
Perceived humanness (CR = .917, AVE = .688)	
extremely inhuman-like – extremely human-like	.811
extremely unskilled – extremely skilled	.873
extremely unthoughtful – extremely thoughtful	.810
extremely impolite – extremely polite	*dropped (.563)*
extremely unresponsive – extremely responsive	.777
extremely unengaging – extremely engaging	.872
Social presence (CR = .908, AVE = .767)	
I felt a sense of human contact with the chatbot	.903
I felt a sense of personalness with the chatbot	.892
I felt a sense of human warmth with the chatbot	*dropped (.596)*
I felt sense of human sensitivity with the chatbot	.831
Service satisfaction (CR = .913, AVE = .777)	
How satisfied are you with the chatbot's advice?	.911
…the way the chatbot treated you?	.851
…the overall interaction with the chatbot?	.881
CR = Composite Reliability, AVE = Average Variance Extracted	

Two items, politeness to measure perceived humanness and perceived human warmth for social presence, were dropped due to factor loadings below .60 (Gefen and Straub 2005). All constructs exhibited sufficient CR (> .80) and AVE (> .50) with respect to the levels proposed by Urbach and Ahlemann (2010). In the final part of the survey, we collected complementary data with regard to demographic information (age and gender) and open-ended feedback on the interaction with the chatbot.

2.5 Results

We analyzed the data from the follow-up survey by means of descriptive statistics and used a t-test to test our three hypotheses concerning the impact of preset answer options on perceived humanness (H1), social presence (H2), and service satisfaction (H3). The dataset contained three invalid responses for the control group that were identified using the control questions presented in the previous section, where participants consistently gave the same answers also for inverted questions. Thus, the sample size was reduced from 80 to 77 participants. We analyzed conversation logs as a manipulation check to understand whether participants in the treatment group used the provided preset answer options and found that in 78% of all possible cases participants actually clicked on the quick reply buttons instead of manually typing a reply. In addition, we checked for moderating effects of age, agender, and prior chatbot experience yet did not find significant effects. Table 23 summarizes the results of our analyses, which were carried out using SPSS version 25. The homogeneity of variance was successfully proven by the Levene tests for all three constructs (perceived humanness $F(75) = 3.25$, $p = 0.075$, social presence $F(75) = 0.49$, $p = 0.487$, service satisfaction $F(75) = 2.11$, $p = 0.151$). We then tested for a significant difference between the control (without preset answer options, necessitating manual typing) and treatment conditions (with preset answer options for every of the three experimental tasks).

Table 23 (Study 3): Descriptive Statistics and t-Test Results

		Condition		t-value (df = 75)	p-value
		Treatment (n = 44)	Control (n = 33)		
Perceived humanness	Mean SD SE	6.65 1.68 0.25	7.47 1.30 0.23	-2.35	0.022
Social presence	Mean SD SE	3.05 1.09 0.16	3.52 0.92 0.16	-2.00	0.049
Service satisfaction	Mean SD SE	4.21 0.81 0.12	4.53 0.75 0.13	-1.73	0.087

SD = Standard deviation, SE = Standard error

With regard to perceived humanness, we found a significant difference between the control and treatment conditions. Thus, our data indicates that the use of preset answer options does indeed reduce the perceived humanness of a CA in a conversation, providing support for our first hypothesis.

Concerning social presence, our results reveal that there is a significant difference between the control and treatment conditions. The data from our experiment thus supports our second hypothesis that the use of preset answer options significantly reduces the sense of human contact in CA interaction.

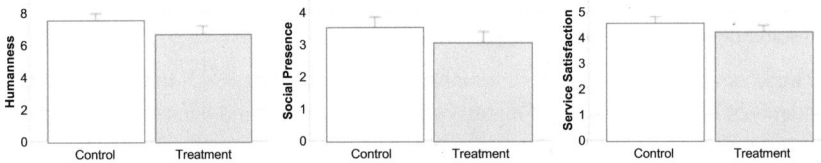

Figure 25 (Study 3): Differences between conditions for the three constructs

Finally, the results do not indicate a significant difference for service satisfaction between the control and treatment conditions. Consequently, we do not find support for the third hypothesis in our data that the use of quick reply elements increases a user's satisfaction with the service encounter due to faster and more convenient interaction. The results for perceived humanness, social presence and service satisfaction are visualized in Figure 25 for both conditions with error bars indicating the 95% confidence interval. Table 24 summarizes the results from the experiment for our three hypotheses.

Table 24 (Study 3): Results for Hypotheses

Hypothesis	Result
H1: A chatbot that provides preset answer options yields a lower level of perceived *humanness* than a chatbot that exclusively relies on manually typed natural language responses by the user.	Supported
H2: A chatbot that provides preset answer options yields a lower level of perceived *social presence* than a chatbot that exclusively relies on manually typed natural language responses by the user.	Supported
H3: A chatbot that provides preset answer options leads to a higher *service satisfaction* than a chatbot that exclusively relies on manually typed natural language responses by the user.	Not supported

2.6 Discussion

In our experiment, we examined the effect of preset answer options on user perceptions of text-based conversational agents in a customer service context. Our results indicate that the use of such elements does reduce the perceived humanness and social presence but does not increase a user's satisfaction with the service encounter. Even though the availability of preset answer options reduces the required efforts for users to manually formulate a reply, the users did not perceive this as an added value in the conversation with the chatbot in our setting. Actually, our results indicated that the use of preset answer options could lead to a lower user satisfaction though the difference between control and treatment was not statistically significant.

These results might seem counter-intuitive at first glance: A CA that offers quick reply elements decreases required manual efforts for the user and aims to reduce the overall time needed to fulfill a customer request. As the speed with which a service request is fulfilled, together with the expertise of customer service and the quality of the reply, influences the perceived customer service performance and customer satisfaction (Setia et al. 2013), one can expect that the use of preset answer options actually increases service satisfaction as formulated in our third hypothesis. However, viewing the results in the light of social response theory allows for a different interpretation: As the CA provided a variety of social cues, such as the name ("Linda"), expressions of emotions through words and emoticons, and through natural language interaction itself, it elicited social responses by the users. Thus, participants anthropomorphized the CA, which is also reflected in the free-form feedback: "The short waiting time in comparison to chats with human service employees is useful and saves a lot of time" and "[...] it would be great if Linda could respond to things like praise or say how she feels at the moment (I know these are gimmicks, but they are fun!)" [translated to English]. The participants viewed the CA as a "virtual human" and compared it to customer service employees rather than to self-service systems, such as on company websites (Meuter et al. 2000). As shown in previous work, this perceived humanness and social presence can be associated with further effects, particularly on service satisfaction (Gnewuch et al. 2018b), user engagement (Schuetzler et al. 2018b), and perceived usefulness (Hassanein and Head 2007). Against this background, the use of answer options reduces the degree to which users anthropomorphize a CA as shown in our experiment. As such elements replace formulating and typing of a natural language message, which users know from digital human-to-human communication and represents a social cue (Fogg 2003), with something that resembles elements known from graphical interfaces, they decrease how human-like the users perceive the CA. In parallel, it changes how users view the agent and how satisfied they are with the encounter.

2.6.1 Implications for the Design of Conversational Agents

The results of our study have two main implications for the design of text-based conversational agents, in particular in a company context. First, our insights place emphasis in the importance of perceived humanness as well as social presence and their influence on other factors, such as user satisfaction (Baylor 2009; Gefen and Straub 2004; Hassanein and Head 2007). For designers, our results highlight the need to consider different anthropomorphic design dimensions, e.g. with regard to the human identity and verbal as well as non-verbal cues (Seeger et al. 2018) when implementing a conversational agent besides traditional established dimensions, such as the time required to fulfill a user's request. In the context of our experiment, the degree to which a CA is perceived as human-like and socially present seemed to be even more relevant to the user's service encounter satisfaction than the speed at which a request is fulfilled. Specifically, the partial replacement of formulating and typing a natural language response with a set of preset answers reduced both how human-like a CA is perceived as well as how satisfied users were with the service encounter. These results are in line with recent work in the context of CAs like the study by Gnewuch et al. (2018b), who found that dynamically delayed response times of chatbots increase perceived humanness, social presence, and service satisfaction even though the CA's responses might take longer to appear than with static response delays.

Second, our study highlights the need to carefully balance the use of "human versus robot" aspects in the design of conversational agents. While users have the advantage of conversational freedom in natural language interaction without the need to navigate through preset menus or dialogues, this freedom poses a major challenge for the design where high variation of input and flexible interaction flows need to be taken into account and the repertoire of control mechanisms for the designer is dramatically reduced (Brandtzæg and Følstad 2018). As Brandtzæg and Følstad (2018, p. 41) state, the "user interface is to a much greater degree a blank canvas where the content and features of the underlying service are mostly hidden from the user, and where the interaction is more dependent on the user's input".

In this context, the use of preset answer options can be a useful approach to guide and structure the conversation flow towards a specific goal as well as to ensure that the CA can provide adequate and helpful responses. However, as our results indicate, the use of such elements reduces the perceived humanness and social presence in the interaction as well as potentially even decreases user satisfaction. Consequently, we suggest to carefully consider the use of preset answer options by taking into account the need to structure the conversation flow at each specific part of the conversation (to ensure the responsiveness of the agent) with the potentially detrimental impact of such elements on perceived humanness and social presence of the CA.

2.6.2 Limitations and Opportunities for Future Research

Our study is not free of limitations and offers opportunities for future research on CA interaction and design. One limitation of the present work results from the specific context in which our experiment took place, customer service. While the general purpose of preset answers to provide quick and convenient replies is independent from the context in which a CA is used, user motivation, goals and behavior are different across contexts. In particular, a user that does not have a specific question or task in mind, might perceive these buttons differently. For example, a potential customer that has a longer lasting interaction with a CA in a marketing and sales context to explore the product range of a company might view preset answer options and the conversational structure they can provide as helpful. Thus, we suggest that future work explores the use of such elements in different contexts with regard to user satisfaction and perceived humanness, in particular in settings where users might not have a specific task they intent to complete or a specific question to ask.

In addition, the degree of CA anthropomorphism deserves further investigation with regard to the perception of preset answer options. For example, users might perceive preset answer options differently for a CA that is deliberately designed to be machine-like instead of human-like, which can be a suitable design option to induce CA trustworthiness for tasks that are typically carried out by machines (Seeger et al. 2017). We recommend future studies to explicitly investigate how such preset answer options are perceived by users, which we did not consider in our experimental design. Furthermore, we provided a rather specific set of tasks to the participants. Hereby, the CA could be precisely prepared for the user statements and the variation of user input was reduced. The CA that did not provide preset answers was thus able to process the majority of user input without the use of fallback replies. Against this background, future research on CA design could investigate how preset answers are perceived by the user in a dialogue where otherwise some of the requests cannot be adequately processed by the conversational agent.

Additionally, the conversation logs offered few options to analyze and understand user behavior, for example the actual required time to complete the experimental task could not be investigated. We encourage future experimental CA studies to implement complementary conversation data storage instead of relying on the analytical functionality of the natural language processing platform, which may restrict options for log analysis (Diederich et al. 2019b). In addition, our experiment took place in a rather controlled setting in which we deliberately minimized distraction by providing a basic web interface for the conversation. Typical distractions and breaks in the conversation, such as notifications on mobile phones or new content on social media, were excluded from our experiment. Thus, while our online setting had strengths regarding precision and control, it had its weaknesses regarding realism (Dennis and Valacich 2001). We propose that future research explores the use of preset answers in the field, for example by means of a case study with a company that uses a CA on a website or social media.

Finally, we did not differentiate between requirements for specific groups of users in our experiment, particularly with regard to user age, and did not collect information on how they perceive preset answer options. Studies on CAs have shown that users of different age groups interact with and perceive CAs in different ways (e.g. Beer et al. 2015) and thus might have different requirements regarding the design of dialogues. Similarly, cultural aspects with regard to values, beliefs, and behavioral patterns impact how interactive systems are used and need to be taken into consideration when designing a CA on a cross-cultural scale (Pereira and Baranauskas 2015). One approach to deal with these differences could be to actively ask the users at the beginning of a conversation whether she or he prefers to receive preset answers, thus accounting for personal preferences. Hence, we propose the investigation of customization of CAs with regard to the provision of preset answer options as a further opportunity for future research.

2.7 Concluding Remarks

The goal of this study was to investigate the impact of preset answer options in human-CA interaction on perceived humanness, social presence, and service encounter satisfaction, thus adding to the growing knowledge base on the design of and interaction with conversational agents. The results of our online experiment indicate that CAs which use preset answer options decrease perceived humanness and social presence compared to CAs who do not use such design elements. Interestingly, CAs that offer these elements for quick and convenient replies, do not increase service encounter satisfaction according to our results, but might even lead to a decrease in user satisfaction. Therefore, our work indicates that even though users are required to put in extra effort for manual typing, they are more satisfied with the customer service encounter, potentially due to a more 'human' feeling in the interaction. The results support the overall direction in CA design research to enhance perceived humanness as well as social presence by emphasizing that these can even lead to a higher user satisfaction despite the additional manual effort for the users. In addition, our insights can be used to inform the design process of CA in practice by highlighting the potential drawbacks of apparently useful elements and emphasizing the need to design for natural interaction.

III. Exploring the Potential of Human-Like Design

The first and second chapters of Part B served to organize and assess existing knowledge (B.I) as well as to advance our understanding regarding the impact of limited conversational capabilities and the mitigation of associated negative effects on user perception of CAs (B.II).

To complement these insights, the following chapter (B.III) contributes to closing two specific research gaps related to the potential of anthropomorphic CA design. Studies 4 and 5 investigate two aspects of CA design that are particularly relevant in company settings. First, Study 4 proposes and evaluates a design approach to emulate empathetic communication in professional encounters based on sentiment analysis (Liu 2010, 2012) to improve the social conversational capabilities of enterprise CAs. Second, Study 5 combines anthropomorphic design with elements from persuasive system design (Oinas-Kukkonen and Harjumaa 2009) to craft compelling CAs, which can be particularly useful in contexts, such as a marketing and sales (Hanus and Fox 2015; Watanabe et al. 2015).

1. Study 4: Emulating Empathetic Behavior in Online Service Encounters with Sentiment-Adaptive Responses – Insights from an Experiment with a Conversational Agent

Table 25: Fact Sheet of Study 4

Title	Emulating Empathetic Behavior in Online Service Encounters with Sentiment-Adaptive Responses: Insights from an Experiment with a Conversational Agent
Authors	Stephan Diederich*[1], Max Janßen-Müller[2], Alfred Benedikt Brendel[1], Stefan Morana[3] 1) Chair of Information Management, University of Göttingen, Platz der Göttinger Sieben 5, 37073 Göttingen, Germany 2) University of Bremen, Bibliothekstraße 1, 28359 Bremen 3) Institute of Information Systems and Marketing, Karlsruhe Institute of Technology, Kaiserstraße 89-93, 76133 Karlsruhe, Germany *Corresponding author. Tel.: +49 551 3921170. E-Mail: stephan.diederich@stud.uni-goettingen.de
Outlet	International Conference on Information Systems (ICIS), Munich, Germany, 2019
Abstract	Conversational agents currently attract strong interest for technology-based service provision due to increased capabilities driven by advances in machine learning and natural language processing. The interaction via natural language in combination with a human-like design promises service that is always available, fast, and with a consistent quality and at the same time resembles a human service encounter. However, current conversational agents exhibit the same inherent limitation that every interactive technology has, which is a lack of social skills. In this study, we make a first step towards overcoming this limitation by presenting a design approach that combines automatic sentiment analysis with adaptive responses to emulate empathy in a service encounter. By means of an experiment with 112 participants, we evaluate the approach and find empirical support that a CA with sentiment-adaptive responses is perceived as more empathetic, human-like, and socially present and, in particular, yields a higher service encounter satisfaction.
Keywords	Conversational Agent; Empathy; Interactive Service Technology, Social Response Theory, Anthropomorphic Design

1.1 Introduction

Emerging technologies, in particular driven by machine learning and natural language processing, continue to rapidly transform customer interactions (Marinova et al. 2017) and the service interface evolves from being human-driven to becoming technology-dominant (Larivière et al. 2017). Innovating and automating service provision through interactive, natural language technology currently attracts strong interest in theory and practice alike (Wünderlich and Paluch 2017). So-called conversational agents (CAs), defined as software with which users interact through natural language, are explored at the service interface, for example to provide customer service (Gnewuch et al. 2017; De Keyser et al. 2019), support sales (Chattaraman et al. 2012) or offer financial advisory (Dolata et al. 2019). In the context of technology-enabled service systems (Marinova et al. 2017), CAs as a technological component have the potential to provide service that is always available, easy to use, and faster than human customer service yet offers the feeling of a personal contact (Verhagen et al. 2014). Recent success stories by the railroad company Amtrak, where the CA "Julie" answered over 5 million customer questions in its first year (NextIT 2018), or the airline KLM, where "BlueBot" helps to respond to increasing volumes of service requests and reduces workload of the hotline (Vogel-Meijer 2018), underline the potential of CAs for service provision. From a theoretical perspective, CAs are a particular interesting phenomenon as the human-like characteristics of such agents, such as the interaction via natural language, trigger social responses by users (Nass et al. 1994; Reeves and Nass 1996). As the human-like design of CAs can contribute to a positive perception and service experience (Gnewuch et al. 2018b), different studies aim to increase the human-likeness, for example with the disclosure of artificial feelings or with the representation of the CA with a name or gender (Cowell and Stanney 2005).

Despite this potential, present CAs share the same inherent limitation of any other service technology: A lack of human social skills, which in turn limits their potential for service provision (Larivière et al. 2017; Yan et al. 2013). In particular a lack of empathy, comprising the ability to recognize a customer's affective state and respond in an appropriate manner in a service encounter, poses restrictions for technology-based service design (Larivière et al. 2017). Empathy is often seen as a basis of social cooperation and prosocial behavior (Leite et al. 2013) and can contribute to service encounter satisfaction (Yan et al. 2013). Yet, the limited social capabilities of interactive service technology have contributed to the assumption that empathy is reserved exclusively for human service provision (Frey and Osborne 2017; Yan et al. 2013). In our study, we challenge this assumption and explore the design and perception of empathetic service agents with the following question (RQ): *How does empathetic behavior of a conversational agent in a service context affect customer perception compared to a non-*

empathetic agent? We simulate empathy in a two-step approach by using automatic sentiment analysis to approximate a user's emotional state and providing sentiment-adaptive responses in real-time during a service encounter. By means of an experiment with a CA in a customer service context and 112 participants, we assess the impact of sentiment-adaptive responses on user perception of the CA.

Our research makes three contributions: First, we make an initial step towards overcoming social limits of current service technologies by proposing a basic design approach for sentiment-adaptive conversational service agents. Second, our study sheds light on the role of empathy in service provision with interactive technology, which was considered to be primarily relevant for human service provision in the past. Third, we contribute to human-like CA design by presenting empathy as a social cue that leads to a more human-like perception of conversational agents. We continue by providing an overview of related work on CAs in general as well as in a service context, and describe the role of empathy in service encounters. Then, we introduce our research design and present the results of our experiment. We afterwards discuss the implications of these results for designing CAs in service encounters, describe limitations of our work and propose opportunities for future research in this area.

1.2 Related Work and Theoretical Background

The idea to interact with software through natural language dates back decades to the 1960s, when the first CA, called ELIZA, was developed by Joseph Weizenbaum (1966). While these early CAs executed simple pattern matching to provide responses to users (McTear 2017), CAs now exhibit significantly improved capabilities, in particular due to advances in natural language processing and machine learning (Følstad and Brandtzæg 2017). With these increased capabilities, they currently attract significant interest in research (McTear 2017) as well as practice (Oracle 2016) and a variety of different CAs emerged in the last few years (Diederich et al. 2019a). Present-day CAs can be distinguished by three main dimensions: the mode of interaction, the embodiment and their application context. With regard to the interaction mode, users can interact with CAs via spoken language, often referred to as digital or voice assistants, or written text, often described as chatbots, or both (Schroeder and Schroeder 2018). Regarding the embodiment, or the representation of the CA (Seeger et al. 2018), CAs can have a physical embodiment, such as service robots, a virtual interactive or static avatar (Wünderlich and Paluch 2017), or be disembodied. Finally, CAs can be able to converse about a variety of topics or fulfill different tasks, such as Cleverbot (2018) or be domain-specific (Gnewuch et al. 2017), such as for customer service (Verhagen et al. 2014), financial advisory (Dolata et al. 2019) or team collaboration (Elson et al. 2018). In the context of this study, we focus on a text-based CA with a virtual embodiment for customer service.

1.2.1 Conversational Agents in the Context of Service Systems

As the capabilities of CAs continue to improve, their application in service systems becomes increasingly versatile. While customer service is one of the primary application areas at the moment where CAs can fulfill requests like providing product information or handling complaints (Gnewuch et al. 2017), they can be expected to support or even fully assume tasks currently performed by human service personnel (Marinova et al. 2017; Verhagen et al. 2014), such as financial advisory (Dolata et al. 2019). Against this background, CAs that use machine learning to continuously improve their performance over time meet recent calls from service researchers, such as Beverungen et al. (2017) or Larivière et al. (2017), to explore how different types of artificial intelligence can be embedded in service systems. As technological components of service systems, which can be defined as "configurations of people, technologies, and other resources that interact with other service systems to create mutual value" (Maglio et al. 2009, p. 395), CAs have the potential to bridge the gap between service technology (which is always available yet lacks a feeling of personal interaction), such as self-service online portals, and human service employees (who offer a personal contact to a service provider yet have limited availability). In particular, CAs with a human-like design can elicit feelings of social presence and personalization that are not present in typical online service provision (Verhagen et al. 2014). Furthermore, conversational agents have the potential to provide a steady level of service quality as well as efficiency and thus overcome inherent human performance variability (Larivière et al. 2017). Overall, the evolving capabilities of CAs will require service providers to evaluate which types of service can be better provided by human employees, (self-)service technologies or conversational agents and to reflect on the human-technology mix for service provision to foster an appealing customer journey (Larivière et al. 2017).

1.2.2 Empathy in Service Encounters

In the context of service encounters, empathy can be understood as the caring, individualized attention that a firm provides its customers (Parasuraman et al. 1985). In a human-to-human service encounter, empathy can be expressed both in verbal communication, for example by indicating understanding of a customer's request and feelings, as well as in non-verbal communication, such as with nodding or through frequent eye contact (Gabbott and Hogg 2004). In general, empathy is considered to influence the perceived service quality alongside the dimensions responsiveness, assurance, reliability and tangibles (Bolton and Drew 2002; Parasuraman et al. 1985, 1988). A prevalent assumption of technology in a service encounter is that it dehumanizes the service interaction as it "cannot provide the empathy a human agent can provide (Yan et al. 2013, p. 7). Understanding a conversation partners emotional state and taking it into account during the encounter is considered to be one of the main factors that differentiate service provision by humans and technology (Larivière et al. 2017). While service provision through technology, such as in the form of self-service portals, has advantages regarding service availability and fulfillment speed, it is usually associated with a lack of personal and emotional interaction due to the social limits of technology (Frey and Osborne 2017). Hence, we suggest to make a first step towards overcoming the social limits of interactive service technology by emulating empathetic behavior of a CA through the use of sentiment analysis and sentiment-adaptive responses.

1.2.3 Social Response Theory and Anthropomorphic CA Design

Recent IS research on CAs draws on Social Response Theory to study user-CA interaction (Diederich et al. 2019c) and inform the design of such artifacts (Gnewuch et al. 2017; Gnewuch et al. 2018b). Social Response Theory posits that humans mindlessly apply social rules and expectations to anything, including computers, which demonstrates human-like traits or behavior (Nass and Moon 2000; Reeves and Nass 1996). Nass and Moon (2000) explain how humans overuse social categories (e.g. gender) and social behaviors (e.g. reciprocity), hypothesizing that "the more computers present characteristics that are associated with humans, the more likely they are to elicit social behavior" (Nass and Moon 2000, p. 7). Due to the fact that CAs usually exhibit a variety of social cues (Feine et al. 2019a), including turn-taking, the use of self-references or having a name, they trigger substantial social responses in users.

These social responses pose opportunities for human-like CA design, yet at the same time foster high user expectations as users would rather compare the CA to a human customer service employee than to a computer system (Følstad and Brandtzæg 2017). Different studies have stated that a higher degree of perceived humanness is often associated with a positive impact on other factors, such as trustworthiness (Schroeder and Schroeder 2018), perceived competency (Araujo 2018), authenticity (Wünderlich and Paluch 2017), or service encounter satisfaction (Gnewuch et al. 2018b) despite potential feelings of uncanniness and eeriness when interacting with a human-like technological artifact (MacDorman et al. 2009). Consequently, many scholars explore different approaches to design CAs as human-like as possible. For the design of human-like CAs, Seeger et al. (2018) provide a conceptual framework which distinguishes three dimensions: Human identity, nonverbal communication, and verbal communication. In this framework, human identity includes cues which serve to identify a human being in computer-mediated communication, such as a name or avatar (Cowell and Stanney 2005). Nonverbal communication refers to any expression of emotional states not directly conveyed in the language itself, such as blinking dots to simulate thinking and typing a response or the use of emoticons (Wang et al. 2008) to express emotions. Third, verbal communication includes the spoken or written sentences itself and cues, such as greetings, small talk and anecdotes (Bickmore and Picard 2005).

In the context of this study, we investigate the effect of a verbal social cue (affective responses) to make CAs display empathy.

1.3 Hypotheses

While various studies have been conducted on empathy in human-computer interaction (e.g. Leite et al. 2013; Niewiadomski and Pelachaud 2010) and human service encounters (e.g. Yan et al. 2013), to the best of our knowledge little empirical research has been conducted on how the empathetic behavior of an artificial virtual agent is perceived by a user in a service context and whether it affects service encounter satisfaction. Different studies on CA design emphasize that CAs should have the capacity to adequately display emotions (e.g. McQuiggan and Lester 2007). However, we still lack an understanding regarding the impact of synthetically displaying empathy in human-CA service encounters. As a first step towards designing interactive service technology that is capable of understanding and adequately showing affective communication behavior, we propose the combination of automatic sentiment analysis and adaptive responses to emulate empathy. Sentiment analysis makes use of the fact that texts written by humans convey valuable information about their emotional state (Liu 2012) and are capable of accurately extracting positive or negative polarity in written text (Liu 2010). Based on the extracted polarity, a CA can provide tailored responses and thus simulate empathy. Hence, we first hypothesize as follows:

H1: A CA that provides sentiment-adaptive responses in a service encounter yields a higher level of perceived empathy than a CA that sends static responses independent of the sentiment.

In the context of human-like design, researchers explore the use of various cues that are intended to contribute to the human-likeness of CAs. For example, Gnewuch et al. (2018b) propose an approach to dynamically delay response times of an agent to simulate thinking and typing of replies and find that such delays lead to a higher perceived human-likeness than immediate responses in a service encounter. Thus, the authors suggest that dynamic response delay represents a cue for human-like design as it can contribute to simulating human communication behavior. Similarly, Araujo (2018) finds that giving a CA a human name and using personalized greetings contribute to perceived humanness. In line with these studies, we consider the display of empathy by understanding a person's affective state and reacting adequately as an essential part of human communication that significantly influences how we perceive each other (Davis 2015). Thus, we suggest that empathetic communication contributes to perceived humanness as follows:

H2:   A CA that provides sentiment-adaptive responses in a service encounter yields a higher level of perceived humanness than a CA that sends static responses independent of the sentiment.

Social cues in the form of avatars or emotions have been found to not only influence the perceived human-likeness of an agent, but to also have an impact of the social presence one feels when interacting with technology (Gefen and Straub 2004). Social presence was originally understood as "the degree of salience of the other person in a mediated communication and the consequent salience of their interpersonal interactions" (Short et al. 1976, p. 65) and has been shown to likewise exist without actual human contact (Gefen and Straub 2004). The concept has been studied in different contexts, such as avatars (Von Der Pütten et al. 2010) or virtual agents (Qiu and Benbasat 2009), with researchers discovering different cues, such as human photos or the use of emotional statements directed towards the user, equally contribute to perceptions of social presence (Hassanein and Head 2007). In line with our view of empathy as a social cue, we argue that empathetic responses convey a feeling of higher social presence than static statements:

H3:   A CA that provides sentiment-adaptive responses in a service encounter yields a higher level of social presence than a CA that sends static responses independent of the sentiment.

Finally, different studies on the role of empathy in human-CA interaction, often with physically or virtually embodied agents, highlight positive effects on further factors. For example, Bickmore and Picard (2005) and Liu and Picard (2004) describe positive effects of suitable expressions of emotion on perceptions of persuasiveness and credibility. Similarly, Brave et al. (2005) found that an agent that is perceived as empathetic is considered to be significantly more caring, likable, trustworthy and supportive. Overall, these studies indicate that adequate displays of empathy by an artificial agent contribute to a better perception of the agent by its user. In the context of human service encounters, empathy has been shown to be associated with greater perceptions of service quality and higher customer satisfaction (Caruana et al. 2000; Mohr and Bitner 1991; Price et al. 1995). Service employees that display empathy are perceived as approachable (Parasuraman et al. 1985), caring (Johnston 1995), and additionally make an effort to understand consumers' needs (Wels-Lips et al. 1998). In addition, Feine et al. (2019b) find a significant correlation between subjectively measured service encounter satisfaction and scores from a sentiment analysis of customer dialogues, underlining the potential of sentiment detection in the context of service provision with CAs. Thus, we hypothesize that an empathetic CA fosters a comparable effect in a human-technology encounter with regard to the overall satisfaction with the provided service.

H4:   Customers are more satisfied with a service encounter when the CA gives sentiment-adaptive, empathetic responses than with a CA that gives static, sentiment-independent responses.

Figure 26 visualizes the hypotheses regarding the impact of sentiment-adaptive responses on perceived empathy, perceived humanness, social presence, and service encounter satisfaction in our model.

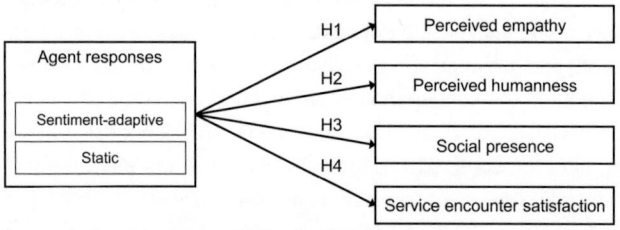

Figure 26 (Study 4): Research Model

1.4 Method

We tested the four hypotheses in an online experiment that took place over a span of two months at the beginning of 2019. For the experiment, we selected a between-subjects design to prevent carryover effects (Boudreau et al. 2001) and chose a customer service context with a fictitious telecommunications company to provide participants with an intuitively understandable service encounter setting. In the following, we describe our data collection procedure and sample, the two experimental configurations with a focus on the design of sentiment-adaptive responses, and the measures as well as underlying items used in the survey after the interaction with the virtual service agent.

1.4.1 Data Collection Procedure and Sample

At the beginning of the experiment, the participants received a briefing website in which the context (service encounter), the structure of the experiment (interaction with CA as service agent and subsequent survey) as well as the experimental task were explained. We provided every participant with the exact same sets of information for the experiment (Dennis and Valacich 2001) and participants were assigned randomly to the control or treatment configuration. Every participant was presented with a fictitious mobile phone invoice and asked to contact the customer service chatbot of the company, find out why the invoice amount was much higher than usual and afterwards file a complaint for an incorrect invoice.

After completing the task, the participants received a link to the online survey from the agent. In total, the experiment took around 10 minutes per participant. With an a priori power analysis using G*Power (Faul et al. 2007), we determined a sample size of at least

102 subjects (effect size = .50, alpha = .05, power = .95). We recruited 112 participants via personal networks, comprising mainly information systems students, and mailing lists, who were not compensated for their participation. We identified six invalid responses with inverted control questions and excluded them from the analysis as participants provided straight line answers, thus reducing the sample size from 112 to 106 participants. The participants' age ranged from 17 to 68 years (mean: 25.6 years) and our sample had a share of 32% female persons. Most of the participants indicated that they never use digital assistants, such as Siri or Alexa (n = 57) and indicated that they never use CAs (n = 70).

1.4.2 Control and Treatment Configurations

We prepared two instances (control instance with static responses, treatment instance with sentiment-adaptive responses) of one CA using the design platform for natural language software Dialogflow by Google (2019). We further implemented a custom-built web interface to provide convenient access to the CAs and minimize distraction. Both CAs received the same training phrases, i.e. exemplary statements which customers might make during the service encounter that indicate a user's intent and trigger a reply. The CAs were able to process different variations of sentences with the same meaning and could extract parameters, such as invoice numbers, and use them throughout the dialogue for paraphrasing. Furthermore, both CAs were designed to state that they did not understand a user's request at one point in the service encounter to explicitly provoke the user in addition to the expensive mobile phone invoice.

The CAs received different cues for human-like CA design according to the three dimensions (human identity, verbal, non-verbal) as suggested by Seeger et al. (2018) to establish a baseline for perceived humanness and social presence: With regard to the human identity, we equipped the CA with the name "Sarah" (Cowell and Stanney 2000), a female gender (Nunamaker et al. 2011) and a comic avatar representing a female customer service employee. Concerning verbal communication, the CA was designed to use self-references, such as "I fully understand...", (Sah and Peng 2015), turn-taking and a personal introduction ("Hello, my name is Sarah and I am part of the customer service team. How can I help you?") as well as polite greeting in the form of a welcome message (Cafaro et al. 2016). Regarding the non-verbal human-like CA design dimension, we implemented blinking dots in combination with dynamic response delays depending on the length of the preceding message as suggested by Gnewuch et al. (2018b) to simulate thinking and typing of replies by the CAs.

Overall, both instances of the CA were identical except for the use of sentiment analysis and adaptive replies (Figure 27).The treatment instance additionally detected the sentiment of a user statement in the background using the automatic sentiment analysis provided by Aylien (2019) and adapted its response to the detected sentiment at three points in the encounter: When the user describes the service request (1), after the CA presents the elements of the invoice (2), and, finally, when the participant complaints about the subscription for mobile games included in the invoice amount (3). If the automatic sentiment analysis determined a positive or neutral sentiment of the participant's message, the treatment instance used the same responses as the control instance. In case of a negative sentiment, the agent added an empathetic statement before the response at the respective interaction point. The empathetic responses aimed to simulate empathetic behavior that a human service agent would most likely show by indicating understanding of the customer's affective state and politely apologizing for the inconvenient situation.

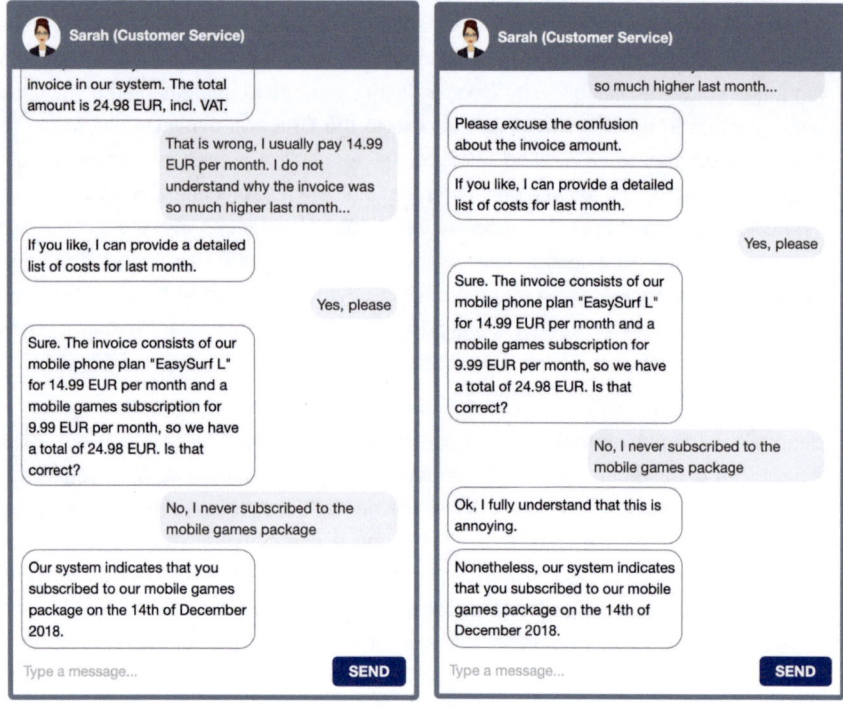

Figure 27 (Study 4): Interface with Static (left) and Adaptive Configurations

The architecture used in this experiment consisted of four components (Figure 28) that were connected via webservices. Once the user entered a query in the web interface it was transmitted to the agent implemented on Google Dialogflow. Dialogflow then detected the user's intent from the statement based on a set of predefined intents (e.g. file invoice complaint) and extracted parameters (e.g. invoice number) that were for example used for paraphrasing by the agent. Next, Google Dialogflow forwarded the detected intent name, parameters, and user statement to a custom fulfillment component.

If Dialogflow was not able to successfully detect a user intent from a statement, it directly sent a context-specific fallback response back to the web interface (e.g. "Unfortunately, I did not understand your response. Please provide the invoice number so we can take a look at the amount for last month"). In case of successful intent detection, the fulfillment component then transmitted a request for sentiment analysis to the external text analytics provider Aylien (2019) and received information on the polarity (negative, neutral, positive) of the original user statement. The fulfillment component then selected the agent's response for this intent and identified polarity (static response in case of positive or neutral polarity, empathetic response in case of negative polarity) and forwarded it to Dialogflow. Finally, Dialogflow sends the response to the Web Interface, which displayed it to the user after the dynamic response delay and indicator (blinking dots) to simulate thinking and typing (Gnewuch et al. 2018b).

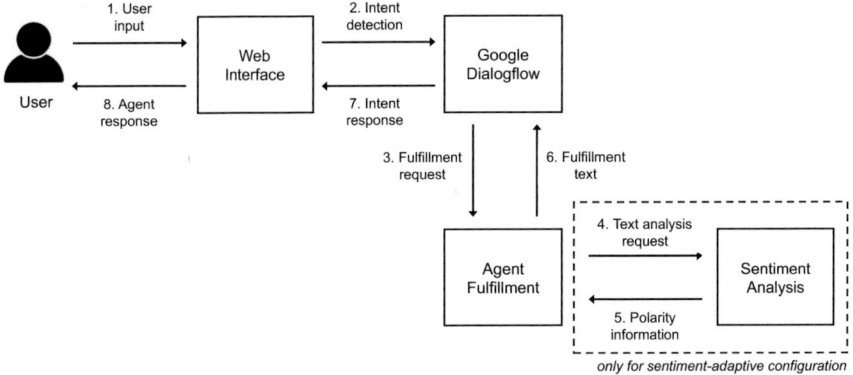

Figure 28 (Study 4): Agent Architecture

To ensure that the real-time sentiment analysis did not delay the CA's responses, we tested whether the sentiment analysis and adaptation of responses lead to higher response times than the dynamic response delays. The test indicated that the designed delays did always exceed the time required for analyzing the sentiment of the previous user statement. Table 26 provides an overview of the static as well as sentiment-adaptive responses used in the interaction.

Table 26 (Study 4): Static and Sentiment-Adaptive Responses

Service interaction point	Static response	Sentiment-adaptive response (for negative sentiment)
Interaction point #1: Description of service request	"To view the invoice, please provide your customer and invoice numbers as well as your date of birth for authentication"	"I understand your concern and would be happy to take a look at your invoice. To view the invoice, please provide your customer and invoice number as well as your date of birth for authentication."
Interaction point #2: Presentation of invoice elements	"If you like, I can provide a detailed list of costs for last month."	"Please excuse the confusion about the invoice amount. If you like, I can provide a detailed list of costs for last month."
Interaction point #3: Complaint about games subscription	"Our system indicates that you subscribed to our mobile games package on the 14th of December 2018."	"Ok, I fully understand that this is annoying. Notwithstanding, our system indicates that you subscribed to our mobile games package on the 14th of December 2018."

1.4.3 Manipulation Check

After the experiment, we conducted a manipulation check to ensure that participants in the treatment condition actually triggered and received empathetic replies. We reviewed conversation logs to identify responses where a negative polarity was identified at the three interaction points in the service encounter. At the first interaction point, where the participant described its request at the beginning of the service encounter, 41% of the responses were neutral and 59% empathetic. At interaction point two after the elements of the incorrect invoice were presented, 14% of the agent's responses were neutral and 86% empathetic. Finally, at the third interaction point where the participant complains about the mobile games subscription, the CA replied neutrally in 28% of the responses and empathetically in 72% of the responses. Overall, around 72% of responses in the treatment instance were empathetic, i.e. the CA detected a negative sentiment and tailored its response accordingly. Thus, the treatment CA did indeed make use of sentiment-adaptive responses nearly three out of four times in the interaction.

1.4.4 Measures

Following the encounter with the virtual service agent, the participants completed a survey in which we measured how the participants perceived the virtual agent and whether they were satisfied with the service encounter. For the design of the questionnaire, we used established measurement instruments from previous studies that were used in the context of technology-driven service encounters (Gnewuch et al. 2018c; Yan et al. 2013). We measured four constructs corresponding to our hypotheses: Perceived empathy (Yan et al. 2013), perceived humanness (Holtgraves and Han 2007), social presence (Gefen and Straub 1997) and service encounter satisfaction (Verhagen et al. 2014). All constructs were measured with two to six items each. As suggested in the original studies, we used a 9-point semantic differential scale to measure perceived humanness and a 7-point Likert scale to measure the constructs perceived empathy, social presence, and service encounter satisfaction. Furthermore, we added two control questions to the survey by inverting two items, one for perceived humanness and one for social presence to check whether participants provided straight line responses in the questionnaire. In the final part of the survey, we collected demographic information (gender and age), information on the frequency of use of digital assistants (e.g. Siri or Alexa) and chatbots on websites and social media ranging from never over monthly to weekly to daily. We further asked for free form feedback for the service encounter and the experiment. Table 27 summarizes the four constructs, items and factor loadings including Cronbach's α, composite reliability (CR) and average variance extracted (AVE). Two items were dropped from the analysis due factor loadings lower than .60 as proposed by Gefen and Straub (2005). All constructs showed sufficient Cronbach's α (larger than .80), CR (larger than .80) and AVE (larger than .50) with respect to the levels proposed by Urbach and Ahlemann (2010) and were thus included in the analysis.

Table 27 (Study 4): Constructs, Items, and Factor Loadings

Constructs and items	Loadings	Scale and source
Perceived empathy (α = .847, CR = .849, AVE = .738)		
The agent gives customers individual attention.	.860	7-point Likert scale (Yan et al. 2013)
The agent gives customers personal attention.	.858	
Perceived humanness (α = .917, CR = .917, AVE = .689)		
How human-like did you perceive the agent?	.811	
How skilled do you perceive the agent?	.870	9-point semantic differential scale (Holtgraves and Han 2007)
How thoughtful do you perceive the agent?	.825	
How polite do you perceive the agent? (dropped)	*(0.549)*	
How responsive do you perceive the agent?	.817	
How engaging do you perceive the agent?	.826	
Social presence (α = .861, CR = .858, AVE = .602)		
I felt a sense of human contact with the agent.	.777	
I felt a sense of personalness with the agent.	.814	7-point Likert scale (Gefen and Straub 1997)
I felt a sense of sociability with the agent (dropped)	*(0.490)*	
I felt a sense of human warmth with the agent.	.729	
I felt sense of human sensitivity with the agent.	.781	
Service satisfaction (α = .848, CR = .851, AVE = .659)		
How satisfied are you with the agent's advice?	.781	7-point Likert scale (Verhagen et al. 2014)
...the way the agent treated you?	.721	
...the overall interaction with the agent?	.920	

1.5 Results

We analyzed the survey data by means of descriptive statistics and t-tests to understand the relation between static or sentiment-adaptive agent responses and perceived empathy (H1), perceived humanness (H2), social presence (H3), and service encounter satisfaction (H4). The analyses were carried out using the statistical computing software R and SPSS version 25. Table 28 summarizes our results for the four hypotheses. We first checked for homogeneity of variance and the Levene tests indicated equal variances for perceived humanness (F = 5.20, p = 0.055), social presence (F = 1.42, p = 0.236), and service encounter satisfaction (F = 0.244, p = 0.622). For perceived empathy, the Levene test showed unequal variances (F = 5.20, p = 0.025). Thus, we used Student's t-tests to analyze for differences between the conditions regarding perceived humanness, social presence and service encounter satisfaction (homogeneous variances) and Welch's t-test for perceived empathy (non-homogeneous variance). All t-tests were performed one-sided to examine whether sentiment-adaptive responses (treatment group) positively affected customer perception of the CA in comparison to static responses (control group).

Our data reveals that participants in the treatment group perceived the CA as more empathetic (M = 4.28, SD = 1.27) than participants in the control group (M = 3.39, SD = 1.65), $t(97.4)$ = -3.14, p = .001. Thus, the data supports our first hypothesis that a CA with dynamic, sentiment-adaptive response is perceived as more empathetic than a CA that provides static, neutral responses. Concerning perceived humanness, the survey data indicates a significant difference between the control (M = 4.29, SD = 1.97) and treatment groups (M = 5.35, SD = 1.49), $t(104)$ = -3.12, p = .001, providing support for our second hypothesis that a CA with sentiment-adaptive responses is perceived as more human-like than a CA with static replies.

Table 28 (Study 4): Descriptive Statistics and t-Test Results

		Condition		t-value (df)	p-value	Result
		Control (n = 53)	Treatment (n = 53)			
Perceived empathy	Mean SD SE	3.39 1.65 0.23	4.28 1.27 0.17	-3.14 (97.4)	.001	H1 supported
Perceived humanness	Mean SD SE	4.29 1.97 0.27	5.35 1.49 0.20	-3.12 (104)	.002	H2 supported
Social presence	Mean SD SE	2.92 1.34 0.18	3.74 1.26 0.17	-3.23 (104)	< .001	H3 supported
Service satisfaction	Mean SD SE	3.97 1.37 0.19	4.70 1.29 0.18	-2.61 (104)	.003	H4 supported

SD = Standard deviation, SE = Standard error

B. Studies on Anthropomorphic CAs

Furthermore, participants in the treatment group reported a higher social presence ($M = 3.74$, $SD = 1.26$) than participants in the control group ($M = 2.92$, $SD = 1.34$), $t(104) = -3.23$, $p < .001$, providing support for the third hypothesis. Finally, participants that interacted with the sentiment-adaptive CA showed a higher service encounter satisfaction ($M = 4.70$, $SD = 1.23$) than participants that were assigned to the CA with non-empathetic responses ($M = 3.97$, $SD = 1.37$), $t(104) = -2.61$, $p = 0.03$). Thus, we find support for the fourth hypothesis, highlighting that participants who interacted with the sentiment-adaptive CA were more satisfied with the service encounter than participants that engaged in a conversation with the static CA in the control configuration.

Next, we conducted additional robustness tests. We analyzed for differences between the control and treatment groups with regard to demographics. We found no significant differences in age ($t(69.1) = -1.92$, $p = 0.059$), gender ($\chi^2(1) = 0.17$, $p = 0.679$), frequency of use for digital assistants like Siri or Alexa ($\chi^2(3) = 0.06$, $p = 0.996$), and frequency of use for chatbots on social media or company websites ($\chi^2(3) = 5.81$, $p = 0.121$) between the two groups. Overall, the results of our tests indicate that the differences in perceived empathy, perceived humanness, social presence, and service encounter satisfaction are not explained by differences in demographics or CA experience between the two experimental groups. Furthermore, we conducted a multiple linear regression to investigate whether the frequency of use for digital assistants or chatbots on websites and social media had an impact on perceived empathy, perceived humanness, social presence, and service satisfaction yet the results were not significant. In addition, we performed post-hoc power analyses using G*Power (Faul et al. 2007), which suggested that all tests have sufficient power for the given sample size ($power_{empathy} = .916$, $power_{perceived\ humanness} = .899$, $power_{social\ presence} = .925$, $power_{service\ satisfaction} = .836$). Figure 29 visualizes the differences between the control and treatment group with regard to the four measured constructs with the error bars indicating the 95% confidence interval.

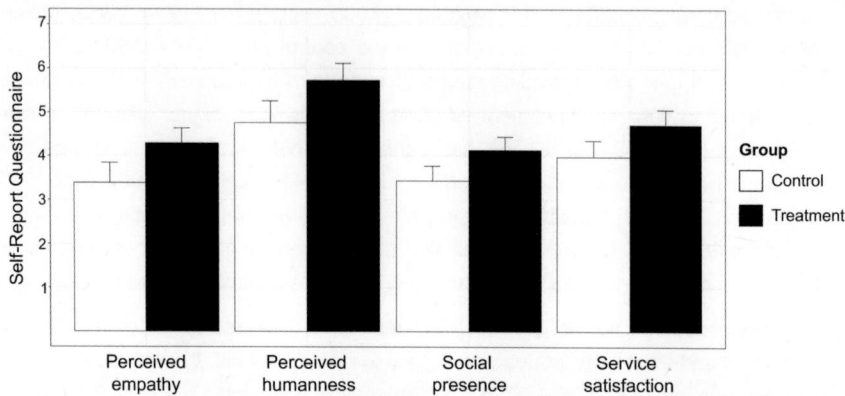

Figure 29 (Study 4): Differences for the Constructs between the Groups

We further conducted a post-hoc exploratory moderator analysis, examining whether the relation between static or sentiment-adaptive responses and empathy, perceived humanness, social presence, and service satisfaction was moderated by age, gender or frequency of use of digital assistants or chatbots. The participants' age and frequency of use were not identified as moderators.

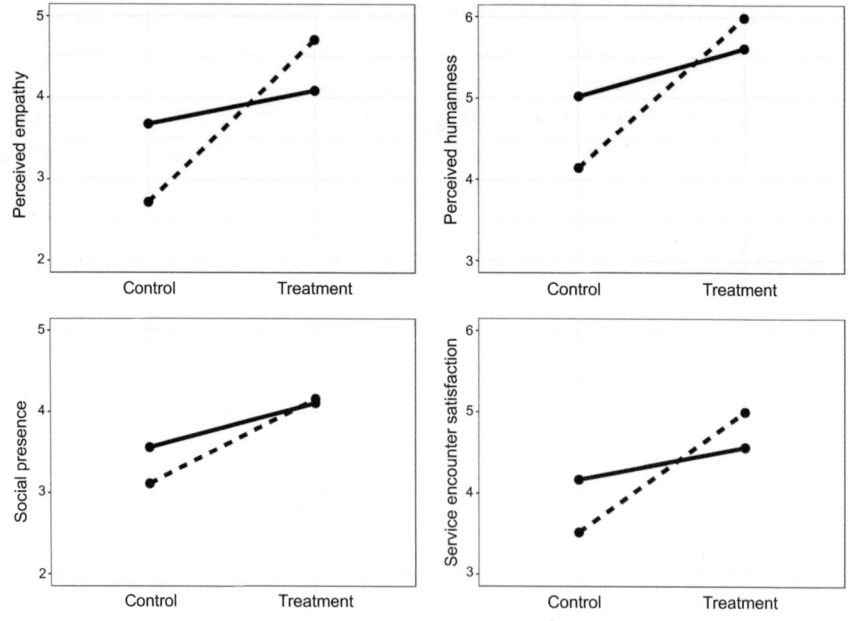

Figure 30 (Study 4): Mean Values by Gender (Dotted: Female Participants)

However, the interaction term between the group and gender explained a significant increase in variance in empathy ($\Delta R^2 = .058$, $F(1, 102) = 6.868$, $p = .010$), thus the participant's gender moderated the relationship between the experimental group and empathy. The potential moderations by gender with regard to the relation between the experimental group and perceived humanness ($\Delta R^2 = .027$, $F(1, 102) = 3.118$, $p = .080$), social presence ($\Delta R^2 = .009$, $F(1, 102) = 0.992$, $p = .322$), and service encounter satisfaction ($\Delta R^2 = .034$, $F(1, 102) = 3.837$, $p = .053$) were not statistically significant. Figure 30 visualizes the relationship between experimental group, gender, and empathy, humanness, social presence, and service satisfaction.

1.6 Discussion

Our results provide empirical support that sentiment-adaptive responses increase perceived empathy, perceived humanness, social presence, and service encounter satisfaction in comparison to static responses. In the following, we discuss implications of our results for service provision with CAs and their human-like design, state limitations of our work, and outline opportunities for future research.

1.6.1 Implications for CAs in Service Encounters and their Design

The results of our experiment demonstrate how detecting a user's affective state and providing empathetic responses contributes to a better perception of the CA and overall satisfaction with the service encounter, even when the actual request cannot be directly fulfilled by the system. Against this background, the real-time identification of negative sentiments in an interaction and the provision of empathetic responses can help to reduce customer frustration and overcome social limits of current interactive service technology (Yan et al. 2013). The fundamental idea of our sentiment-adaptive design, comprising the combination of sentiment analysis and adaptive responses, can be adapted by practitioners implementing CAs for service provision and its components (e.g. provider for sentiment analysis or CA platform used for intent detection) can be exchanged to meet different organizational requirements, such as for architectural standards or concerning data protection.

In addition, the automatic identification of sentiment in the dialogue can be used not only to provide tone-aware responses, but could also enable a better transition of the service encounter with the virtual agent to human service personnel by forwarding service requests of potentially frustrated customers. As the design of CAs that are able to deal with a high variety of user input remains a challenging endeavor (Følstad and Brandtzæg 2017), it can be expected that CAs will have to forward service requests, particularly the ones that are more complex or did not occur frequently in the past, to human service personnel. Thus, a real-time sentiment analysis of the human-CA dialogue can not only be used to increase customer satisfaction with the service encounter, but also opens up further options for designing service encounter transitions in a way that remains appealing and convenient for the customer (Lemon and Verhoef 2016). Future CAs for service provision could for example apply automatic compensation strategies in case a frustrated user is recognized, similar to approaches of human service employees nowadays.

Concerning the human-like design of such service agents, our experiment shows that users indeed anthropomorphize CAs in a service context in line with Social Response Theory (Nass and Moon 2000; Reeves and Nass 1996), highlighting the potential of this technology to (partially) overcome current limitations of human service employees (availability, consistent quality, response time) and self-service technologies (lack of personal contact). While empathy was considered in the past to be primarily relevant for human service encounters and not for service provision via technology due to its inherent social limits (Yan et al. 2013), our results indicate a necessity to rethink how we design and position technology in a service context and emphasize the potential of human-like CA design (Seeger et al. 2018). In the context of continuously increasing capabilities of CAs, we expect that thinking carefully about the role of CAs between existing interactive service technology and human service provision will become even more relevant in the future, urging managers to reflect on which services are better provided by humans and which by different types of seemingly intelligent technology (Scherer et al. 2015).

Finally, our analysis of gender-related moderation effects highlights the importance of empathy in human-CA interaction in particular for female customers. According to our findings, empathetic communication seemed to be relatively more important for women than for men regarding perceptions of empathy and humanness of the service agent as well as with regard to service satisfaction. Female participants in the control group perceived the agent as less empathetic and human-like and were less satisfied with the service encounter than male participants. However, female participants in the treatment group rated the CA as more empathetic and human-like and indicated a higher service satisfaction than male participants in the same experimental group (Figure 30). These results are in line with studies on human service provision. For example, Chiu (2002) as well as Chiu and Wu (2002) investigated gender-related differences between the affective and cognitive components of attitude towards service quality (Zajonc and Markus 2002). In this distinction, cognitive components refer to "what we know" whereas the affective components describe "what we feel" for a particular product or service (Zanna and Rempel 1988). Their findings suggest that the affective component is perceived as more important for service quality than the cognitive component for female customers while there are no differences in the relative importance these components of service quality for male customers (Chiu 2002). Thus, our results suggest that existing findings concerning empathy in human service encounters hold true for service provision with human-like CAs. Consequently, CA designers could explore varying interaction styles to account for the gender-related differences in communication and perception of quality.

1.6.2 Limitations and Opportunities for Future Research

Our work is not free of limitations. First, our exploratory design with the automatic sentiment analysis and sentiment-adaptive verbal responses for statements with a negative polarity, offers opportunities for future design-oriented CA studies in a service context. While our study places emphasis on detecting and addressing negative emotions in the service encounter, future studies can explore whether positive feelings in an interaction can be reinforced by adaptive CA behavior as well, thus contributing to a better perceived service experience. Furthermore, the empathetic responses in our experiment were exclusively verbal without the use of non-verbal communication. Exploring the use of sentiment-adaptive non-verbal communication, such as facial expressions of a virtually embodied service agent or the use of emoticons (Beale and Creed 2009) to express empathy, represents a promising research endeavor.

In addition, our experiment was conducted in an online setting where we benefitted from control yet lacked realism (Dennis and Valacich 2001). We provided the participants with a set of rather specific tasks, which in turn allowed for a better design of the communication behavior of the CA as the variation of user input was limited. Thus, we propose future research to investigate the design of sentiment-adaptive responses of CAs in the field where user input exhibits a potentially higher variability and fallback responses or transitions between service encounters with CAs and human personnel need to be carefully designed to ensure a high-quality user experience.

Furthermore, our research design and sample did not account for cultural differences among participants that could moderate the relation between sentiment-adaptive responses and the four measured constructs. Future studies could explore a culturally informed design as for example suggested by Pereira and Baranauskas (2015) to account for cultural differences related to the importance and display of empathy.

Finally, the CA that we designed with the selected set of human-like cues was perceived positively by the participants. However, recent research on CA design indicated potentially unintended outcomes of combining human-like design cues to maximize humanness (Seeger et al. 2018), such as a high degree of uncertainty concerning the human or technological nature of the service agent or unrealistic expectations towards the agent's capabilities (Wünderlich and Paluch 2017). Similarly, Schroeder and Schroeder (2018) found that increasing human-likeness does not linearly increase with trust, but that users may feel threatened at one point.

In this context, the theory of Uncanny Valley (Mori 1970) describes a sharp drop of affinity for a human-like object, where the attention of a user shifts from the human-like qualities to the aspects that seem to be inhuman (MacDorman et al. 2009). Thus, we suggest that future studies investigate the risks associated with increasing anthropomorphism by combining sentiment-adaptive responses with other social cues, such as a representation by means of an interactive avatar and name, to determine if and where a human-like CA could elicit negative responses (e.g. feelings of eeriness or uncanniness) in service encounters.

1.7 Concluding Remarks

Interactive service technology in the form of CAs promises to provide service that is always available, easy-to-use and resembles human-to-human service encounters. Yet, the social capabilities of current CAs with regard to recognizing and adequately reacting to a customer's affective state are limited. To make a first step towards overcoming the social limits of conversational service agents, we proposed and evaluated the use of sentiment-adaptive responses in a customer service context. Our findings provide empirical evidence that a sentiment-aware CA leads to a higher perceived empathy, perceived humanness, social presence, as well as service encounter satisfaction in comparison with CAs operating with static responses. In addition, our results suggest that existing findings from human service provision concerning gender-related differences between the importance of cognitive and affective components for perceived service quality hold true for service provision with interactive technology, offering new design options for increasing service satisfaction through varying communication behavior.

Our study contributes to designing CAs as an emerging, innovative technology for service provision in three ways: First, we suggest a design approach for emulating empathy in conversational service agents through the combination of automatic sentiment analysis and sentiment-adaptive verbal responses. Second, our results place emphasis on the potential of affective communication in interactive service technologies, which was primarily considered to be relevant for human service encounters in the past, as it contributes perceived empathy, perceived humanness, social presence, and, in particular, service encounter satisfaction. Finally, our results add to the growing knowledge base on human-like CA design by displaying how empathy represents a social cue, which can effectively contribute to a more human-like perception of such virtual agents in service encounters.

2. Study 5: Promoting Sustainable Mobility Beliefs with Persuasive and Anthropomorphic Design – Insights from an Experiment with a Conversational Agent

Table 29: Fact Sheet of Study 5

Title	Promoting Sustainable Mobility Beliefs with Persuasive and Anthropomorphic Design: Insights from an Experiment with a Conversational Agent
Authors	Stephan Diederich*[1], Sascha Lichtenberg[1], Alfred Benedikt Brendel[1], Simon Trang[2] 1) Chair of Information Management, University of Göttingen, Platz der Göttinger Sieben 5, 37073 Göttingen, Germany 2) Chair of Information Security and Compliance, University of Göttingen, Platz der Göttinger Sieben 5, 37073 Göttingen, Germany *Corresponding author. Tel.: +49 551 3921170. E-Mail: stephan.diederich@stud.uni-goettingen.de
Outlet	International Conference on Information Systems (ICIS), Munich, Germany, 2019
Abstract	Sustainable mobility behavior is increasingly relevant due to the vast environmental impact of current transportation systems. With the growing variety of transportation modes, individual decisions for or against specific mobility options become more and more important and salient beliefs regarding the environmental impact of different modes influence this decision process. While information systems have been recognized for their potential to shape individual beliefs and behavior, design-oriented studies that explore their impact, in particular on environmental beliefs, remain scarce. In this study, we contribute to closing this research gap by designing and evaluating a new type of artifact, a persuasive and human-like conversational agent, in a 2x2 experiment with 225 participants. Drawing on the Theory of Planned Behavior and Social Response Theory, we find empirical support for the influence of persuasive design elements on individual environmental beliefs and discover that anthropomorphic design can contribute to increasing the persuasiveness of artifacts.
Keywords	Sustainable Mobility; Persuasive Design; Conversational Agent

2.1 Introduction

Sustainable mobility behavior becomes more and more important nowadays due to the extensive environmental impact of current transportation systems (Vergragt and Brown 2007) as well as the increasing variety of transportation modes (Willing et al. 2017). On the individual level, people in urban areas now have various mobility modes at their disposal, in particular shared ones, such as for cars, bicycles or e-scooters (Rodrigue et al. 2013). However, it is still up to the individual to decide which (sustainable) mobility mode to use, a decision that is influenced not only by pragmatic questions of availability and travel time but also by the salient beliefs one holds regarding the different modes and their environmental impact (Donald et al. 2014). According to the Belief-Action-Outcome framework by Melville (2010), this belief precedes an individual's action (e.g. to choose a car or bicycle for travel), which ultimately leads to a certain outcome (e.g. adding to CO_2 emissions or not). Information systems (IS) have been recognized for their potential to influence individual beliefs and actions towards sustainable behavior (vom Brocke et al. 2013; Butler 2011; Elliot 2011; Malhotra et al. 2013). In the context of environmental sustainability, studies investigate how IS can promote sustainable mobility behavior with the use of e-bikes (Flüchter and Wortmann 2014; Froehlich et al. 2009), encourage efficient energy use (Corbett 2013a; Fitzpatrick and Smith 2009; Loock et al. 2013), or create transparency for different types of environmentally friendly actions (Pitt et al. 2011). However, studies that explore the opportunity to promote eco-friendly beliefs and behavior through IS design are still scarce (Henkel and Kranz 2018; Seidel et al. 2017), focus primarily on action-formation (Brendel et al. 2017) and the question of how individual environmental beliefs can be influenced through IS design in Melville's research agenda (2010, RQ5) remains largely unanswered.

In this study, we contribute to closing this research gap by designing and evaluating an artifact that we envisage to positively influence individual sustainability beliefs regarding the use of shared e-bikes in an organizational setting. In contrast to prevalent studies that present persuasive designs of mobile apps or websites in the context of environmental sustainability, we design a conversational agent (CA) with which users interact through natural language. CAs, driven by machine learning and natural language processing, currently attract strong interest in research and practice alike (McTear 2017; Oracle 2016), both in the form of digital assistants (e.g. Siri or Alexa) as well as chatbots on company websites and social media (Baier et al. 2018). From a theoretical perspective, CAs represent an interesting phenomenon as users show substantial social responses to the human-like representation and behavior of such agents, which in turn offers new opportunities for the anthropomorphic design of such agents (Seeger et al. 2018) and their persuasiveness (Adler et al. 2016).

In this study, we combine insights from human-like CA design with prescriptive knowledge from persuasive systems for environmental sustainability to explore the following research question: *How can persuasive and human-like design of conversational agents positively shape individual beliefs towards sustainable mobility behavior?*

To address this question, we design a conversational agent and investigate to which extent it impacts individual behavioral, normative, and control beliefs (Ajzen 1985, 1991) in the context of organizational e-bike sharing by means of an online experiment with 225 participants and a 2x2 between-subjects design. Our study makes three main contributions: First, we empirically demonstrate how the design of an artifact can shape individual beliefs for sustainable mobility at the example of e-bikes, thus augmenting the prevalent research focus on action-formation. Second, we present a conversational agent as a new technological artifact that triggers social responses by users and offers new opportunities for anthropomorphic design. Third, we show how prescriptive knowledge from persuasive system design and human-like design can be combined to build an artifact that exhibits a greater degree of persuasiveness. The remainder of this paper follows the communication schema for experimental research proposed by Dennis and Valacich (2001): We first describe individual environmental beliefs and their formation, persuasive system design and anthropomorphic CA design as well as Social Response Theory as the research background of our study. Then, we develop our hypotheses and present our research design, comprising the data collection procedure and sample, the experimental conditions as well as the measures used in the questionnaire. Afterwards, we present our results, discuss theoretical and practical implications as well as outline limitations and opportunities for future research before concluding with some final remarks.

2.2 Research Background and Related Work

Every individual action, such as choosing the car or bicycle for short distance travel, is influenced by personal beliefs. In the context of sustainability, these beliefs can encourage environmentally friendly behavior, in particular when individuals believe that they can take efficient countermeasures to mitigate a threat to personally valued objects like oceans or rainforests (Henkel and Kranz 2018; Steg et al. 2005). Individual beliefs are influenced by a variety of societal and organizational factors (Melville 2010). Societal factors include for example family life or political discourses that shape our beliefs about the state of the planet and the impact of human behavior on it. Organizational factors comprise aspects, such as corporate vision statements, sustainability campaigns or information systems that create transparency regarding the environmental impact of the organization and promote sustainable behavior. Against this background, the Theory of Planned Behavior (Ajzen 1985, 1991) helps to understand the relation between individual environmental beliefs and actions (De Groot and Steg 2007; Melville 2010). According to

Ajzen (1991), three types of salient beliefs influence individual action: First, *behavioral beliefs* link behavior to outcome and describe that if an outcome is favorable from the individual's perspective she or he will have a positive attitude towards performing the behavior, which increases the likelihood of actually performing it. For example, if one believes contributing to the reduction of CO_2 emissions, even on a very small scale, is a favorable outcome, she or he will have a generally positive attitude towards riding a bicycle instead of taking a car. The second type of belief, *normative beliefs,* considers that humans are social beings and suggests that the key people around an individual with their behavioral expectations influence individual behavior. Staying with the example of bicycles as a sustainable mobility mode, behavioral expectations could stem from colleagues at work that expect one to use a bicycle for short distance travel. Third, *control beliefs*, comprise an individual's belief about factors that may facilitate or hinder performing a specific behavior. The concept of perceived behavioral control is related to self-efficacy (Bandura 1977, 1996) and includes for example if one feels to make a worthwhile contribution to reducing CO_2 emissions by taking a bicycle for a short ride or whether it contributes to individual health. In the following, we will use this distinction between *behavioral, normative,* and *control beliefs* for a more granular understanding of the relation between our artifact's design and individual environmental beliefs.

2.2.1 Persuasive Design for Pro-Environmental Beliefs and Behavior

The idea that technology can influence human beliefs and behavior has been established for around two decades now and is based on the paradigm of computers as social actors (Fogg and Nass 1997; Nass and Moon 2000). Research in the area of persuasive design seeks to account for the social response people show to computers (Reeves and Nass 1996) and uses different design elements to shape user perception and promote desired behavior. Fogg (2003) distinguishes five types of social cues in persuasive design: physical (e.g. face, movement), psychological (e.g. humor, empathy), language (e.g. interactive language, spoken language), social dynamics (cooperation, praise), and social roles (e.g. teammate, guide). Designers are thus equipped with cues that can be used for persuasive design in a variety of application domains, such as education, health or environmental sustainability (Langrial et al. 2012).

In the domain of green IS, persuasive design offers the opportunity to promote individual and organizational environmentally friendly beliefs and behavior (Brauer et al. 2016; Shevchuk and Oinas-Kukkonen 2016), thus contributing to more sustainable processes and practices (Dedrick 2010; Gholami et al. 2016; Marett et al. 2012). While design-oriented studies in this domain are limited (Brendel et al. 2017; Henkel and Kranz 2018), different researchers have started to explore persuasive design for green IS and indicate a positive impact on individual behavior. For example, Loock et al. (2013) design a web portal to motivate customers to reduce their electricity consumption with the use of goal setting. Their results show a positive impact of default goal setting on energy conservation as long as the default goal is not set too low or too high with regard to a self-set goal and identify a moderating effect of feedback on goal attainment. Similarly, Fitzpatrick and Smith (2009) explore technology-enabled feedback on domestic energy consumption and present design concerns to build systems that provide effective consumption feedback to promote behavior change. Extending this fact-orientated feedback on sustainability behavior, Flüchter and Wortmann (2014) investigate the role of additional normative feedback on the use of e-bikes for commutes. Flüchter and Wortmann (2014) design an information system that facilitates a competition for e-bike use and creates transparency regarding the user's own ranking in this challenge. The authors argue that while commuting competitions might be useful to encourage sustainable user behavior, they might also lead to unintended negative effects regarding individual intrinsic motivation (decreased enjoyment of e-bikes) and perceived autonomy (increased feeling of being controlled in the competition). Shevchuk and Oinas-Kukkonen (2016) review these and other applications in published research to identify elements of persuasive design used in such artifacts. These design elements fall into the categories of primary task support (e.g. self-monitoring or personalization), dialogue support (e.g. praise, rewards, or reminders), credibility support (e.g. trustworthiness or expertise), and social support (social facilitation, cooperation, or competition). Admitting that Green IS is still a rather young domain, Shevchuk and Oinas-Kukkonen (2016) find that few studies explore design in the context of sustainability and its impact on individual beliefs and actions despite its relevance and potential (Malhotra et al. 2013).

2.2.2 Anthropomorphic CA Design and Social Response Theory

Studies that present prescriptive knowledge for systems which promote pro-environmental belief and behavior change primarily focus on web-based systems (e.g. Loock et al. (2013)) or mobile applications (e.g. Pitt et al. (2011)) with traditional, graphical user interfaces. With substantial technological progress in the areas of natural language processing and machine learning, so-called conversational agents (CAs) currently attract strong interest in both theory and practice (Diederich et al. 2019a; McTear et al. 2016; Oracle 2016). Based on the fundamental idea of human-computer interaction via natural language, CAs are now studied in various application areas, such as customer service (e.g. Diederich et al. 2019c, Wünderlich and Paluch 2017), marketing and sales (e.g. Hanus and Fox 2015), healthcare (e.g. Sebastian and Richards 2017), or education (e.g. Graesser et al. 2017; Le and Wartschinski 2018) and different forms of CAs have emerged. Humans can now interact with CAs using written (e.g. chatbots) or spoken natural language (e.g. personal assistants like Siri or Microsoft Cortana) and CAs can be disembodied (Araujo 2018), have a virtual embodiment (Wünderlich and Paluch 2017) or a physical embodiment, such as in the form of service robots (Stock and Merkle 2018).

The human-like characteristics of CAs, both in form, such as a human name, and function, for example participating in a dialogue with turn-taking, trigger mindless social responses by users (Feine et al. 2019b; Verhagen et al. 2014) as postulated in Social Response Theory (Fogg and Nass 1997; Nass and Moon 2000) where the intensity of such responses varies according to the degree of human-likeness of the CA (Gong 2008). Emerging studies on CA design find that a higher degree of humanness is associated with different positive effects, such as on service encounter satisfaction (Gnewuch et al. 2018b), perceived social presence (Pereira et al. 2014), trustworthiness (Araujo 2018) and persuasiveness (Gong 2008).

For the human-like design of CAs, Seeger et al. (2018) present a conceptual framework that comprises three dimensions (Table 30): The first dimension, *human identity*, includes anthropomorphic cues regarding the representation of the agent, for example by means of an avatar (Gong 2008) or demographic characteristics like a human name (Cowell and Stanney 2005) or gender (Nunamaker et al. 2011). The second dimension, *verbal cues*, comprises the choice of words and sentences and the way the CA converses with a user. Exemplary cues in this dimension include for example self-references ("I think that..." (Sah and Peng 2015)), self-disclosure of artificial thoughts and emotions ("In my experience, riding the bicycle to work instead of taking the car does make a difference for the environment" (Schuetzler et al. 2018b)) or variability in syntax and word choice (Seeger et al. 2018) instead of repeating the same sentences in a conversation. The third dimension, *non-verbal cues* includes non-verbal communication that conveys information about an individual's attitudes or emotional state (Ekman and Friesen 1969). Anthropomorphic cues in this dimensions include dynamic response times depending on message length and complexity to indicate thinking (Gnewuch et al. 2018b) or blinking dots to simulate the typing of responses by the artificial agent (de Visser et al. 2016) as well as the use of emoticons to express emotions in a dialogue (Mayer et al. 2006).

Table 30 (Study 5): Dimensions for Anthropomorphic CA Design and Cues

Anthropomorphic Design Dimensions		
Human identity	Verbal cues	Non-verbal cues
• Avatar (Gong 2008) • Human name (Cowell and Stanney 2005) • Gender (Nunamaker et al. 2011)	• Self-references (Sah and Peng 2015) • Self-disclosure (Schuetzler et al. 2018b) • Personal introduction and greeting (Cafaro et al. 2016) • Variability in syntax and word choice (Seeger et al. 2018) • Politeness through words (Mayer et al. 2006)	• Dynamic response times (Gnewuch et al. 2018b) • Blinking dots (de Visser et al. 2016) • Politeness through emoticons (Mayer et al. 2006)

2.3 Hypotheses Development

Our research seeks to contribute to a better understanding of the relation between CA design and individual beliefs regarding sustainable mobility with a focus on two dimensions: persuasive and anthropomorphic design. Specifically, we hypothesize that persuasive (Shevchuk and Oinas-Kukkonen 2016) and human-like (Seeger et al. 2018) design elements in conversational agents contribute to stronger behavioral, normative, and control beliefs (Ajzen 1991) of individuals regarding the environmental sustainability of e-bike use.

Drawing on the computers as social actors paradigm (Fogg and Nass 1997; Nass and Moon 2000), it has been found that technology influences individual beliefs and behavior (Fogg 2003). Similar to human persuasion approaches, technology can shape user attitudes and behavior through different approaches ranging from humor, empathy, and praise to using social dynamics like cooperation and competition. Oinas-Kukkonen and Harjumaa (2009) organize these persuasive elements in a framework that provides prescriptive knowledge by means of specific design principles and exemplary instantiations. The researchers propose four categories that group design elements into primary task support (e.g. tailoring of information and personalized design), dialogue support (e.g. praise or rewards), credibility support (e.g. trustworthiness or expertise), and social support (e.g. social facilitation or normative influence) (Oinas-Kukkonen and Harjumaa 2009; Shevchuk and Oinas-Kukkonen 2016). These design elements have the potential to reinforce, change or shape beliefs and behavior of individuals by increasing the persuasiveness of artifacts (Lehto et al. 2012). Thus, we formulate our first hypothesis as follows:

H1: Persuasive design elements have a positive impact on perceived persuasiveness of the agent.

Furthermore, conversational agents as a specific type of IT artifact with which users interact through natural language offer various possibilities for human-like design. Equipping the agent with a human identity including a name, gender and avatar (Cowell and Stanney 2005; Gong 2008), verbal cues like expressions of emotions (Wang et al. 2008) or the use of self-references (Sah and Peng 2015), and non-verbal cues, such as dynamic response delays for thinking and typing (Gnewuch et al. 2018b) can contribute to users perceiving the agent as more human-like despite its apparent artificial nature. Against this background, we hypothesize that such cues contribute to users perceiving the agent as more human-like:

H2: *Human-like design cues have a positive impact on perceived humanness of the agent.*

Emerging studies that explore the human-like design of conversational agents suggest that perceived humanness can increase the persuasiveness of the agent. For example, Harjunen et al. (2018) find that participants in an experiment accepted virtual offers more when the agent showed human-like behavior by smiling or touching with a haptic glove. Similarly, Adler et al. (2016) show that a CA which showed (positive) emotions, exhibits a higher degree of perceived persuasiveness than a CA that does not make emotionally-loaded statements. Thus, we hypothesize:

H3: *Perceived humanness has a positive impact on perceived persuasiveness of the agent.*

Next, we consider the relation between persuasiveness and individual behavioral beliefs. As persuasive design elements, such as praise for e-bike use in combination with positively highlighting the individual environmental contribution (Oinas-Kukkonen and Harjumaa 2009), link behavior (e-bike use) to an actual, favorable outcome (contribution to our environment), we hypothesize that persuasiveness has a positive impact on behavioral beliefs in the fourth hypothesis:

H4: *Perceived persuasiveness positively impacts individual behavioral beliefs regarding the environmental impact of e-bike use.*

Additionally, we suggest that persuasive design can increase individual normative beliefs by showing the sustainable behavior of normative referents of the individual user, such as family, friends, and colleagues. Elements from the persuasive design category of social support (Oinas-Kukkonen and Harjumaa 2009), such as social comparison, social facilitation or competition/cooperation, can make collective desired behavior transparent and indicate the underlying, implicit beliefs by highlighting activities of other users (Flüchter and Wortmann 2014). Thus, we propose that perceived persuasiveness positively affects individual normative beliefs regarding the use of e-bikes:

H5: Perceived persuasiveness positively impacts individual normative beliefs regarding the environmental impact of e-bike use.

Finally, we propose that persuasive design can positively contribute to stronger control beliefs in the context of environmental sustainability by highlighting factors facilitating and diminishing factors that inhibit performance of sustainable behavior. For example, a conversational agent with a persuasive design can provide tailored information (Shevchuk and Oinas-Kukkonen 2016) by highlighting the decreased commute time for business travelers with a e-bike compared to a car during rush hour and emphasize the positive impact on individual health. In this example, decreased commute time for business travelers with little time and contributing to individual health, serve as facilitating factors for commuting with the e-bike instead of the car. Hence, we hypothesize that persuasive design of a CA by means of tailored information (Oinas-Kukkonen and Harjumaa 2009) positively impacts individual control beliefs with regard to the environmental impact of e-bike use.

H6: Perceived persuasiveness positively impacts individual control beliefs regarding the environmental impact of e-bike use.

Overall, we formulate six hypotheses with regard to the relation between anthropomorphic and persuasive conversational agent design and individual behavioral, normative and control beliefs concerning the environmental impact of e-bike use. Figure 31 visualizes the hypotheses in our research model.

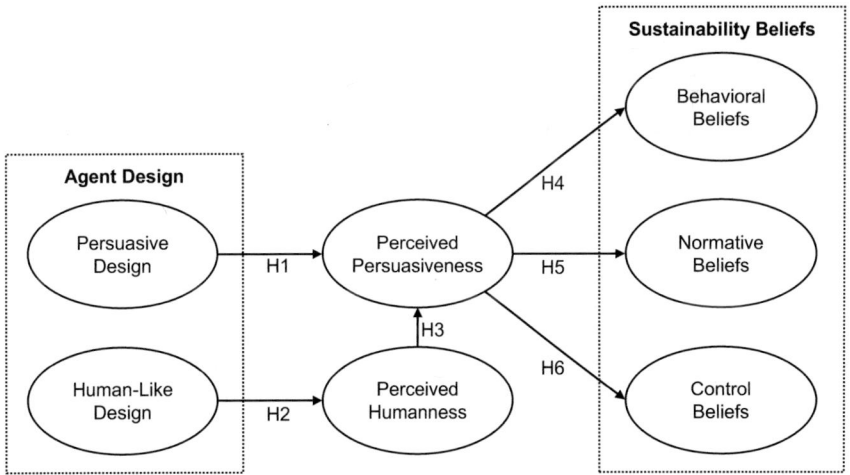

Figure 31 (Study 5): Research Model

2.4 Research Design

To investigate our hypotheses regarding the relation between persuasive, anthropomorphic CA design and sustainability beliefs, we conducted an online experiment in the context of organizational e-bike sharing. The experiment took place in the first quarter of 2019 over a span of three months and is part of a larger design science research project which aims to design an information system that facilitates and promotes e-bike sharing within different organizations. In the following, we describe the experimental conditions, the data collection procedure and sample, and the measures used in our post-experimental survey.

2.4.1 Data Collection Procedure and Sample

The participants of our experiment were asked to interact with a conversational agent to look up and modify a reservation for an e-bike to ride from one company site to another. Every participant received exactly the same information for the experiment (Dennis and Valacich 2001) in the form of a briefing document in which we described the context (e-bike sharing in a company), the structure of the experiment (interaction with a virtual reservation agent followed by a questionnaire) as well as experimental tasks. The document further contained a link that randomly assigned the participant to one of the experimental conditions. Every participant was asked to complete five tasks, independent from his or her intention to use e-bikes: Look up an existing e-bike reservation (task 1) and authenticate with the virtual reservation agent (task 2), find out whether a bike is available at a given company site tomorrow in the afternoon (task 3), modify the existing reservation for tomorrow afternoon (task 4), and request a confirmation of the change via e-mail (task 5).

Although the agent was able to process most of the participant's input regardless of the wording used, we chose a rather specific set of tasks to allow for a relatively structured dialogue and comparability across the experimental conditions, similar to other experimental studies on current conversational agents (e.g. Gnewuch et al. 2018b). After completing the final task, the agent responded with a link to the survey. The experiment took around eight minutes per person. Participants were acquired using the panel company Clickworker (2018) and received a small compensation for their participation. After removing six invalid responses, identified by two attention checks where participants were asked to indicate a specific number, we arrived at a sample size of n = 225 participants ranging from 18 to 49 years old (mean: 32.2 years) and a share of 45.3 % female persons.

2.4.2 Experimental Conditions

We chose a 2x2 experimental design comprising the dimensions persuasive design (neutral/persuasive) and anthropomorphic CA design (machine-like/human-like) as visualized in Table 31. Every participant was randomly assigned to one experimental condition (between-subjects design), thus avoiding carryover effects (Boudreau et al. 2001). To conduct the experiment, we designed and implemented a text-based CA using the natural language processing platform Dialogflow by Google. We integrated the agent using a custom-built web interface to provide access from different devices. The agent was able to understand and process variations of sentences with the same meaning and was able to extract, validate and repeat different parameters, such as reservation numbers or e-mail addresses, to indicate that it understood a user's request.

Table 31 (Study 5): Conditions of the Experimental Design

		Anthropomorphic Design	
		Machine-Like	Human-Like
Persuasive Design	Neutral	Condition 1 Agent without anthropomorphic cues and without persuasive design elements	Condition 2 Agent with anthropomorphic cues and without persuasive design elements
	Persuasive	Condition 3 Agent without anthropomorphic cues and with persuasive design elements	Condition 4 Agent with anthropomorphic cues and with persuasive design elements

After implementing the conversation model, we created four different instances corresponding to our experimental conditions: *Condition 1* consisted of an agent with a neutral and machine-like design, thus the CA did not exhibit additional anthropomorphic cues or persuasive design elements, but provided support for the user in the experimental task. The agent in *condition 2* did not contain persuasive design elements, but included anthropomorphic cues, such as a name, self-references and dynamic response times. *Condition 3* contained an agent without anthropomorphic cues and persuasive design elements. Finally, *condition 4* comprised an agent with human-like cues as well as the aforementioned persuasive design elements. Concerning the dimension anthropomorphic CA design, the human-like design in conditions 2 and 4 contained the anthropomorphic cues shown in Table 31. Regarding the human identity, we equipped the CAs with a comic-like human avatar, a name ("Sarah"), and female gender. With regard to verbal cues, it used self-references and self-disclosure, a personal introduction and greeting ("Hello! My name is Sarah and I am here to help you reserving an e-bike"), different wording of sentences and word choice as well as polite statements. Furthermore, the human-like CA was designed with non-verbal cues by means of dynamic response times and blinking dots to indicate thinking and typing as well as the use of emoticons to express emotions.

The CAs with persuasive design elements in condition 3 and 4 included self-monitoring for e-bike use, praise, social cooperation and facilitation, as well as tailoring (Oinas-Kukkonen and Harjumaa 2009). These elements were distributed among the five experimental tasks as follows: After looking up the existing e-bike reservation (task 1) and authenticating with the agent (task 2), the persuasive CAs provided self-monitoring information in combination with praise ("With this reservation, you already took four e-bike rides this week and traveled more than 6.5 kilometers - without any traffic jam or CO2 emissions. Keep it up!"). After checking the availability of an e-bike, the CAs with persuasive designs highlight that two colleagues will be travelling at the same time to the selected company site (social facilitation). Finally, after requesting a confirmation of the modified reservation, the CAs with a persuasive design thank the user for the contribution to the environment as follows: "Thank you for contributing to the environmental goals of our company – only 29 rides to go until we reach our goal 300 commutes. With your e-bike use, you already reduced CO2 emissions by around 1,100g compared to taking the car and helped to reduce traffic congestion in our city." (praise, tailoring, social cooperation to reach shared organizational environmental goal).

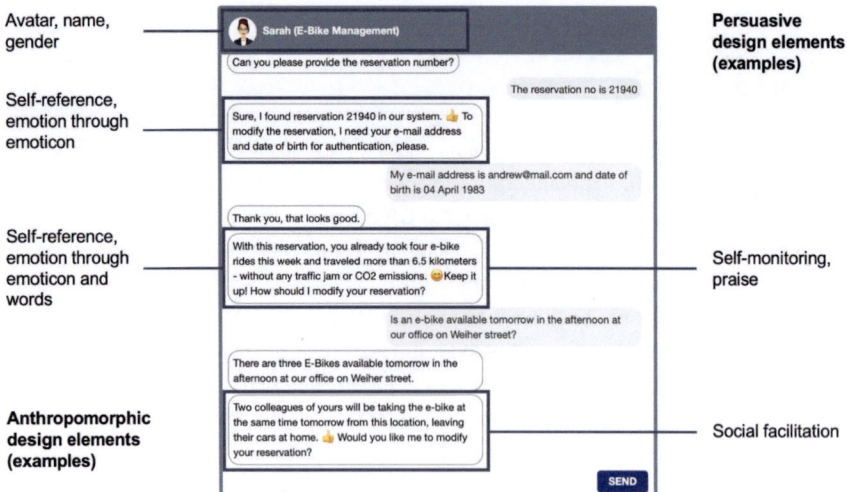

Figure 32 (Study 5): Agent in Condition 4 (Material translated to English)

2.4.3 Measures

After the interaction with the conversational agent, every participant was asked to complete a survey concerning their beliefs with regard the environmental impact of e-bike use and the perception of the agent. For measuring behavioral, normative and control beliefs (Ajzen 1985, 1991), we followed the guideline provided by Ajzen (2006) by first conducting interviews to elicit salient beliefs of participants as a preparation for the survey. We carried out six qualitative interviews with free-form responses in which we identified behavioral outcomes of e-bike use (reduced CO_2 emissions, less traffic congestion, general contribution to our environment), normative referents in the organizational context (supervisor, colleagues), and control factors (positive environmental impact, worthwhile environmental impact).

Next, we used the results from the interviews to adapt and contextualize the instruments by Ajzen (2006) in our survey. We extended these by established measures for perceived humanness (Holtgraves and Han 2007; Holtgraves et al. 2007) and perceived persuasiveness (Lehto et al. 2012). As suggested in the respective studies, perceived humanness was measured on a 9-point semantic differential scale, while all other items were measured on a 7-point Likert scale. Two attention checks were added to the survey. Finally, we collected demographic information (age, gender) and information on the frequency of digital assistant use (e.g. Siri, Alexa, and chatbots) by the participants ranging from daily, weekly, monthly to never.

Table 32 (Study 5): Constructs, Items, and Factor Loadings

Construct	Items	Loading
Behavioral beliefs (Ajzen 1985, 1991) Cronbach's α = .887 CR = .914 AVE = .693 M = 5.910 SD = 1.004	Using a e-bike for commuting will contribute to reducing CO_2 emissions.	.831
	Reducing CO_2 emission through e-bike use is good.	.842
	Using a e-bike for commuting will result in less traffic congestion.	.785
	Reducing traffic congestion through e-bike use is good.	.713
	Using a e-bike for commuting will contribute to our environment	.803
	Contributing to our environment through e-bike use is good.	.815
Normative beliefs (Ajzen 1985, 1991) Cronbach's α = .835 CR = .889 AVE = .668 M = 4.307 SD = 1.262	My supervisor thinks that I should contribute to our environment by taking the e-bike for commutes.	.761
	When it comes to the environmental sustainability of our organization, I want to do what my supervisor thinks I should do.	.789
	My colleagues think that that I should contribute to our environment by taking the e-bike for commutes.	.878
	When it comes to the impact of environmental sustainability of our organization, I want to do what my colleagues think I should do.	.837

Construct	Items	Loading
Control beliefs (Ajzen 1985, 1991) Cronbach's α = .871 CR = .912 AVE = .722 M = 5.429 SD = 1.252	I expect my e-bike use to positively influence the environmental impact of our organization.	.856
	Positively influencing the environmental impact of our organization would enable me to use the e-bike for commuting.	.838
	I expect my e-bike use to make a worthwhile contribution to our environment	.852
	Making a worthwhile contribution to our environment would enable me to take the e-bike for commuting.	.852
Humanness (Holtgraves and Han 2007) Cronbach's α = .892 CR = .919 AVE = .656 M = 6.628 SD = 1.607	extremely inhuman-like – extremely human-like	.791
	extremely unskilled – extremely skilled	.891
	extremely unthoughtful – extremely thoughtful	.829
	extremely impolite – extremely polite	.634
	extremely unresponsive – extremely responsive	.852
	extremely unengaging – extremely engaging	.836
Persuasiveness (Lehto et al. 2012) Cronbach's α = .944 CR = .964, AVE = .899 M = 3.225, SD = 1.654	The agent has an influence on my thinking on environmental sustainability.	.930
	The agent is personally relevant for me.	.954
	The agent makes me reconsider my thinking about sustainable mobility.	.961

CR = Composite Reliability, AVE = Average Variance Extracted, M = Mean, SD = Standard Deviation

Table 32 summarizes the constructs, items, and factor loadings including Cronbach's α, composite reliability (CR) and average variance extracted (AVE). We included all items in the analysis as the factor loadings were larger than .60 as suggested by Gefen and Straub (2005). All constructs showed sufficient values for Cronbach's α (larger than .80), composite reliability (larger than .80) and average variance extracted (larger than .50) with respect to the levels proposed by Urbach and Ahlemann (2010).

2.5 Results

Partial least squares (PLS) was used to test our hypotheses regarding the relation between persuasive and anthropomorphic design and individual sustainability beliefs due to our focus on prediction rather than model fit and the use of latent variables with formative measures (Ringle et al. 2012). All analyses were carried out using SmartPLS 3. As suggested by Chin (1998), the significance of path coefficients was calculated with a bootstrapping resampling method with 5,000 samples. Figure 33 visualizes the path coefficients, R^2 values, and significance levels.

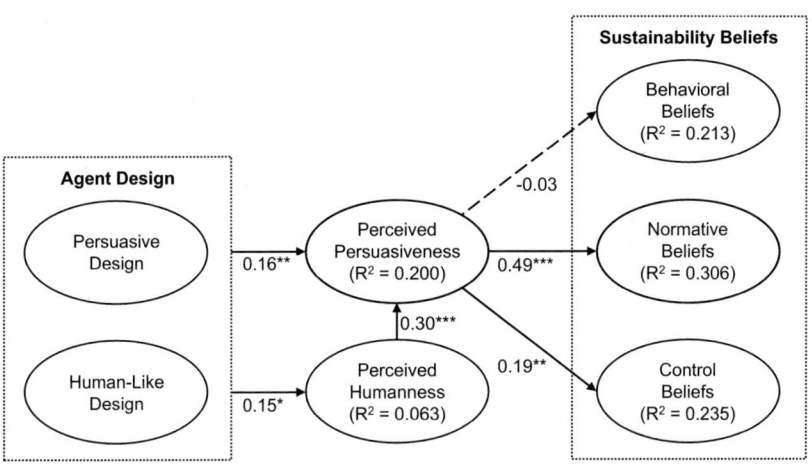

Solid lines indicate significant paths, dashed line non-significant path
*** $p \leq .001$, ** $p \leq .01$, * $p \leq 0.05$

Figure 33 (Study 5): PLS Structural Model (n = 225)

The paths between the CA's design dimensions (persuasive design, human-like, design) and user perceptions regarding persuasiveness and humanness of the agent show significant relationships. Our data indicates that persuasive design positively impacts perceived persuasiveness for environmental belief change (Persuasive Design → Perceived Persuasiveness, $\beta = 0.16$, $p = .007$), thus providing support for H1. Human-like design through anthropomorphic cues has a positive impact on perceived humanness (Human-Like Design → Perceived Humanness, $\beta = 0.15$, $p = .013$), indicating support for H2. In addition, our results show support for H3, stating that perceived humanness positively contributes to perceived persuasiveness (Perceived Anthropomorphism → Perceived Persuasiveness, $\beta = 0.30$, $p < .001$). Finally, two of the three paths between perceived persuasiveness and the three individual sustainability beliefs indicate significant relationships. The data from our post-experimental survey shows no significant relationship between perceived persuasiveness and individual behavioral beliefs (Perceived Persuasiveness → Behavioral Beliefs, $\beta = -0.03$, $p = .327$), thus we do not find support for H4. With regard to the relation between perceived persuasiveness and individual normative beliefs, we observe a significant relationship (Perceived Persuasiveness → Normative Beliefs, $\beta = 0.49$, $p < .001$), indicating support for H5. Finally, our survey data shows a significant path between perceived persuasiveness and individual control beliefs (Perceived Persuasiveness → Control Beliefs, $\beta = 0.19$, $p = .002$). Consequently, we find support for our sixth hypothesis, which states a positive influence of perceived persuasiveness on control beliefs. Table 33 summarizes the hypothesized relationships and their significance.

Table 33 (Study 5): Results of Hypothesis Tests

H.	Relationship	β-value	t-value	p-value	Support
H1	Persuasive Design → Perceived Persuasiveness	0.16	2.49	.007	Yes
H2	Human-Like Design → Perceived Humanness	0.15	2.23	.013	Yes
H3	Perceived Humanness → Perceived Persuasiveness	0.30	5.16	.000	Yes
H4	Perceived Persuasiveness → Behavioral Beliefs	-0.03	0.45	.327	No
H5	Perceived Persuasiveness → Normative Beliefs	0.49	9.13	.000	Yes
H6	Perceived Persuasiveness → Control Beliefs	0.19	2.83	.002	Yes

We also analyzed the effect of the control variables (age, gender, frequency of digital assistant use) on the latent variables and conducted an exploratory post-hoc analysis for moderator effects. Significant paths include age to control beliefs (β = 0.10, p = .038), age to perceived persuasiveness (β = -0.21, p = .001), digital assistant use on behavioral (β = 0.13, p = .014), normative (β = 0.12, p = .025), and control beliefs (β = 0.14, p = .013) as well as on perceived persuasiveness (β = 0.17, p = .004), and gender to control beliefs (β = 0.11, p = .041). In addition, two significant moderator effects were found in our dataset: First, we found that the age of the participants moderated the relationship between human-like design and perceived humanness (β = -0.11, p = .032), indicating that users with higher age did perceive an agent with a human-like design as less anthropomorphic. Similarly, the frequency of digital assistant use moderates the relationship between human-like design and perceived humanness (β = -0.15, p = .009).

2.6 Discussion

Our experiment aimed to explore the relation between persuasive and anthropomorphic design of conversational agents and sustainability beliefs. The results have implications for promoting environmental beliefs of individuals through the design of artifacts in general and conversational agents in particular and provide empirical evidence for the potential of anthropomorphism in the context of persuasive design.

2.6.1 Shaping Environmental Beliefs through Design

We find empirical support for our hypotheses that perceived persuasiveness has a positive impact on individual normative and control beliefs regarding environmental sustainability of e-bike use and sharing, however, our data does not indicate support for the relation between perceived persuasiveness and behavioral beliefs. Concerning normative beliefs, showing the behavior and the implicit beliefs guiding such action of normative referents, in this case colleagues and supervisors, seems to be efficient in shaping individual normative beliefs of users. By means of social facilitation ("two of your colleagues will be using the e-bike tomorrow at the same time") and cooperation towards achieving a shared organizational goal for e-bike use, the agent has the potential to facilitate social influence as also shown in similar studies on environmental sustainability and design (e.g. Baeriswyl et al. 2011; Koo and Chung 2014; Römer et al. 2015). While we were able to show fictitious, positive behavior of the referents, designers need to consider potentially unintended effects of such social support elements in persuasive design, for example normative referents not showing the intended behavior and thus potentially decreasing a user's motivation, the influence of group characteristics (Yim 2011) or a decreased feeling of autonomy for individual employees as e-bike use is made transparent across the organization (Flüchter and Wortmann 2014).

With regard to control beliefs, the persuasive design including tailored information, praise for e-bike use, and highlighting personal benefits positively influenced individual control beliefs. The provision of personalized and tailored information in combination with praise ("you already took four e-bike rides this week and traveled more than 6.5 kilometers" or "with this e-bike use, you contributed to reducing CO2 emissions by 1.100g – keep it up!") indicated the participant that she or he made a positive and worthwhile contribution, which is often challenging in this context as CO2 emissions can be a "mythical" number without a tangible connection to individual lives (Corbett 2013b). In addition, highlighting the individual contribution towards reaching a shared goal for e-bike use can increase the user's feeling of making a worthwhile contribution (Loock et al. 2013) and emphasizing personal benefits (e.g. no need for parking space or waiting in traffic) (Marett et al. 2012) have the potential to further shape individual control beliefs. Thus, designers have different persuasive design elements at their disposal to positively influence perceived behavioral control as a key driver of sustainable behavior (De Groot and Steg 2007).

While our study underlines the potential of persuasive design elements to promote what we consider desirable environmentally sustainable mobility beliefs and behavior, we emphasize the need for creating transparency regarding the persuasion goals of such artifacts. From an ethical point of view, revealing the designer's intention to the artifact's users is essential and persuasion should always be open and be based on truthful information (Oinas-Kukkonen and Harjumaa 2009; Shevchuk and Oinas-Kukkonen 2016). Thus, we consider it the designer's responsibility to take into account intended ethical outcomes as well as reasonably predictable unintended outcomes of persuasive technology in line with the arguments provided by Berdichevsky and Neuenschwander (2002).

2.6.2 Human-Like Conversational Agents in the Context of Persuasive Design

We further find a positive impact of perceived humanness of the conversational agent on perceived persuasiveness as formulated in our third hypothesis, indicating that the human-like design and human perception of such agents does indeed contribute to persuasiveness. Similar studies on anthropomorphic conversational agent design, drawing on the Social Response Theory, find a positive effect of perceived humanness on further aspects, such as perceived competency, social influence, trustworthiness (Araujo 2018; Gong 2008), and service encounter satisfaction (Gnewuch et al. 2018b). As for example perceived trustworthiness of an artifact directly affects its potential for persuasion (Lehto et al. 2012), the human-like design of such agents can enable reaching a higher degree of persuasiveness. Furthermore, praise coming from a human-like CA, to which users show social responses, might mean more to the individual as praise expressed by a machine-like agent (Jucks et al. 2018).

The explorative post-hoc analysis for moderator effects revealed that a user's age ($\beta = -0.11$, $p = .032$), and frequency of digital assistant and chatbot use ($\beta = -0.15$, $p = .009$) moderate the relation between human-like design and perceived humanness. Thus, the effect of a human-like design of a CA on perceived humanness might be smaller for older users and users that frequently use comparable assistants. Furthermore, different studies on anthropomorphic system design highlight the need to consider unintended effects of increasing anthropomorphism of the agent, such as that human-likeness does not linearly increase with trust, but that users might feel threatened at one point (Seeger et al. 2018). Similarly, Wünderlich and Paluch (2017) describe that users can be irritated as they could feel unsure whether the interact with a machine or an actual human.

2.6.3 Limitations and Opportunities for Future Research

Our study is not free of limitations and offers different opportunities for future research. We conducted the online experiment in a rather controlled setting with a set of specific tasks that every participant was asked to complete and a single interaction with the conversational agent. Thus, we benefitted from control yet lacked realism in our research design (Dennis and Valacich 2001). Future research could investigate how CA design influences individual behavioral, normative, and control beliefs with regard to sustainable mobility in the field where users interact with the CA in a variety of tasks.

In addition, observing individual environmental belief change, in particular with regard to behavioral beliefs, over a longer period of time and over multiple interactions with an artifact can be beneficial as successful persuasion takes place incrementally (Oinas-Kukkonen and Harjumaa 2009). A long-term observation can further be useful to analyze whether unintended effects on individual beliefs might occur. For example, Flüchter and Wortmann (2014) found a partially negative perception of social normative feedback in the form of a ranking in an organizational e-bike competition by users after a longer period of time. Furthermore, our work focused on individual sustainability beliefs in-depth but did not research subsequent actions and outcomes (Melville 2010). We believe that investigating the interplay between human-like CA design, individual sustainability beliefs, and their impact on actions and outcomes represents a worthwhile research opportunity as pro-environmental behavior is guided by values and norms (Lindenberg and Steg 2013; Lo et al. 2012). IS researchers can for example draw on the Theory of Planned Behavior (Ajzen 1985, 1991) to gain a better understanding of the relation between persuasive and anthropomorphic design, environmental behavioral, normative, and control beliefs, as well as individual intentions to use and actual mobility behavior. From our point of view, a better understanding of this relation can be useful to inform the design of artifacts that successfully promote environmentally friendly individual behavior. In addition, our research design did not account for socially desirable responding, which represents a further research opportunity in the context of anthropomorphic CA design and might help to better understand if the elicited beliefs are substantial, persist over time and translate in actual sustainable mobility behavior.

Furthermore, while our research makes a first step towards a better understanding between Information System design and environmental belief-formation at the example of sustainable mobility, we did not cover the full range of persuasive design elements (Oinas-Kukkonen and Harjumaa 2009) and our research design did not allow for an analysis of the impact of single persuasive design elements on the three types of individual beliefs (Ajzen 1985, 1991). Thus, future studies can explore the impact of single persuasive design elements on belief types to gain a more precise understanding of the interplay between design and individual (sustainability) beliefs. Additionally, and in line with Shevchuk and Oinas-Kukkonen (2016), we suggest to explore the full range of persuasive design elements, such as tailored and personalized presentation of environmental information, rewards and reminders, and social roles in the context of individual belief and behavior change as a promising opportunity for future studies. Furthermore, our study has shown that combining persuasive and anthropomorphic design can increase the persuasiveness of CAs. However, our data also indicated that the human-like design of the agent used in this experiment only explains a small part of the variance in perceived humanness ($R^2 = 0.063$), thus we propose future research to investigate which factors, related to the CA design or other aspects, influence how human-like a CA is perceived by its users. In addition, while we focused on promoting sustainable mobility behavior, we suggest to adapt the approach used in this study to use cases in domains outside of Green IS, such as health or education. Finally, future research in the context of persuasive, anthropomorphic CAs should explore and critically discuss the ethical questions that arise when designing increasingly human-like, persuasive conversational agents.

2.7 Concluding Remarks

Positively influencing individual environmental beliefs and behavior through the design of technical artifacts is a key concern in the area of green IS and of high practical relevance as it can contribute to more sustainable attitudes and practices (vom Brocke et al. 2013; Melville 2010). In this study, we set out to explore the relation of persuasive and human-like design and behavioral, normative, and control beliefs. By means of an 2x2 online experiment with a conversational agent and 225 participants, we find empirical evidence for the positive impact of persuasive and human-like design on individual environmental control and normative beliefs at the example of organizational e-bike sharing. In addition, our results underline the potential of anthropomorphic design to facilitate a stronger persuasiveness in the context of artifacts that seek to promote sustainable individual beliefs and behavior.

Against this background, our study makes three contributions: First, we empirically show how an artifact's persuasive design can shape individual normative and control beliefs for sustainable mobility. Second, we extend the focus of existing green IS designs on mobile apps and websites with a text-based conversational agent as a new type of artifact that gains increasing interest in research and practice (McTear 2017) and triggers substantial social responses (Seeger et al. 2018). Third, our results indicate how the human-like design of such agents can contribute to the persuasiveness of the artifact, thus increasing the potential to promote sustainable beliefs and behavior through IS design. We encourage future design-oriented studies in this area to further explore the interplay between an agent's design, environmental beliefs and behavior over a longer period of time and in the field as well as to specifically investigate the impact of single persuasive design elements on individual behavioral, normative, and control beliefs in the context of environmental sustainability. Overall, a thorough understanding of effective and efficient designs to positively influence beliefs and behavior on the individual level can allow us to build artifacts that address prevalent challenges in our society and thus strengthen the positive environmental impact of our discipline.

Acknowledgments

This research was supported by the German Federal Ministry for the Environment, Nature Conservation and Nuclear Safety by resolution of the German Bundestag.

IV. Formulating a Nascent Design Theory

The first three chapters of Part B aimed to organize existing prescriptive knowledge on CAs (B.I.) and to contribute to closing selected research gaps in the knowledge base with regard to technological limitations (B.II) and the potential of anthropomorphic CA design in a company context (B.III).

Drawing on these findings, the following chapter (B.IV), containing Study 6, brings together design-oriented knowledge to build and evaluate an anthropomorphic CA for a professional services company based on the DSR approach proposed by Kuechler and Vaishnavi (2008). In addition to presenting the design of the technological artifact, Study 6 proposes a nascent design theory for anthropomorphic CAs that offer a human-like interaction while mitigating negative effects due to limited conversational capabilities.

1. Study 6: Designing Anthropomorphic Enterprise Conversational Agents

Table 34: Fact Sheet of Study 6

Title	Designing Anthropomorphic Enterprise Conversational Agents
Authors	Stephan Diederich*, Alfred Benedikt Brendel, Lutz M. Kolbe Chair of Information Management, University of Göttingen, Platz der Göttinger Sieben 5, 37073 Göttingen, Germany *Corresponding author. Tel.: +49 551 3921170. E-Mail: stephan.diederich@stud.uni-goettingen.de
Outlet	Business and Information Systems Engineering (BISE)
Abstract	The increasing capabilities of conversational agents (CAs) offer manifold opportunities to assist users in a variety of tasks. In an organizational context, particularly their potential to simulate a human-like interaction via natural language currently attracts attention both at the customer interface as well as for internal purposes, often in the form of chatbots. Emerging experimental studies on CAs study the impact of anthropomorphic design ele-ments, so-called social cues, on user perception. However, while these studies provide valu-able prescriptive knowledge on selected social cues, they neglect the potential detrimental influence of the limited responsiveness of present-day conversational agents. In practice, many CAs fail to continuously provide meaningful responses in a conversation due to the open nature of natural language interaction, which negatively influences user perception and often led to CAs being discontinued in the past. Thus, designing a CA that provides a human-like interaction experience while minimizing the risks associated with limited conversational capabilities represents a substantial design problem. This study addresses the aforementioned problem by proposing and evaluating a design for a CA that offers a hu-man-like interaction experience while mitigating negative effects due to limited responsive-ness. Through the presentation of the artifact and the synthesis of prescriptive knowledge in the form of a nascent design theory for anthropomorphic enterprise CAs, this research adds to the growing knowledge base on designing human-like assistants and supports practitioners seeking to introduce them in their organizations.
Keywords	Conversational Agent; Anthropomorphism; Social Response Theory; Theory of Uncanny Valley, Design Science Research

1.1 Introduction

Technological advances, particularly in machine learning and natural language processing, continue to change the way in which we live, work, and interact with each other, thereby expanding the scope for innovation and automation of human activities (Brynjolfsson and McAfee 2016; Davenport and Kirby 2016). One phenomenon in this wave are conversational agents (CAs), defined as software which users interact with through natural language (McTear et al. 2016). Equipped with increasing capabilities to assist users in a variety of tasks (Maedche et al. 2016; Morana et al. 2017), these agents permeate our private and professional lives (Maedche et al. 2019) in different forms, including digital assistants on smartphones (Chattaraman et al. 2018), chatbots on social media (Xu et al. 2017) or as physically embodied service robots (Stock 2018; Stock and Merkle 2018).

CAs currently attract interest in theory and practice alike due to their potential to provide an enjoyable user experience that resembles a human-to-human interaction (Diederich et al. 2019a). From a theoretical perspective, the social cues of such agents, comprising for example the interaction via natural language, the expression of emotions or a human name, trigger social responses by the users (Pfeuffer et al. 2019a). These social response comprise both how users perceive the CA as well as their expectations towards its representation and behavior as posited in Social Response Theory (Nass et al. 1994; Nass and Moon 2000). Different studies highlight that social responses and associated perceptions of anthropomorphism can contribute to a positive user perception of CAs, for example with regard to service satisfaction (Diederich et al. 2019d; Gnewuch et al. 2018b), enjoyment (Lee and Choi 2017) or trust (Araujo 2018). However, several studies at the same time indicate that human-like design may lead to undesired negative effects due to feelings of uncanniness (Wiese and Weis 2019) and that a "more is more" approach does not necessarily lead to increased user perception of anthropomorphism (Seeger et al. 2018). Against this background, the Theory of Uncanny Valley (Mori 1970) posits a sharp drop in affinity for human-like artifacts where a user's attention abruptly shifts from the human-like qualities to its inhuman imperfections (MacDorman et al. 2009).

From a design perspective, a variety of social cues for CAs is available to trigger social responses and stimulate perceptions of anthropomorphism (Feine et al. 2019a). However, while many of these cues can be incorporated in the design with relatively low effort, such as giving the CA a human name (Cowell and Stanney 2005) or using response delays to simulate thinking and typing of a CA (Gnewuch et al. 2018b), sustaining a human-like interaction in an evolving conversation represents a major design challenge. As Følstad and Brandtzæg (2017, p. 41) note, the natural language interface of a CA represents a "blank canvas where the content and features of the underlying service are mostly hidden from the user" and that design to a large extent comprises anticipating user input as well equipping the CA with the ability to provide meaningful responses contingent on what has been communicated (Go and Sundar 2019). In practice, many CAs were discontinued due to their inability to provide meaningful responses and engage in an interactive dialogue (Ben Mimoun et al. 2012), which hinders the usefulness and enjoyment when interacting with such agents compared to systems with graphical interfaces that need to account for a much smaller variety of input (Følstad and Brandtzæg 2017).

Many studies on human-like CA design in IS and HCI are carried out with a focus on selected social cues and by means of experiments (Diederich et al. 2019a) where participants either receive a predefined set of tasks or interact with an actual human in a Wizard-of-Oz setting, thus ensuring responsiveness of the agent during the interaction. These experiments provide valuable insights regarding the impact of specific social cues. However, with the notable exception of Seeger et al. (2018), they neglect the interplay of the social cues incorporated in the design, in particular with the agent's limited conversational capabilities. Against this background, increasing the social cues incorporated in the design might lead to Uncanny Valley effects as users start to focus on the inhuman imperfections of the agent related to its responsiveness, ultimately leading to a negative perception. While several studies on CA design, such as Gong (2008) or Gnewuch et al. (2018b), discuss potential issues related to uncanniness, such experimental designs with highly structured dialogues or Wizard-of-Oz settings are unlikely to yield strong feelings of uncanniness as adequate, natural responses, of the CA are ensured during the conversation. However, situations in practice where limited conversational capabilities of human-like CAs abruptly lead to response failure occur frequently (Følstad and Brandtzæg 2017), potentially leading to the perception of the CA as uncanny. Hence, how the human-like design of a CA can provide utility despite its limited capabilities has yet to be investigated.

With our study, we address this problem and contribute to the knowledge base on anthropomorphic CA design with the following research question: *How can a CA in a professional context be designed to offer a human-like interaction while mitigating feelings of uncanniness due to limited conversational abilities?* Specifically, we bring together prescriptive knowledge for CAs gained mostly in experiments and propose a design for a CA that offers a human-like interaction experience enabled through the combination of social cues with approaches to address the limited responsiveness of present-day CAs. The artifact was created in a design science research (DSR) project over a span of seven months with a large professional services firm and evaluated with a comparative approach to demonstrate that the CA indeed represents an improvement over the extant system with a graphical user interface.

We continue by providing the research background for our study. Then, we introduce our DSR approach and describe the artifact with a focus on design principles as well as present the results from the evaluation. Afterwards, we formulate our design theoretical contribution, state limitations of our work and propose opportunities for future research.

1.2 Related Work and Theoretical Background

Our DSR project contributes to solving the design problem of crafting anthropomorphic CAs while minimizing the risk of negative perception due to limited conversational capabilities. The design is grounded in two theories on user perception of human-like artifacts and the project is carried out based on the DSR approach by Kuechler and Vaishnavi (2008). The overall research background is visualized in Figure 34. In the following, we first describe existing research on human-like CAs and highlight the issue of limited conversational capabilities. Afterwards, Social Response Theory and the Theory of Uncanny Valley are introduced.

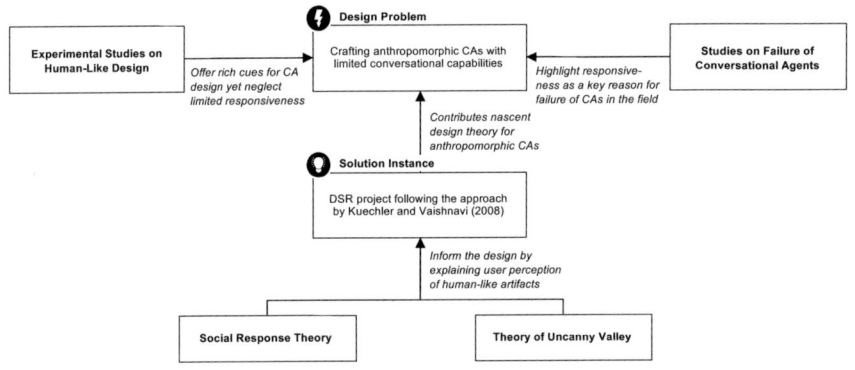

Figure 34 (Study 6): Research Background

1.2.1 Human-like Design of CAs and their Conversational Capabilities

The use of CAs in companies offers the potential to automate and innovate tasks in various application areas. Recent studies have explored text-based CAs, for example in customer service (Wünderlich and Paluch 2017), marketing and sales (Vaccaro et al. 2018), team collaboration (Elson et al. 2018; Toxtli et al. 2018) and human resources (Liao et al. 2018). CAs are typically introduced for two purposes: First, CAs have the potential to provide intuitive access to existing systems via natural language, thus avoiding the need to manually interact with a graphical interface in multiple steps (McTear et al. 2016). Second, CAs can provide the feeling of a human contact in an interaction with a technological artifact (Verhagen et al. 2014). While many studies on CA design suggest crafting a CA as human-like as possible, it is not a design goal per se. For example, Seeger et al. (2017) theorize that the agent's substitution type, i.e. whether the CA substitutes a task previously carried out by a human person or by a computer system, impacts perceived trustworthiness of the agent. In cases where the agent substitutes a human expert, the perceived familiarity with a human-like CA can lead to a more positive evaluation of the CA by the user due the user's knowledge about the familiar human equivalent (Komiak and Benbasat 2006). In cases, however, where the CA substitutes an existing computer system, a less human-like design could lead be perceived as more useful due to the associated superiority of computers in terms of rationality, reliability, and objectivity (Mosier and Skitka 1996). Thus, increasing the humanness of a CA does not necessarily lead to better perception, but needs to follow a careful consideration of the task that it is intended to fulfill.

Emerging design-oriented work on anthropomorphic CAs investigates the impact of different social cues on user perception, often by means of experiments (Diederich et al. 2019a). According to Seeger et al. (2018), anthropomorphic design comprises three dimensions: A human identity, referring to the representation of the CA, verbal cues, including the choice of words and sentences, and non-verbal cues, comprising the non-verbal communication behavior of the CA. With regard to a human identity, Gong (2008) for example finds empirical evidence in an experiment that agent representations with images which exhibit a higher anthropomorphism increases the social responses shown by the users. Concerning non-verbal cues, Gnewuch et al. (2018b) for example explore response times and find that dynamic delays positively impact humanness, social presence, as well as user satisfaction even though they lead to a higher waiting time for the user. Related to the third dimension, verbal cues, Schuetzler et al. (2014) for example found that even modest adjustments to an agents responses with regard to syntax and word variability lead to a more positive evaluation of a CA. Overall, these and similar experiments highlight a variety of social cues that is available to make a CA appear as human-like as possible (Feine et al. 2019a).

While extant studies on anthropomorphic CAs provide valuable insights on the impact of selected social cues on user perception, they do not consider the interplay of social cues with each other, except for the work by Seeger et al. (2018), and with further aspects of the agent's design, in particular its limited responsiveness. In these studies, participants either received a set of rather narrowly defined tasks or interacted with an actual human in a Wizard-of-Oz setting to ensure that the agent could provide meaningful responses in the conversation. However, the limitations of present-day CAs with regard to responsiveness are a substantial, practical design issue which often leads to unfulfilled user expectations (Luger and Sellen 2016) and CAs being discontinued (Ben Mimoun et al. 2012). Table 35 provides an overview of exemplary experimental research on CA design and studies that highlight responsiveness as a key issue as well as positions the contribution of this study.

B. Studies on Anthropomorphic CAs

Table 35 (Study 6): Overview of Exemplary Studies on CA Design

Study	Research Method	Key Results
Gnewuch et al. (2018b)	Online experiment with **predefined conversation** (given tasks)	Dynamic response delays of the CA to indicate thinking and typing increase perceived humanness, social presence, and service satisfaction.
Gong (2008)	Laboratory experiment with **predefined conversation** (given reply options)	Higher anthropomorphism of agents' facial images increases social response by users regarding to social judgment, homophily, competence, trustworthiness and social influence.
Schuetzler et al. (2014)	Laboratory experiment with **predefined conversation** (given tasks)	Modest interactive and responsive communication of the CA significantly increases perceived humanness and engagement of the agent.
Burmester et al (2019)	Laboratory experiment **(Wizard-of-Oz)**	Interactive communication (e.g. remembering user input or suggesting ideas) by the agent and a human name increase the natural feeling in a conversation.
Wang et al. (2008)	Laboratory experiment **(Wizard-of-Oz)**	Politeness leads to increased learning performance, providing empirical support for CAs as social actors and emphasizing the need for social intelligence.
This study	*Design science research*	*Design of anthropomorphic CAs in a professional context that mitigates negative effects due to limited capabilities.*
Ben Mimoun et al. (2012)	Performance analysis and expert interviews	Main reasons for failure of CAs in the field are limitations of the agents to manage and **provide meaningful information** to complete a user's request.
Luger and Sellen (2016)	Semi-structured interviews	**User expectations are often not in line with the system's actual capabilities**, design should indicate the systems potential and limitations.

1.2.2 Social Response Theory and the Theory of Uncanny Valley

A key theory underlying the interaction with and design of IT artifacts with human-like characteristics is Social Response Theory (Nass and Moon 2000; Reeves and Nass 1996). Social Response Theory posits that humans mindlessly respond to social cues from artifacts and apply social rules as well as expectations to anything that demonstrates human-like traits or behavior (Nass and Moon 2000; Reeves and Nass 1996). Nass and Moon (2000) discovered in a set of experiments that humans overuse social categories, such as gender, and social behaviors, such as reciprocity, and hypothesized that "the more computers present characteristics that are associated with humans, the more likely they are to elicit social behavior" (Nass and Moon 2000, p. 7). The social cues incorporated in an artifact's design lead users to anthropomorphize technology, i.e. to have perceptions of humanness in the interaction. In addition, different studies indicate that the availability of social cues leads to perceptions of social presence (e.g. Gnewuch et al. 2018b; Diederich et al. 2019d), defined as the sense of human contact embodied in a medium (Gefen and Straub 1997). This is in line with further studies that indicate a positive impact of small adjustments on social presence, such as adding human images or personalized messages, to websites (Cyr et al. 2009; Gefen and Straub 2003). While perceptions of humanness and social presence have been shown to positively impact desired factors, such as trustworthiness (Schroeder and Schroeder 2018), perceived competency (Araujo 2018) or authenticity (Wünderlich and Paluch 2017), the social cues at the same time foster expectations regarding the artifact's (human-like) characteristics and behavior that need to be accounted for in the design (Diederich et al. 2019c). In the context of CA design, these perceptions of humanness often lead to expectations regarding the agent's abilities that are not in line with its capabilities (Luger and Sellen 2016).

A related theory for human-like artifacts is the Theory of Uncanny Valley (Mori 1970), originally from the field of robotics. The Theory of Uncanny Valley hypothesizes on the relationship between an artifact's humanoid appearance and the emotional responses by humans. The theory suggests that there is no linear relationship between the degree of human-likeness of an object and positive emotional responses to it, but that a sharp drop in affinity exists at a particular point. MacDorman et al. (2009, p.2) describe this as a shift of attention from the human-like qualities to the aspects that seem to be inhuman; stating that "as something looks more human it looks also more agreeable, until it comes to look so human that we start to find its nonhuman imperfections unsettling". While there is no clear measure or metric for the notion of "affinity" in the theory (Seymour et al. 2018), or "Shinwakan" in the original Japanese wording (Mori et al. 2012), uncanniness is described as negative feelings associated with strangeness of nonhuman imperfections of artifacts (MacDorman et al. 2009).

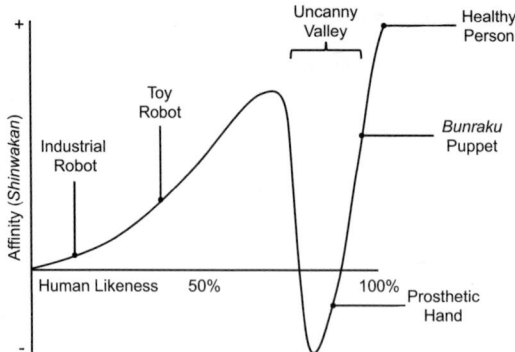

Figure 35 (Study 6): The Uncanny Valley (Mori et al. 2012)

Against the background of these theories, crafting anthropomorphic CAs represent a substantial design challenge. On the one hand, designers have various social cues at their disposal to make the agent appear human-like and thus benefit from positive effects associated with perceptions of humanness and social presence by the users (Knijnenburg and Willemsen 2016), such as on perceived enjoyment (Qiu and Benbasat 2010). On the other hand, maximizing the human-likeness of an agent increasingly poses the risk of disappointing users and fostering feelings of uncanniness (Luger and Sellen 2016; Ben Mimoun et al. 2012), in particular when the CA does not provide meaningful responses due to its limited conversational capabilities and is thus not able to fulfill user expectations regarding its human-like behavior.

1.3 Research Approach

Generating knowledge and improving the understanding of a problem through the building and application of a designed artifact is the paradigm underlying design science research (Hevner 2007; Hevner et al. 2004). With a fundamental orientation towards problem solving and an engaged relationship between academics and practitioners (Gregory and Muntermann 2014), DSR seeks to build artifacts that solve relevant issues for society, organizations or individuals (Walls et al. 1992) via for instance applying existing kernel theories and deriving design principles (Iivari 2015; Walls et al. 1992). In this research, we address a specific design problem (a human-like CA for simulating job interviews) by building an artifact in a specific context (a professional service firm) and, through the design and evaluation, generate prescriptive knowledge in the form of a nascent design theory (Gregor and Jones 2007) to address a specific design problem. Our research project is based on the DSR framework by Kuechler and Vaishnavi (2008) and is illustrated in Figure 36.

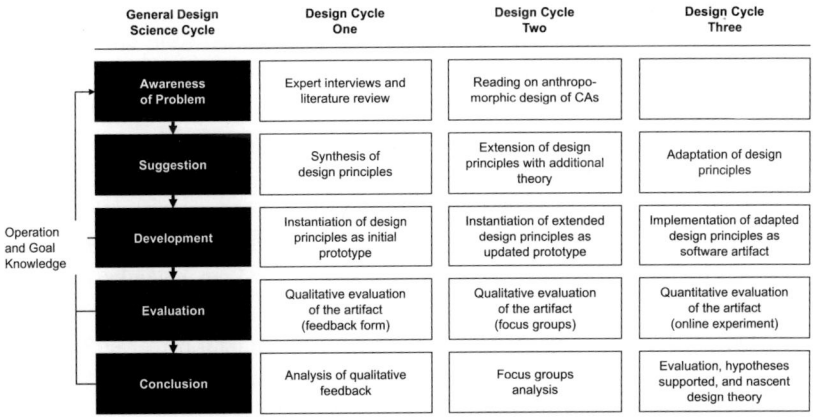

Figure 36 (Study 6): Design Cycles and Research Activities

We conducted three design cycles. In the first design cycle, we gained an in-depth understanding of the opportunity to innovate the recruiting process through a discussion with a senior HR manager of the case company. We then conducted six semi-structured interviews with members of the HR department and potential job candidates using initial meta-requirements extracted from the literature as a guideline. Specifically, we asked two recruiting specialists with extensive job interview experience from the HR department as well as four job candidates that were preparing for the recruiting process about their requirements for the form and function of a CA in the context of interview preparation. The interviews lasted for 14 to 26 minutes and the requirements were coded using an iterative approach, which was started with a preliminary list of meta-requirements identified in the literature. The list of codes (meta-requirements) was extended when a new requirement was stated in the interviews. An overview of exemplary codes (meta-requirements) and quotes from the interviews can be found in the appendix (Table 42). Afterwards, we reviewed further literature on CA design to refine and extend the elicited meta-requirements as well as to formulate preliminary design principles. After the interviews and reading, we had an initial list of meta-requirements (MR1-6) and three preliminary design principles (DP1-3). We then instantiated the principles in an early prototype. After preparing the prototype, we invited seven potential job applicants known to the HR department to interact with the prototype and provide qualitative feedback in a free-form survey. The qualitative feedback was coded with an open and iterative approach where the issues stated by the participants where finally assigned to three categories (see appendix for the categories and exemplary quotes). The results mainly indicated shortcomings regarding the rather "inhuman" feeling in the conversation (for example, one participant stated that "you immediately realize that the same responses are used repeatedly" or that the agent "only understands straight-forward responses, creative replies are not appreciated"), which led us to initiate a second cycle.

In the second cycle we added two meta-requirements (MR7-8) to address the issues described in the interviews regarding the rather mechanical nature of the interaction. After further reading of CA literature, in particular on anthropomorphic design, we added a fourth design principle. Then, we instantiated the design principle with a set of anthropomorphic cues identified in the literature in an updated prototype. We evaluated the prototype with two focus groups, one consisting of four representatives of the HR department and one consisting of three members of the so-called talent pool of the company that contained promising job candidates known from marketing events. During the focus group sessions, we discussed and noted strengths and weaknesses of our adapted design. While the updated prototype was in general perceived as positive by both focus groups, a lack of context-dependent support, guidance and agent responsiveness was reported during the interview simulation. Consequently, we engaged in a third design cycle in which we adapted our design principles to account for context-specific fallback handling and guiding users, such as by providing suggestions or hints in the conversation. Furthermore, we used dialogue data from the previous cycle to improve the CA's capabilities. A visualization of the evolution of our design can be found in the appendix.

1.4 Artifact Design and Implementation

Throughout the design cycles, we gained an in-depth understanding of the opportunity for innovation, elicited eight meta-requirements and derived four design principles. Then, we instantiated the design principles, formulated testable propositions, and evaluated the artifact.

The overall motivation for our DSR project stemmed from the idea to provide a new tool that supports applicants in their interview preparation at the professional services company. At the case company, the candidates, mostly recent graduates from university, apply for consultant positions and have to undergo a larger recruiting process comprising several interviews. As these job interviews are standardized and case-study based, which is common for companies of that size and in that industry, applicants can prepare themselves through practicing online case studies. These cases involve the structuring of a business problem, estimating and calculating numbers, and presenting as well as defending the solution and take usually half an hour for completion. Existing training systems typically consist of Q&A forms with a transparent structure and multiple-choice questions. While those systems can be helpful to understand the basic course of interviews, they lack realism due to their obvious structure and do not offer the feeling of a personal interaction like in a human dialogue. Against this background, we considered an anthropomorphic text-based CA as a promising opportunity to improve existing solutions in this application domain (Gregor and Hevner 2013).

1.4.1 Meta-Requirements and Design Principles

We identified meta-requirements (MR) that comprise the fundamental conversational capabilities of anthropomorphic CAs as well as approaches to address the agent's limited responsiveness, both by mitigating and handling situations where the agent is not able to provide a meaningful reply, and a human-like interaction experience. To address these meta requirements, we formulated four design principles (DP), as visualized in Figure 37. In the context of this study, we consider design principles not to lead to a certain effect in a deterministic manner but rather consider them as opening up potential for action (Chandra et al. 2015). Our approach for design principle formulation thus follows the suggestions by Chandra et al. (2015) and Seidel et al. (2017) to incorporate material- and action-oriented information as well as, if relevant, boundary conditions stemming from user characteristics or implementation settings.

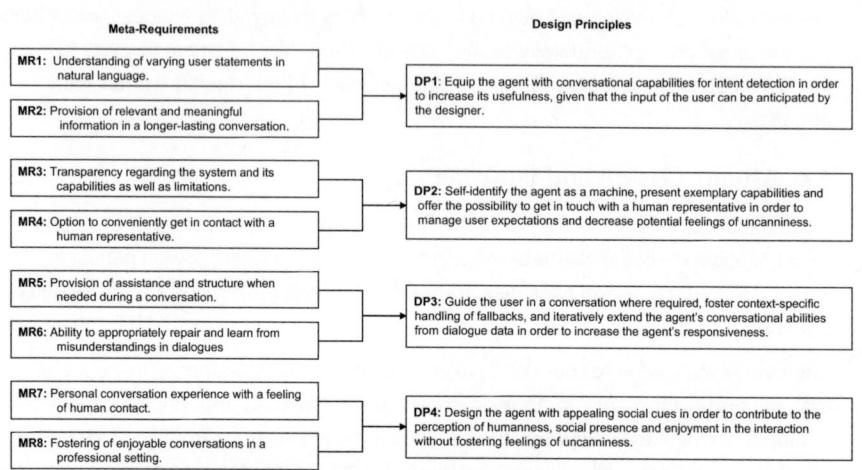

Figure 37 (Study 6): Meta-Requirements and Design Principles

MR1-2 and DP1 refer to the essential conversational abilities of the agent. As user input in a natural language interaction has a much higher variety than input in graphical user interfaces (Følstad and Brandtzæg 2017), the agent needs to be able to accurately detect the intent in a user's statement, given that it can be anticipated by the designer. This variety comprises both the different intents with which a user approaches the agent as well as different formulations for the same intent. After detecting the intent, the agent needs to provide a meaningful response, for example through integration in business systems where the requested information is stored (Gnewuch et al. 2017) or by directly embedding information in the agent's processing logic. Understanding a person's intent and providing a reply that fits the conversational context and contains relevant information contingent on what has already been communicated (Go and Sundar 2019) are fundamental requirements for text-based CAs and essential for the agent to be a useful tool for the user (Følstad and Brandtzæg 2017). Against this background, one interviewee described that the agent needs to be able to "logically connect what has been communicated in the conversation" and must not "forget everything that has been said and just offer the same reply". Thus, we formulate DP1 to provide the agent with capabilities to detect user intents and provide meaningful responses in a conversation.

MR3-4 and DP2 describe a need for transparency regarding the agent's capabilities and limitations as well as the possibility to conveniently contact an actual human person in case it encounters a request that it is not able to complete. As users anthropomorphize CA, they form expectations towards the system that are similar to humans instead of computer systems and which substantially differ from the agent's actual capabilities (Dzindolet et al. 2003). Consequently, the design of the agent should reveal the system's capabilities throughout the interaction (Luger and Sellen 2016). In this context, one participant highlighted that the agent should "clearly delineate areas in which it can provide as good replies as possible". In addition, creating transparency whether the user interacts with a human or machine (Wünderlich and Paluch 2017) and self-disclosure of the CA (Saffarizadeh et al. 2017) were found to positively impact the perception of CAs and mitigate feelings of uncanniness. Against this background, one interviewee stated that he appreciates if an anthropomorphic system sympathetically states that "it is a computer but it also has certain human characteristics". DP2 thus comprises the self-disclosure of the CA as a machine, the presentation of exemplary capabilities, as well as the possibility to get in touch with a human representative in situations where the agent fails to provide a meaningful response in order to decrease potential feelings of uncanniness.

MR5-6 and DP3 address the ability of the agent to provide structure where needed as well as to recover from misunderstandings to contribute to agent responsiveness. Due to the varying user input, the agent needs to be able to guide the conversation towards a specific goal, for example by suggesting responses (Diederich et al. 2019c) or creating transparency for the conversation flow (Gnewuch et al. 2017) in order to avoid situations of limited responsiveness. In addition, the agent should provide context-specific assistance to the user (Maedche et al. 2016). For case-study based interviews, this includes assisting the user with calculations by indicating how close the user's estimate is to the correct value or repeating important information for the solution. Furthermore, as misunderstandings are always possible in dialogues, the agent needs to be able to recover, for example by clarifying a statement or asking for reformulation, and be iteratively trained to learn from conversation data over time (Følstad and Brandtzæg 2017).

MR7-8 and DP4 refer to the anthropomorphic design and comprise meta-requirements concerning the feeling of a personal contact as well as enjoyment. The agent is supposed to offer an experience that resembles a human-to-human dialogue to elicit positive effects associated with humanness and social presence (Araujo 2018). Regarding a human interaction experience, one interviewee emphasized that the agent should for example adequately provide positive, motivating feedback (e.g. "you can do it") and thus contribute to "taking away the fear for the actual recruiting day". Furthermore, due to the non-linear relationship between human-like design and user affinity towards an artifact as postulated in the Theory of Uncanny Valley (Mori 1970), the fourth design principle emphasizes the need to find an appealing combination of social cues (Seeger et al. 2018), which in combination with the agent's limited conversational capabilities is able to foster a human-like interaction. As the agent will most likely encounter unexpected user input at some point in a conversation (Følstad and Brandtzæg 2017), a high degree of humanness can also increase user expectations and lead to substantial disappointment if the agent fails provide a meaningful, relevant response (Ben Mimoun et al. 2012). Thus, DP4 addresses a combination of social cues that balances the need for a human conversation experience with the actual conversational capabilities of the agent (Gnewuch et al. 2017). In addition, the agent should foster an enjoyable conversation, for example by using praise (Diederich et al. 2019e; Wang et al. 2008) as well as polite statements (Mayer et al. 2006).

1.4.2 Implementation of the Artifact

We built the artifact and instantiated the design principles using Google Dialogflow and a custom-built web interface (Figure 38). Dialogflow provided the natural language processing capabilities, in particular for intent detection, while the web interface was developed to provide convenient access. We collaborated with the HR department to better understand a case-study based interview and to design the conversation, in particular to model the different intents with which users approach the agent (DP1) on Google Dialogflow. The agent was designed to self-identify itself and highlight exemplary capabilities (DP2). To address the high variability of input and the reported lack of guidance, we created fallback responses that fit the conversational context and implemented guidance to help the user to arrive at the solution (e.g. by indicating errors in calculations or repeating assumptions), as well as extended the capabilities from dialogue data (e.g. by using unanticipated user input as training phrases). We further implemented suggestions to guide the user and increase the responsiveness of the agent in parts of the conversation where user input varied substantially (DP3).

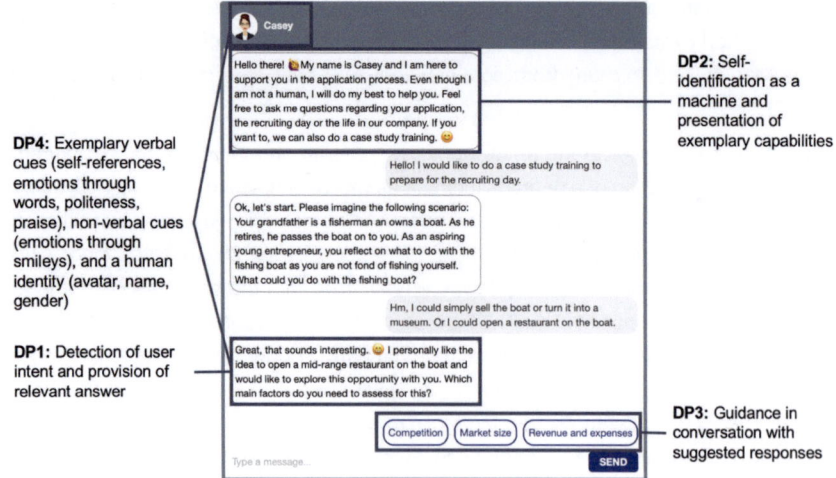

Figure 38 (Study 6): Instantiated Design Principles (Material translated)

To address the requirements for an enjoyable, and professional interaction similar to a human-to-human conversation, we selected a set of social cues for anthropomorphic design (Table 36) and organized them using the design framework by Seeger et al. (2018). Due to the non-linear relationship between the human-like design and positive emotional responses (Mori et al. 2012), we first reflected on the desired human traits the users described and then purposefully chose cues that we expected to support these characteristics. After identifying the cues in the extant literature, we aligned the selected cues with HR and marketing staff of the company.

Table 36 (Study 6): Social Cues incorporated in the Artifact

Desired Traits	Dimensions and Cues for Anthropomorphic Design		
	Human Identity	Verbal Cues	Non-verbal Cues
Essential human-like representation and behavior	• Name (Cowell and Stanney 2005) • Avatar (Gong 2008) • Gender (Nunamaker et al. 2011)	• Turn-taking (Gong 2008) • Syntax and word variability (Seeger et al. 2018) • Self-references and self-disclosure (Schuetzler et al. 2018b)	• Dynamic response times (Gnewuch et al. 2018b) • Blinking dots (de Visser et al. 2016)
Supportive demeanor		• Empathy and support (McQuiggan and Lester 2007) • Praise through words (Diederich et al. 2019e)	• Praise through emoticons (Wang et al. 2008)
Enjoyable and professional		• Personal introduction and greeting (Cafaro et al. 2016) • Politeness through words (Mayer et al. 2006)	• Politeness through emoticons (Mayer et al. 2006)

1.5 Evaluation

Every design cycle was accompanied by an evaluation of the artifact. Drawing on the FEDS framework proposed by Venable et al. (2016), we selected a Human Risk & Effectiveness strategy for our project due to the major design risks stemming from the user perception of the artifact. We implemented the evaluation strategy with two naturalistic and formative evaluations in the first two cycles by means of qualitative feedback and focus groups (Figure 39), focusing on selected aspects of our design (mechanical nature of the interaction in cycle one, lack of context-dependent support and limited agent responsiveness in cycle two). Afterwards, we conducted a summative evaluation by means of an online experiment with two goals. First, the experiment was intended to show that a human-like CA was perceived as more useful and enjoyable than the extant training system, i.e. that anthropomorphic design in this context is of value to the user. Second, the experiment aimed to evaluate whether the human-like design and approach to address the limited responsiveness does actually lead to perceptions of humanness and social presence as well whether it induces increased feelings of uncanniness. For the purpose of the experiment, the HR department provided a list of members of their talent pool, comprising potential applicants that were known from marketing events. Overall, we invited 226 members via e-mail of which 72 participated in the experiment (response rate 31.8%). Participation in the experiment took around 25 minutes per participant without compensation. The sample consisted of 18 female participants (25%) and the average age was 24.9 years (min = 21 years, max = 36 years). In the following, we present the hypotheses we formulated, the design of the experiment and measures, as well as the results from the evaluation.

1.5.1 Derivation of Constructs and Testable Propositions

In line with the suggestions by Gregor and Jones (2007), we formulate testable propositions for our proposed design. We follow the idea that these propositions can exhibit a comparative logic similar to "if a system or method that follows certain principles is instantiated then it will work, or it will be better in some way than other systems or methods." (Gregor and Jones 2007, p. 327). In our context, the propositions aim to validate that our proposed anthropomorphic CA design works better than the existing training system with a graphical user interface.

First, the objective of the DSR project was to design a CA that helps the candidates to prepare for their job interviews at the company. Thus, the overall utility of the CA with its human-like appearance is defined by the extent to which this design is perceived as more useful for the interview preparation than the existing online systems. The usefulness of a CA in a natural language interaction to a large extent depends on its ability to understand a user's request and provide a meaningful reply contingent on what has already been communicated (Go and Sundar 2019; Wünderlich and Paluch 2017) as reflected in the DP1. Against the background of the agent's proposed conversational capabilities and the overall idea that an anthropomorphic CA is suitable to better simulate a job interview than the extant training system with a graphical user interface, we thus hypothesize:

H1: *If a CA follows the proposed design, then it is perceived as more useful than the extant system with a graphical user interface.*

Complementary to this utilitarian perspective, we consider enjoyment as a relevant hedonic variable as indicated in MR8. Enjoyment is characterized by its non-goal orientation, that is the pleasure users perceive in the use of a system per se (Junglas et al. 2013). As the proposed CA design is intended to contribute to an enjoyable user experience (DP4) through an appealing combination of social cues (Liao et al. 2018), such as praising the user where adequate or offering a personal introduction, we hypothesize that the interaction with the CA is perceived as more enjoyable than with the extant system that does not contain such cues:

H2: *If a CA follows the proposed design, then it is perceived as more enjoyable than the extant system with a graphical interface.*

Third, we hypothesize that the CA exhibits a higher level of humanness and social presence as the extant training system due to the rich social cues as posited in Social

Response Theory. While the idea that users anthropomorphize a CA more than the existing online training system might seem obvious at first glance, the cues might also be detrimental as users could focus more on the inhuman imperfections instead of its human-like qualities (MacDorman et al. 2009) as indicated in the Theory of Uncanny Valley. Thus, in line with the suggestions by Seeger et al. (2018), we propose that the selected combination of social cues (DP4) in our design provides an appealing human-like experience and fosters feelings of social presence:

H3: *If a CA follows the proposed design, then it yields a higher perceived humanness than the extant system with a graphical interface.*

H4: *If a CA follows the proposed design, then it yields a higher feeling of social presence than the extant system with a graphical interface.*

Finally, the human-like design could lead to unintended perception of the artifact as uncanny due to the non-linear relationship between human-likeness and affinity (Mori 1970). As the selected social cues are intended to foster a higher level of perceived humanness and associated user expectations regarding the CA's behavior, they could also lead users to focus on its nonhuman imperfections (MacDorman et al. 2009). Against this background, we suggest that the deliberate selection of social cues depending on the desired human traits (DP4) in combination with self-identification of the CA as a machine and the presentation of exemplary capabilities leads to the CA having a low level of uncanniness:

H5: *If a CA follows the proposed design, then it exhibits a low level of uncanniness.*

1.5.2 Experimental Design and Measures

The propositions for our design were tested by means of an online experiment with a between-subjects design (Boudreau et al. 2001). Participants were invited to interact with a new tool to support their preparation for the recruiting day and were assigned either to the extant online training system with the graphical user interface (control) or the CA (treatment). Both the CA and the extant online training system included the same set of questions for the case-study based job interview. Participants in the control condition interacted with the extant training system in a multiple-choice manner while participants in the treatment condition interacted via natural language. After participation in the training, the job candidates completed a survey.

We adapted established instruments from previous studies that correspond to our hypotheses. Table 37 shows the constructs, items, and factor loadings as well as Cronbach's α, composite reliability (CR) and average variance extracted (AVE) for perceived usefulness, enjoyment, social presence, and uncanniness. To measure perceived humanness, we asked participants to indicate how very inhuman-like to very human-like they perceived the tool on a 9-point semantic differential scale as similarly done by Holtgraves and Han (2007). Three items were dropped from the analysis due factor loadings lower than .60 as proposed by Gefen and Straub (2005). All constructs showed sufficient Cronbach's α (larger than .80), CR (larger than .80) and AVE (larger than .50) with respect to the levels proposed by Urbach and Ahlemann (2010).

Table 37 (Study 6): Constructs, Items, and Factor Loadings

Constructs and Items	Loadings	Scale and Source
Perceived Usefulness (α = .937, CR = .937, AVE = .714)		
The tool would enable me to faster prepare for the interviews.	.882	
The tool would improve my performance in the interviews.	.762	
The tool would increase my productivity in interview preparation.	.824	7-point Likert scale (Davis 1989)
The tool would increase my effectiveness in interview preparation.	.823	
The tool would make it easier for me to prepare for the interviews.	.880	
The tool would be useful to prepare for the interviews.	.891	
Enjoyment (α = .901, CR = .907, AVE = .709)		
I think the interaction with the tool is interesting.	.864	
I think the interaction with the tool is enjoyable.	.820	7-point Likert scale (Koufaris 2002)
I think the interaction with the tool is exciting.	.887	
I think the interaction with the tool is fun.	.793	
Social Presence (α = .841, CR = .838, AVE = .564)		
I felt a sense of human contact with the tool.	.685	
I felt a sense of personalness with the tool.	.716	7-point Likert scale (Gefen and Straub 1997)
I felt a sense of sociability with the tool (dropped)	*(0.457)*	
I felt a sense of human warmth with the tool.	.787	
I felt sense of human sensitivity with the tool.	.810	
Uncanniness (α = .847, CR = .843, AVE = .645)		
I perceived the tool as eerie.	.677	7-point Likert scale (MacDorman et al. 2009; Tinwell and Sloan 2014)
I perceived the tool as inhuman-like (dropped)	*(.599)*	
I perceived the tool as strange.	.804	
I perceived the tool as unappealing.	.911	

1.5.3 Results

The survey data was analyzed by means of descriptive statistics and one-sided t-tests for the comparative evaluation of the artifact. First, we checked for variance homogeneity. The Levene tests indicated unequal variance for perceived usefulness, thus we used Welch's t-test for the analysis. The remaining constructs exhibited equal variance and were analyzed using Student's t-tests. Our data indicated that participants indeed perceived the agent as more useful (H1), more enjoyable (H2), more human-like (H3), and socially present (H4) than the extant online training system. A one sample t-test against the fixed value of 3 showed that the CA exhibited a low level of uncanniness (H5). Additionally, no significant difference for the ratings for uncanniness between the anthropomorphic CA and the extant system with the graphical user interface, for which one would naturally expect a low level of uncanniness as it contains only very few social cues, was found. Table 38 shows the results of the evaluation.

Table 38 (Study 6): Descriptive Statistics and t-Test Results

		Condition		t-value (df)	p-value	Result
		Control (n = 35)	Treatment (n = 37)			
Perceived Usefulness	Mean SD SE	4.52 1.44 0.24	5.05 1.12 0.18	-1.73 (64.3)	.045	H1 supported
Enjoyment	Mean SD SE	4.10 1.37 0.23	4.79 1.25 0.21	-2.25 (70)	.014	H2 supported
Humanness	Mean SD SE	3.60 1.97 0.33	4.76 1.75 0.29	-2.63 (70)	.005	H3 supported
Social Presence	Mean SD SE	2.54 0.94 0.16	3.38 1.08 0.18	-3.49 (70)	.001	H4 supported
Uncanniness[1]	Mean SD SE	3 (fixed value)	1.82 0.87 0.14	-8.22 (36)	<0.001	H5 supported
	Mean SD SE	1.96 0.88 0.15		0.69 (70)	.247	

SD = Standard deviation, SE = Standard error

1) First row depicts one sample t-test of the CA against fixed value of 3, second row shows the t-test comparing control and treatment group

1.5.4 Evaluation of Agent Responsiveness

In addition to the evaluation of user perception of the designed artifact, we analyzed the changes in responsiveness of the agent throughout the three design cycles. Using data provided by Google Dialogflow on the successful detection of user intents in the conversations as well as the use of fallback responses in case no intent was matched to the user's query, we investigated the impact of our design adaptions (Table 39).

We observed a decreasing interaction time and fallbacks per interaction and minute across the cycles. In particular, our design adaptation in the last cycle, where we added more specific user guidance in the conversation by means of context-specific hints as well as selected response suggestions and improved the agent's conversational abilities based on training with existing dialogue data, led to a substantial increase in agent responsiveness. Furthermore, the percentage of users successfully completing the interview training increased from 42.9% to 89.2%.

Table 39 (Study 6): Evolution of Agent Responsiveness across Design Cycles

Design Cycle	Avg. Minutes per Interaction	Avg. Fallbacks per Interaction	Avg. Fallbacks per Minute	Completion Rate
1	33.6	10.80	0.53	20.0%
2	28.7	10.00	0.42	42.9%
3	22.6	1.16	0.06	89.2%

1.6 Discussion

The DSR project presented in this study aimed to address the problem of crafting anthropomorphic conversational agents in a professional context that have limited conversational capabilities as given in present-day technology. In the following, we discuss implications of our results for designing anthropomorphic CAs and summarize the generated prescriptive knowledge in the form of a nascent design theory.

1.6.1 Implications for Anthropomorphic Conversational Agent Design

Our research contributes to the knowledge base for anthropomorphic CA design by proposing and evaluating a design for a human-like agent in a professional context that leverages existing prescriptive knowledge on social cues and at the same time mitigates potential detrimental effects on user perception due to the limited conversational capabilities of present-day natural language technology. Thus, it contributes to overcoming limitations of existing experimental IS and HCI studies on anthropomorphic CA design (e.g. Schuetzler et al. 2014; Gnewuch et al. 2018b; Burmester et al. 2019) as well as to addressing the issue of limited conversational capabilities of CAs in practice (Luger and Sellen 2016; Ben Mimoun et al. 2012). Specifically, the anthropomorphic design proposed in this study has been shown to foster a human-like interaction experience while mitigating and addressing response failures. In line with research on CA design flaws (Luger and Sellen 2016; Ben Mimoun et al. 2012), the insights from the evolution of our design throughout the three cycles emphasized the importance of meaningful responses by the agent in a conversation, in particular as users expect the agent to conform to human conversation behavior due to the rich social cues as posited in Social Response Theory (Nass and Moon 2000; Reeves and Nass 1996). While anticipating user input and conversation flows remains a substantial design challenge due to the open nature of natural language interaction (Følstad and Brandtzæg 2017), our proposed design addresses the currently limited agent responsiveness and thus fosters user perception of social presence and humanness while avoiding feelings of uncanniness. The combination of DP2 (self-identification and presentation of capabilities to manage user expectations as well as providing contact to an actual human person in situations of response failure) and DP3 (offering structure by providing response suggestions and transparent conversation flows as well as using context-specific fallbacks and iteratively training the agent from emerging dialogue data) represents an efficient approach to mitigate as well as address limited conversational capabilities of present-day CAs. In this context, our evaluation of agent responsiveness showed a considerable progress from design cycle 2 to cycle 3 after we added and instantiated DP3, which reduced the number of fallback responses per minute (0.42 to 0.06) as well as more than doubled the percentage of successfully completed interactions (42.9% to 89.2%). Thus, the use of response suggestions in situations where input varied substantially and often led to fallback replies, in combination with context-specific fallbacks, allowed to successfully steer the conversation in a way that the CAs limited conversational capabilities are (in most cases) not revealed and a user's attention is not drawn to the inhuman imperfections of the agent, avoiding potential feelings of uncanniness related to the Uncanny Valley (Mori et al. 2012).

Furthermore, the evaluation of our design showed that a human-like CA in the specific context of interview preparation is perceived more positively by users than the extant training system with a graphical user interface. Specifically, users perceived the designed CA as more useful and enjoyable than the existing system. The designed artifact can thus be more abstractly considered as an improvement, representing a new solution for a known problem (Gregor and Hevner 2013) in a specific application domain. Drawing on the idea that anthropomorphic design is not a goal per se, but beneficial for tasks typically attributed to actual humans (Seeger et al. 2017), we argue that a human-like design in this context is particularly useful as the task at hand (conducting a job interview training) consists of human-to-human interaction.

1.6.2 Towards a Nascent Design Theory

We presented a situated instantiation in the form of an artifact and formulated more general knowledge in the form of constructs, design principles and testable propositions. Table 40 summarizes these contributions using the components suggested by Gregor and Jones (2007).

Table 40 (Study 6): Nascent Design Theory for Anthropomorphic Enterprise CAs

Component	Description
Purpose and scope	The objective of the text-based enterprise CA is to offer the feeling of a human contact in a professional dialogue while minimizing feelings of uncanniness, particularly due to limited conversational abilities.

Component	Description
Constructs	Six constructs were derived that are relevant for the design: Usefulness (Davis 1989), enjoyment (Koufaris 2002), humanness (Holtgraves and Han 2007), social presence (Gefen and Straub 1997), uncanniness (MacDorman et al. 2009; Tinwell and Sloan 2014), and agent responsiveness.
Principles of form and function	Through a review of CA literature and interviews, we derived four theoretically grounded DPs, which were qualitatively and quantitatively evaluated: **DP1:** Equip the agent with conversational capabilities for intent detection in order to increase its usefulness, given that the input of the user can be anticipated by the designer. **DP2:** Self-identify the agent as a machine, present exemplary capabilities and offer the possibility to get in touch with a human representative in order to manage user expectations and decrease feelings of uncanniness. **DP3:** Guide the user in a conversation where required, foster context-specific handling of fallbacks, and iteratively extend the agent's abilities from dialogue data in order to increase the agent's responsiveness. **DP4:** Design the agent with appealing social cues in order to contribute to the perception of humanness, social presence and enjoyment in the interaction without fostering feelings of uncanniness.
Artifact mutability	The CA improves over time as unanswerable user input is monitored and used to continuously extend the agent's conversational abilities.
Testable propositions	With a comparative logic, we formulate five propositions to evaluate the design: **H1:** *If a CA follows the proposed design, then it is perceived as more useful than the extant system with a graphical user interface.* **H2:** *If a CA follows the proposed design, then it is perceived as more enjoyable than the extant system with a graphical interface.* **H3:** *If a CA follows the proposed design, then it yields a higher perceived humanness than the extant system with a graphical interface.* **H4:** *If a CA follows the proposed design, then it yields a higher feeling of social presence than the extant system with a graphical interface.* **H5:** *If a CA follows the proposed design, then it exhibits a low level of uncanniness.*
Justificatory knowledge	The overall design is grounded in Social Response Theory (Nass and Moon 2000), the Theory of Uncanny Valley (Mori 1970), and related work on CAs.
Principles of implementation	We provide an example of how to instantiate the design in the form of an artifact, particularly the selected cues can be used in future CA designs.
Expository instantiation	Two artifacts are presented with different instantiations (prototype with 3/4 DPs, major version with 4/4 DPs which was released by the case company).

1.7 Limitations and Opportunities for Future Research

Our research exhibits four main limitations and offers opportunities for future studies on anthropomorphic CA design. First, we selected a comparative approach for the evaluation, which allowed to evaluate the artifact as a whole in comparison to the extant training system with a graphical user interface. Under consideration of the different DSR genres suggested by Peffers et al. (2018) and our research objective to formulate a nascent design theory, we position our work in the genre of "IS Design Theory" (Gregor and Jones 2007) rather than an "Explanatory Design Theory" (Baskerville and Pries-Heje 2010) where systematic manipulation of design variables is favorable. Against this background, our evaluation was suitable to demonstrate that the designed artifact indeed represents an improvement over the status quo (extant training system with graphical user interface) in the sense of Gregor and Hevner (2013) including a higher level of utility manifested in the constructs. However, it does not allow to explain the impact of single design principles on user perception and performance of the CA. Notwithstanding, the positive impact of adding and instantiating DP3 to address the limited responsiveness can be observed in our analysis of dialogue data (Table 39). Thus, we suggest future studies to investigate the impacts of the three remaining design principles (DP1, DP2, DP4) on user perception of the CA. Additionally, the evaluation did not include varying degrees of anthropomorphism of the CA but focused on a specific combination of social cues as shown in Table 36 and its interplay the agent's conversational capabilities. Thus, we propose to adapt the design theory in future studies and craft anthropomorphic CAs with different variations of social cues and evaluate changes in user perception.

Second, with regard the CA's responsiveness, our evaluation highlighted a positive effect of adding user guidance in situations where response failure occurs as well as using context-specific fallback handling and continuous training from dialogue data (DP3) to address the limited conversational capabilities of the agent. As failure to provide a meaningful reply in a conversation represents a major design issue for anthropomorphic CAs, we suggest to further investigate the impact of response failure on user perception the agent, for example by deliberately altering the number of fallback replies in a (professional) conversation and measuring changes in user perception with regard to humanness, social presence, and uncanniness of the agent as well as to systematically explore different fallback replies.

Third, the summative evaluation of our artifact is based on a sample size of 72 participants. The participants in this evaluation can be considered suitable as they represent actual potential job applicants from the case company's talent pool. However, despite the statistically significant results for the hypotheses tests, the evaluation of our design could be strengthened by increasing the sample size with further participants.

Fourth, our measurement approach exhibits two main limitations. First, we measured perceived humanness with a single item as done in other studies on anthropomorphism (e.g. MacDorman 2006; Holtgraves and Han 2007). As described by Bartneck et al. (2009) alternative, multi-item measurement instruments for anthropomorphism exist, such as the six items used by Powers and Kiesler (2006) that could further increase consistency and reliability of the results. Second, we collected demographic information of the participants but did not gain information on further contextual aspects that could influence user perception of the anthropomorphic CA. For example, experience with chatbots or with the task at hand could have a (moderating) effect on for example perceived humanness or usefulness of the agent. Thus, future studies on anthropomorphic CAs could explore which contextual factors related to the user or the given task impact the perception of the agent.

1.8 Concluding Remarks

Anthropomorphic conversational agents continue to gain substantial interest in companies to automate and innovate different tasks while providing the feeling of a human contact in the interaction. However, the limited conversational capabilities of present-day CAs often lead to situations where a meaningful response cannot be provided by the agent, which abruptly remind users that they are actually interacting with a machine and thus are detrimental to a human-like interaction experience and associated positive effects.

The present study contributes to solving this problem by designing and evaluating an artifact as well as formulating a nascent design theory for anthropomorphic and communicative CAs in a professional context that allows to benefit from a human-like interaction experience while mitigating and addressing situations in which the agent's limited conversational capabilities come to light. We invite researchers and designers to apply, evaluate and extend the proposed design theory to improve our understanding of how to craft human-like technological artifacts while deliberately minimizing negative effects due to the limited capabilities of machines.

1.9 Appendix

Table 41 (Study 6): Participants in qual. Requirements Elicitation and Evaluation

Design Cycle	Research Method	Pseudonym	Gender	Role and Individual Background
1 Awareness of Problem	Semi-structured interviews on requirements and iterative coding	HR01	Female	Head of Global HR Marketing & Recruiting at Company, Educational Background in Marketing
		HR02	Female	Senior Expert HR at Case Company, Educational Background in Marketing
		TP01	Male	Master Student of Information Systems at German University, Member of Company's Talent Pool
		TP02	Male	Bachelor Student of Business Administration at German University, Member of Company's Talent Pool
		TP03	Female	Student of Medicine at German University, Member of Company's Talent Pool
		TP04	Male	Master Student of Business Administration at German University, Member of Company's Talent Pool
1 Evaluation	Free form feedback in survey after interaction with 1st prototype and open coding	TP11	Male	Master Student of Business Administration at Danish University, Consultant Intern at Company
		TP12	Male	Master Student of Business Administration at German University, Member of Company's Talent Pool
		TP13	Female	Master Student of Business Administration at Swiss University, Member of Company's Talent Pool
		TP14	Male	Bachelor Student of Economics at German University, Member of Company's Talent Pool
		TP15	Male	Master Student of Business Administration at German University, Consultant Intern at Company
		TP16	Male	Bachelor Student of Engineering at German University, Member of Company's Talent Pool
		TP17	Male	Master Student of Political Science at German University, Member of Company's Talent Pool
2 Evaluation	Two focus group sessions with 2nd prototype interaction and gathering of strengths and weaknesses of the artifact	HR21	Female	Head of Global HR Marketing & Recruiting at Company, Educational Background in Marketing
		HR22	Female	Senior Expert HR at Company, Educational Background in Marketing
		HR23	Female	Junior Expert HR at Company, Educational Background in Business Administration
		HR24	Female	Expert for Marketing at Company, Educational Background in Marketing
		TP21	Male	Master Student of Information Systems at German University, Member of Company's Talent Pool
		TP22	Male	Master Student of Business Administration at German University, Member of Company's Talent Pool
		TP23	Female	Student of Medicine at German University, Member of Company's Talent Pool

Table 42 (Study 6): Meta-Requirements and Quotes from Interviews (translated)

Meta-Requirement	Exemplary Quote(s) and Source
User Understanding (MR1)	"the bot should be able to answer detailed, follow-up questions that could come up in a specific topic area as long as they can be anticipated" – TP04 "it should understand context-specific questions for the recruiting process [..], for example, what are typical questions on the interview day?" – TP03
Informative Responses (MR2)	"the bot somehow represents the company's image, so questions should be answered informatively" – TP01 "the bot has to be able to remember and logically connect what has been communicated in the conversation [..]. It needs to understand and address what I have said, it should not always offer the same standardized reply" – TP04
System Transparency (MR3)	"In my opinion showing what the bot can do is good as people otherwise have the expectation that it is like Siri and can answer every kind of question […] It would be useful if the bot says I can answer this and answer that at the beginning" –HR02 "The bot should say that it is here to only help and support [the user for the recruiting day], also without tracking individual performance or the like" – HR01 "It would be great if the bot would identify itself as a machine in a sympathetic, playful way" – TP01 "I think it is more appealing if the bot clearly describes that it is a computer but it also has certain human characteristics" – TP02 "the expectation gap is a problem [..] I'm always disappointed if I ask Siri something and she does not understand me. It should clearly delineate areas in which it can provide as good replies as possible" – TP01
Exit Option (MR4)	"Personally, I find it helpful if for example e-mail addresses of HR contacts are provided" – TP02 "In the best case, the bot immediately responds with contact data of an actual person that I can approach with my question" –TP03
Support in Conversation (MR5)	"I don't know if this is technically possible, but it would be great to have the opportunity to state a solution and then receive feedback whether it is correct and whether the solution approach is suitable" – TP02
Conversation Repair and Fallback (MR6)	"the bot should indicate that it is not able to answer the specific question – in a sympathetic way to reduce a user's disappointment" – TP01 "in the best case, the bot would support the reformulation of the user's request that would then allow it to understand the user" – TP01 "[if the bot cannot answer a question] it should politely state something like I am sorry that I cannot offer a reply, please feel free to contact us under…" – TP04

Table 43 (Study 6): Prototype Issues and Free-Form Feedback (translated)

Primary Issue	Exemplary Quote(s) and Source
Mechanical and inhuman feeling in the interaction	„it is not very human-like, you realize that the replies repeat themselves frequently and that follow-up questions are not possible. In comparison to a real-life job interview with a consultant, the bot is not able to respond to spontaneous questions" – TP11 „the chatbot is a bit too friendly, in my opinion it uses too many smileys" – TP15 "it is clear that the technology is still far away from simulating real human behavior [in a job interview]" – TP12 "the quantitative and multiple-choice parts of the interviews are okay; however, it lacks flexibility in the interaction for the more creative interview questions" – TP15 "the bot's name is strange, I would use a normal human name and image – TP15 „the job interview is too mechanic, a case-study interview is about (creatively) approaching business problems. This opportunity is currently missed" – TP17 "the bot's image is unappealing, I would use the image of an actual employee" – TP15
Lack of responsiveness	"the computer obviously reacts to keywords, which often leads to misunderstandings" – TP12 "I had to reply manually multiple times until the chatbot understood that I wanted to do a case-study interview [..] this could lead to very frustrated users and immediately diminished the human-like interaction (if it misunderstands me already at the beginning, how can it be able to do a job interview with me?)" – TP16 "the bot only understands straight-forward responses, creative approaches are not appreciated" – TP17
Further technical issues with web interface	„the input field does not allow to make line breaks; the field is extended continuously which makes you lose the overview" – TP12 "a long delay exists when pressing "Enter" after adding input, which led me to enter a response multiple times" – TP12 "the computer should recognize when the user starts entering a second statement and then wait for the message to be sent. This would be more in line with a natural chat dialogue" – TP15

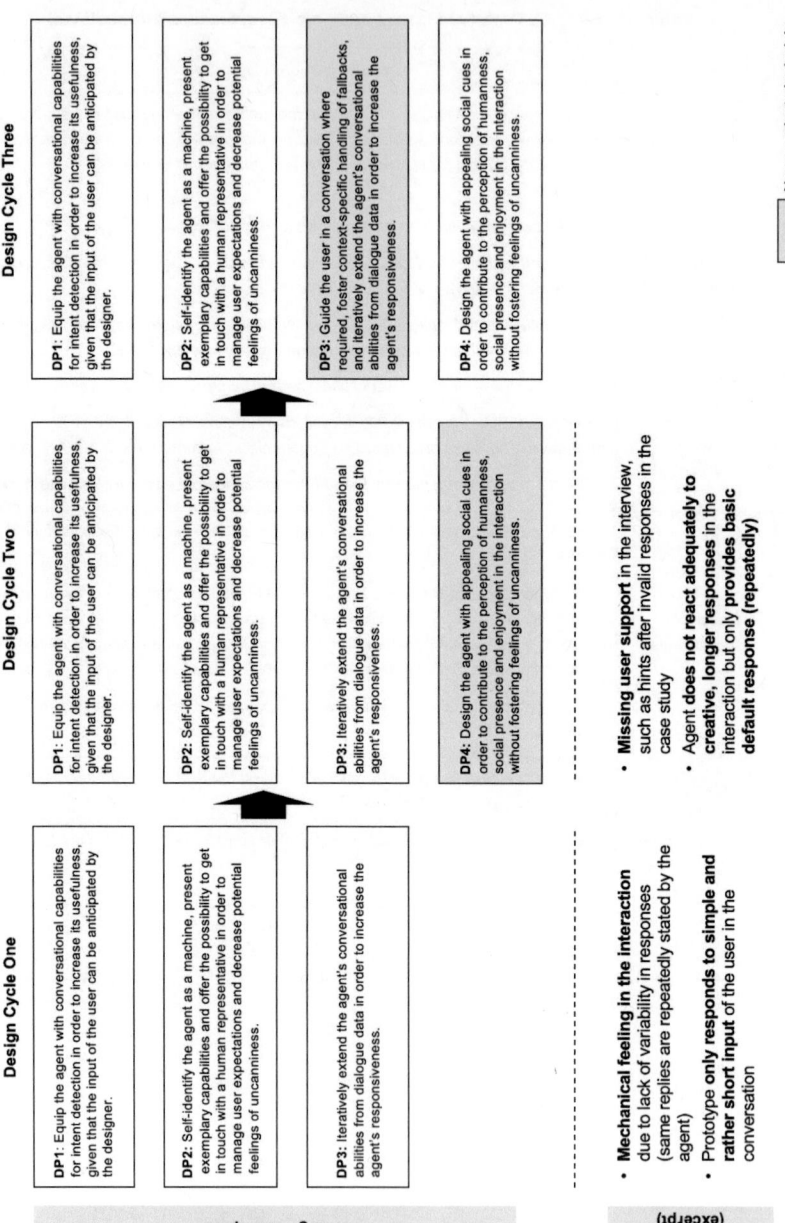

Figure 39 (Study 6): Evolution of Design Principles and Qualitative Feedback

C. Contributions

This cumulative thesis aims to advance our understanding of the anthropomorphic design of conversational agents in a company context. To achieve this research objective, four research questions were formulated with a focus on organizing and assessing existing knowledge (RQ1), investigating specific aspects of CA design (RQ2, RQ3), and subsequently bring together prescriptive knowledge in a nascent design theory as well as provide an exemplary instantiation in the form of a concrete technological artifact (RQ4).

The first Chapter in this part (C.I) recapitulates the findings for each of the research questions and synthesizes them in a design framework for human-like enterprise CAs. The next chapter (C.II) discusses the implications of this work for research and practice. Afterwards, the limitations of this work as well as opportunities for future research are presented (C.III). Finally, this thesis closes with concluding thoughts about the design of and human interaction with increasingly human-like natural language software (C.IV).

I. Findings and Results

This chapter summarizes the key findings of each study structured along the four main research questions. Moreover, the results of the studies are related to each other and brought together in a conceptual framework.

I.1 Findings for the Status Quo of Conversational Agent Research

The first research question (RQ 1) aimed to assess the state of research on the design of and human interaction with conversational agents in a company context. Study 1 (Table 44) addresses this question through organizing the currently rather dispersed knowledge base on CA design, bringing together existing prescriptive knowledge, as well as identifiying research gaps.

Table 44: Findings of Study 1

Title	On the Design of Enterprise Conversational Agents: A Synthesis of IS and HCI Research
Addressed Question	What is the status quo of research on the design of and human interaction with conversational agents in a company context?
Main Contribution	Overview of the status quo of CA research through a design theoretical lens, synthesis of existing prescriptive knowledge, and identification of research gaps

Through a systematic literature review (vom Brocke et al. 2009; Webster and Watson 2002) of 69 articles, the first study organized existing prescriptive knowledge on CAs using a design-theoretical lens (Gregor and Jones 2007). With regard to the first design theory component, the purpose and scope of an artifact, current research focuses on CAs on the automation of processes and tasks at the customer interface particularly in the areas of service provision (e.g. Wünderlich and Paluch 2017; Gnewuch et al. 2018b) and marketing and sales (e.g. Hanus and Fox 2015; Vaccaro et al. 2018). Emerging studies address further application areas, such as team collaboration (Toxtli et al. 2018), human resources (Liao et al. 2018), and data analytics (Fast et al. 2017).

Concerning the entities of interest when designing enterprise CAs, scholars investigate different constructs related to the design of such artifacts (e.g. responsiveness, self-disclosure, representation, or modality) as well as regarding the perception of such artifacts (e.g. trust, human likeness, and social presence). These aspects of a CA's design and its perception by users are linked through initial principles of form and function. For example, Gnewuch et al. (2017) suggest to provide the CA with conversational abilities to deliver messages of situation-dependent length and segmentation and users and Saffarizadeh et al. (2017) places emphasis on the potential of CA self-disclosure in order to increase the users' willingness to disclose information. Further researchers highlight aspects related to the mutability of CAs, for example by iterative refinement of responses to improve the CAs capabilities (Schuetzler et al. 2018b) or adjusting to individual human behavior in the context of decision-making (Elson et al. 2018). In addition, various design- and perception related propositions are formulated in the reviewed studies and tested particularly in experimental research. For example, Adler et al. (2016) suggest that a CA which uses an emotional persuasive strategy is more successful in its persuasion than one that uses a rational one or Schroeder and Schroeder (2018), comparing communication modes with CAs, propose that voice-based communication leads to a higher willingness to share personal information than text-based communication. Finally, with regard to the justificatory knowledge described in the reviewed studies, researchers particularly draw on Social Response Theory and the CASA paradigm, the Theory of Uncanny Valley, as well as theories from human interaction and behavior, such the Self-Determination Theory.

In summary, various design theoretical components are available to craft CAs in organizations. While these studies provide helpful, initial insights into selected aspects of CA design, several research gaps and opportunities were identified in the extant knowledge base. Three of these research gaps are particularly relevant for designing enterprise CAs. First, several studies highlight the importance of responsiveness of a CA. However, since response failure is unlikely to be avoided during evolving natural language conversations in practice (Følstad and Brandtzæg 2017), the interplay with other (human-like) qualities of a CA's design as well as the mitigiation of a determintal impact needs to be investigated. Second, studies indicate the positive potential of selected aspects of a CAs design in a company context, for example with regard to emotion-awareness or persuasion. Further research can build on these initial studies to explore how it can be leveraged in the context of anthropomorphic enterprise CA design. Furthermore, the assessment of the contribution types (Gregor and Hevner 2013) in the reviewed studies highlighted CAs as an emerging research topic where existing prescriptive knowledge is rather context-specific and immature. The studies present situated implementations of CAs, operational principles and architectures in specific contexts as well as insights from experimental research that focuses on context-independent relationships among specific constructs. Thus, further research is needed that provides less specific as well as comprehensive prescriptive knowledge for enterprise CAs through the design and evaluation of such artifacts in real-life settings.

I.2 Findings for Technological Limitations and their Impact

The second research question placed emphasis on understanding the impact the limited conversational capabilities of present-day enterprise CAs (RQ 2.1) as well as to explore how a negative effect of such limitations on the judgment of CAs by users can be mitigated (RQ 2.2).

To better understand the impact of limited conversational capabilities (RQ 2.1), manifested in the form of response failure of a CA during a conversation, Study 2 was conducted. The title of the study, the addressed research question, and the main contribution is summarized in Table 45.

Table 45: Findings of Study 2

Title	Not Human After All: Exploring the Impact of Response Failure on User Perception of Anthropomorphic Conversational Service Agents
Addressed Question	How does failure to provide a meaningful response influence user perception of anthropomorphic CAs in a professional encounter?
Main Contribution	Insights into the impact of modest response failure of a CA on user perception with regard to humanness and uncanniness of the CA as well as familiarity with the artifact and satisfaction with the service encounter.

The findings of Study 2 offer three main insights: First, modest response failure, i.e. the inability of a CA to provide a meaningful reply for one or two times during a conversation in which the agent is ultimately able to successfully complete a customer's request, has a substantial negative impact on user perception of the CA with regard to humanness and uncanniness. The qualitative feedback where the human-like CA was described as "incomplete" or participants criticized that "they had to ask for order cancellation a thousand times" provided further support for the results from the quantitative data and highlighted that such response failure was immediately realized by participants.

Second, a sharp drop in user affinity towards an anthropomorphic CA as postulated in the Theory of Uncanny Valley (Mori 1970; Mori et al. 2012) could not be observed. While response failure of both CAs in the experimental setting (one machine-like agent with few social cues, one human-like agent with many cues) had substantial negative effects on user perception, the human-like CA with many cues did not receive a strong negative evaluation as indicated in the theory. In fact, the human-like CA with response failure received similar ratings concerning humanness, uncanniness, familiarity, and service satisfaction as the machine-like counterpart that did not exhibit response failure.

Third, Study 2 revealed that the perception of humanness (uncanniness) in a professional interaction with a CA has a positive (negative) impact on familiarity and service encounter satisfaction as two relevant outcome variables. In particular, the assessment of direct effect sizes (Cohen 1988) indicated a large effect of the perception of humanness on both service satisfaction and familiarity. Thus, Study 2 provides empirical evidence for the positive impact of anthropomorphic CA design and associated perception of humanness in a customer service encounter, adding further support to emerging studies in this research area (e.g. Wünderlich and Paluch 2017; Gnewuch et al. 2018b).

In summary, Study 2 indicates that response failure has a negative impact on the perception of CAs by users, however, the effect is not as strong as postulated in the Theory of Uncanny Valley (Mori 1970; Mori et al. 2012) and, in particular, a CA with a human-like design and modest response failure still received a rating comparable to a machine-like CA without such failure. Thus, in combination with the positive impact of humanness on service satisfaction and familiarity, it can be concluded that a human-like design is beneficial in a service context despite potential modest response failure, which, however, still should be avoided as far as possible in a natural language interaction (Følstad and Brandtzæg 2017).

Based on this improved understanding of the impact of response failure in a professional conversation, Study 3 aimed to investigate the use of preset answer options as a potential mitigation approach. Specifically, preset answer options can be provided by a CA to steer the conversation and increase the probability that the CA can process the next input of the user, thus avoiding potential response failure due to the high variety of user input in a natural language interaction (Følstad and Brandtzæg 2017). Table 46 summarizes the title, question and main contribution of Study 3.

Table 46: Findings of Study 3

Title	Design for Fast Request Fulfillment or Natural Interaction? Insights from an Online Experiment with a Conversational Agent
Addressed Question	How do preset answer options of text-based CAs influence user perception?
Main Contribution	Insights on the impact of preset answer options (i.e. quick replies) in a professional conversation on user perception with regard to humanness, social presence, and service encounter satisfaction.

Study 3 provided two main findings concerning the use of preset answer options: First, answer options are, despite their potential to mitigate response failure, detrimental to the perception of humanness and social presence of a CA. As suggested answer options resemble elements known from graphical user interfaces, they reduce the intuitive feeling of natural language interaction as a social cue. Second, the use of preset answer options, which allowed participants to faster and more conveniently complete their service request without the need for manual typing, did not significantly increase the satisfaction with the service encounter despite the importance of fulfillment speed in service encounters (Setia et al. 2013). Thus, Study 2 highlights the need to design anthropomorphic CAs for natural language interaction with only careful use of preset answer options due to their detrimental impact on the perception of human-likeness of an agent. Together, the two studies emphasize a negative impact of response failure due to limited conversational capabilities on user perception of CAs, however not as strong as postulated in the Theory of Uncanny Valley, and at the same time highlight the need for a moderate use of preset answer options to mitigate response failure as they decrease the intuitive feeling of in an interaction with a CA. Thus, CA designers should strive for a conversation design that balances a natural language interaction with selective use of preset answer options in situations where response failure is likely to occur. In doing so, designers can contribute to the perception of humanness in a CA which in turn can positively influence further outcome variables like satisfaction with the service encounter or familiarity with the CA.

I.3 Findings for the Potential of Anthropomorphic Design

Complementary to understanding the impact of limited conversational capabilities and how to mitigate a negative effect on user perception, the third research question focuses on the potential of anthropomorphic CA design. Specifically, it places emphasis on two particularly relevant aspects of human-like CAs in professional settings: Empathy, which is for example important in the context of customer service provision (Larivière et al. 2017), and persuasion, which can be helpful in for CA providing product recommendations or acting as an additional sales channel (Hanus and Fox 2015).

Table 47: Findings of Study 4

Title	Emulating Empathetic Behavior in Online Service Encounters with Sentiment-Adaptive Responses: Insights from an Experiment with a Conversational Agent
Addressed Question	How does empathetic behavior of a CA based on sentiment-adaptive responses affect customer perception compared to a non-empathetic agent?
Main Contribution	Design approach for a CA that emulates empathetic communication behavior through sentiment-adaptive responses and evaluation of user perception of the CA regarding perceived empathy, humanness, social presence and service satisfaction.

Study 4 proposes a design approach that combines the use of automatic sentiment analysis of textual user input (Liu 2010, 2012) with adaptive responses. Based on Google Dialogflow as a platform for CA design and Aylien (2019) as a provider for sentiment analysis, the CA adapts its response depending on the sentiment score of the preceding user statement. The evaluation of this design approach by means of an online experiment showed that participants indeed perceived the CA with the sentiment-adaptive design as more empathetic, socially present, and human-like than a CA that provided static responses. Thus, the basic design approach, which adjusted the CA's responses at three points in a customer service encounter, already contributed to the anthropomorphic perception of the agent by users. Furthermore, the experiment also showed that the sentiment-adaptive design increased the overall satisfaction with the service encounter, which is in line with existing studies on empathy in human-to-human customer service provision (Yan et al. 2013). Interestingly, the analysis of gender-related moderation effects revealed the relative importance of empathy in human-CA service encounters particularly for female participants. Our study therefore not only provided further support for social responses to human-like CAs as postulated in Social Response Theory (Nass and Moon 2000), but also indicated the potential to consider user-related differences (e.g. age) in the design of CAs, for example by varying interaction styles or the representation of the agent.

With regard to persuasion, Study 5 explores the combination of anthropomorphic CA design with persuasive system design. Drawing on the Theory of Planned Behavior (Ajzen 1985, 1991), the study investigates the impact of anthropomorphic and persuasive design on the persuasiveness of a CA in relation to individual behavioral, normative, and control beliefs in the exemplary context of sustainable mobility.

Table 48: Findings of Study 5

Title	Promoting Sustainable Mobility Beliefs with Persuasive and Anthropomorphic Design: Insights from an Experiment with a Conversational Agent
Addressed Question	How can persuasive and human-like design of conversational agents positively shape individual beliefs towards sustainable mobility behavior?
Main Contribution	Design approach for a CA that combines social cues with elements from persuasive system design to increase the persuasiveness of the artifact in the exemplary context of sustainable mobility.

Study 5 finds that the perception of humanness in a CA (fostered through different social cues) positively contributes to the persuasiveness (enabled through different persuasive design elements) of the agent. Furthermore, showing the behavior of normative referents in the interaction (e.g. the CA stating that colleagues will also be taking the e-bike to ride to work tomorrow or highlighting that other users are looking at this product as well), influenced the normative beliefs of participants. In addition, persuasive design elements (e.g. the CA praising the user for booking an e-bike and highlighting her or his positive impact to our environment) showed a significant positive impact on individual control beliefs. Thus, in line with Social Response Theory (Nass and Moon 2000) and further studies on the social influence of human-like CAs (Araujo 2018), Study 5 highlights the potential of combining anthropomorphic CA design with elements from persuasive system design (Oinas-Kukkonen and Harjumaa 2009) to increase the persuasiveness of such technological artifacts.

In sum, Studies 4 and 5 highlight the potential of empathy and persuasion in the context of anthropomorphic CA design to influence user perception with regard to desirable outcome variables, such as persuasiveness, empathy, and service encounter satisfaction. Furthermore, both studies provide empirical evidence for the strong social responses humans show to anthropomorphic CAs in the sense of Nass and Moon (2000). In particular, even subtle adaptations of a CAs design (e.g. adding empathetic responses or selectively expressing praise) had significant effects on user perception.

I.4 Findings for a Nascent Design Theory

After organizing existing knowledge on CA design and investigating technological limitations as well as the design of empathetic and persuasive CAs in experimental research, the final step of this research endeavor remains to bring together the gained prescriptive knowledge, instantiate it in a real-life artifact and company setting as well as to synthesize the findings in a nascent design theory (Gregor and Jones 2007). In doing so, the fifth research question is addressed by Study 6 (Table 49).

Table 49: Findings of Study 6

Title	Designing Anthropomorphic Enterprise Conversational Agents
Addressed Question	How can a CA in a professional context be designed to offer a human-like inter-action while mitigating negative effects due to limited conversational capabilities?
Main Contribution	Nascent design theory for anthropomorphic enterprise conversational agents and exemplary instantiation in a concrete technological artifact for a large professional service company.

Study 6 designs an anthropomorphic CA for a professional services company that fosters a human-like interaction and at the same time mitigates potential negative effects due to limited conversational capabilities as given in present-day CAs. The CA in this study aims to support job candidates in their preparation for the recruiting day through the simulation of a case study-based job interview. In particular by offering the feeling of an enjoyable, human-like interaction and more realistically simulating the interview situation, the CA intends to improve the existing solution in this domain (Gregor and Hevner 2013).

Based on the DSR approach by Kuechler and Vaishnavi (2008), the text-based CA is designed in three iterations, each consisting of research activities to better understand the (partial) design problem, finding and designing (partial) solutions, as well as evaluating the (intermediary) artifact and adding new findings to the knowledge base. Study 6 finally proposes a design approach that combines purposefully selected social cues to elicit positive social responses (Nass and Moon 2000) and the perception of anthropomorphism with measures to cope with the limited conversational capabilities of present-day natural language technology, thus avoiding potential feelings of uncanniness (Mori 1970; Mori et al. 2012). Specifically, these measures comprised the self-identification as a machine, the presentation of exemplary capabilities, an exit option to get in touch with a human representative as well as the selective use of preset answer options and context-specific fallbacks. The final evaluation round provides empirical evidence that participants perceive the CA more useful, enjoyable, human-like and socially present than the extant system without increasing feelings of uncanniness. In addition, the evaluation of agent responsiveness (i.e. assessment of response failure) shows substantial progress throughout the design cycles due to iterative training of the agent's conversational capabilities combined with the aforementioned measures. Study

6 synthesizes these findings in a nascent design theory (Gregor and Jones 2007) for anthropomorphic text-based CAs in a company context that aim to offer a human-like interaction without fostering feelings of uncanniness due to limited conversational capabilities. The resulting theory can be applied, evaluated and extended in future design-oriented research on human-like CAs.

After recapitulating the findings from the six studies included in this cumulative thesis, Table 50 summarizes the main findings for each of the four formulated research questions.

Table 50: Main Findings for each Research Question

Chapter	Research Question	Main Findings
Chapter I: Assessing the Status Quo	RQ 1: What is the status quo of research on the design of and human interaction with CAs?	• Extant research offers insights for the design and perception of CAs with regard to specific aspects and indicates potential as well as challenges of CA design • However, currently available prescriptive knowledge is dispersed and context-specific, thus more comprehensive, abstract and field-proven design knowledge is desirable
Chapter II: Understanding Technological Limitations	RQ 2.1: How does response failure influence user perception of human-like CAs in a professional encounter?	• Failure of a CA to provide a meaningful response decreases (increases) the perception of humanness (uncanniness) in a service encounter • However, a human-like design is still perceived better than a machine-like design with (in contrast to the effect suggested in the Theory of Uncanny Valley) • Perception of humanness in a CA positively impacts familiarity with the artifact and service satisfaction
	RQ 2.2: How do preset answer options of text-based CAs influence user perception?	• Preset answer options can mitigate response failure, but are detrimental to the perception of humanness as they reduce the natural feeling of the interaction • The use of preset answer options increases the speed with which a customer's request is fulfilled, however, does not significantly increase service satisfaction • Thus, the conversation design for a CA should focus on fostering a natural interaction and preset answer options should be only where required to mitigate response failure
Chapter III: Exploring Potential of Human-Like Design	RQ 3.1: How does empathetic behavior of a CA based on sentiment-adaptive responses affect customer perception compared to a non-empathetic agent?	• Empathetic communication behavior by a CA can be emulated through the combination of adaptive responses with automatic sentiment analysis • A sentiment-adaptive CA design contributes to the perception of empathy, humanness, and social presence as well as leads to a higher satisfaction • Gender-related differences regarding the importance of empathy known from human-human service provision exist in similar form for human-CA interaction

Chapter	Research Question	Main Findings
	RQ 3.2: How can persuasive and human-like design of conversational agents positively shape individual beliefs?	• The perception of humanness through social cues increases the persuasiveness of CAs, complementing existing elements from persuasive system design • Persuasive, human-like CAs are suitable to influence individual normative beliefs • Similarly, such CAs can exert social influence through for example through praise or highlighting the benefits of desirable user behavior
Chapter IV: Formulating a Nascent Design Theory	RQ 4: How can a CA in a professional context be designed to offer a human-like interaction while mitigating negative effects due to limited conversational capabilities?	• A human-like interaction experience can be fostered through the purposeful selection of social cues with regard to the desired human traits and characteristics • The detrimental effect of limited conversational capabilities can be mitigated through measures like the self-identification of the CA as a machine or guiding users with preset answer options where required • A CA that follows the proposed design can yield a positive user perception concerning aspects like enjoyment or usefulness and at the same time avoid feelings of uncanniness in the interaction

I.5 Synthesis of Findings: A Conceptual Framework for the Design of and Interaction with Anthropomorphic CAs in a Company Context

The six studies provided new insights for the design of and interaction with human-like conversational agents in a company context, thereby adding to the growing knowledge base for this emerging technology. The empirical investigations underlined the potential of anthropomorphic design and associated perceptions of humanness in the interaction with natural language artifacts, such as for increasing customer satisfaction in service encounters (Study 3, Study 4), improving the persuasiveness of CAs (Study 5) or fostering feelings of enjoyment in the interaction (Study 6). However, this research at the same time indicated that CAs, which are not able to fulfill high user expectations, swiftly lead to an adverse user perception as for example highlighted by the significant negative impact of modest response failure (Study 2). The qualitative feedback collected in Study 2 emphasizes this effect on user perception as one participant described that she or he "had to ask for a thousand times" when the agent exhibited response failure for two times in a conversation.

In short, the studies highlight both the potential of anthropomorphic CA design in a company context as well as the risks associated with increasing the human-likeness of such artifacts. In particular, the results show that finding an appealing, human-like CA design through purposefully combining social cues and coping with limited capabilities represents a complex endeavor (Study 6).

To better understand the interplay of the various aspects influencing the interaction of humans with human-like CAs, viewing such artifacts as components of socio-technical systems is helpful. Socio-technical systems essentially consist of humans seeking to accomplish a task in a specific context and the technology that the user uses to carry out the task (Goodhue and Thompson 1995; Heinrich et al. 2011). Based on the idea that the interplay of social and technical aspects influences the outcomes and perception of technology, Zhang and Li (2005) assess the evolution of HCI research in the IS discipline with a focus on *humans* and their characteristics (e.g. demographics), *context* (e.g. social-, organizational-, or group-related), *technology* (e.g. features and properties) as well as the resulting *perception and outcomes* stemming from the interaction. Viewing the interaction of humans with anthropomorphic CAs through this conceptual lens allows to organize and better understand how people perceive such artifacts and how this perception is affected by the design (Figure 40).

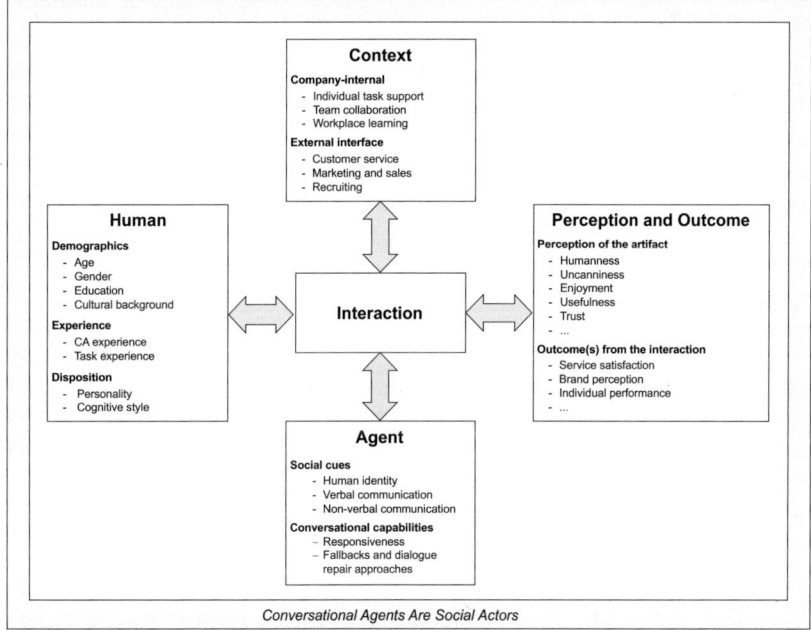

Figure 40: Framework for the Design of and Interaction with Human-Like CAs

Surrounding the framework is the understanding of CAs as social actors in the sense of Nass and Moon (2000). As the studies incorporated in this thesis and emerging research on anthropomorphic CAs (e.g. Araujo 2018; Seeger et al. 2018) have demonstrated, users show social responses to CAs due to their human-like traits and characteristics, particularly due to the interaction via natural language. These social responses comprise both how users perceive these agents (e.g. with feelings of humanness or uncanniness and consciously comparing them to human (service) employees instead of machines) as well as the expectations users have towards such artifacts, which are often out of line with the system's actual capabilities and the reason for failure of CAs in the past (Luger and Sellen 2016; Ben Mimoun et al. 2012). Thus, designers of anthropomorphic CAs should be aware of the social responses CAs trigger through their design, which are often the driver behind positive or negative perception of this technology (Gnewuch et al. 2017).

With regard to the first component, the *human*, the presented studies and further research has highlighted that individual characteristics with regard to demographics, experience, and disposition influence the perception of a CA. For example, the moderator analysis in Study 5 revealed that the age of the participants influenced the perception of humanness fostered by social cues (i.e. a higher age decreased the effect of social cues on the perceived human-likeness of the CA). Concerning the gender, Study 4 for example provided empirical evidence for diverging perceptions of empathetic communication behavior by a CA across female and male participants. Additional characteristics with regard to demographics, such as education or cultural background (Bartneck et al. 2009; Pereira and Baranauskas 2015) influence the perception of CAs. Finally, the experience with natural language technology and personal disposition (e.g. personality) impact user perception and should thus be considered when designing CAs. In this context, Al-Natour et al. (2006) for example found that perceived personality similarity of an shopping assistant with the users leads to a better evaluation. Furthermore, interaction with a CA over time in turn influences individual experience both with CAs as well as with the task at hand, which then shapes future interactions (Al-Natour and Benbasat 2009).

Concerning the second component, the *context*, the studies presented customer service (Study 2, Study 3, Study 4) and recruiting (Study 6) as two exemplary professional contexts in which CAs can be used. Different studies highlight further application areas both internally, such as individual task support (Liao et al. 2018), team collaboration (Seeber et al. 2019) or education (Fryer et al. 2019), and at the customer interface like for marketing and sales (Vaccaro et al. 2018). From these specific contexts, in particular the requirements for the conversational capabilities of a CA can be derived. For example, the conversational capabilities of the CA designed in Study 6 were inspired by a typical case-study based job interview structure and content provided by the professional services company. Similarly, the conversational capabilities of a customer service CA can be collected from the types of service requests it is intended to fulfill and with which users might approach the agent. In addition to the requirements for the dialogue, the context can provide guidance for the desired perception of the artifact and outcome of the interaction. For example, the CA in Study 6 was explicitly designed to provide an enjoyable interaction and to represent a useful tool in the context of interview preparation.

The third component, *agent*, refers to the design of the CA itself and in particular encompasses the social cues incorporated in the artifact as well as its conversational capabilities. As emerging studies on anthropomorphic CA design, such as Seeger et al. (2018) or Feine et al. (2019a), point out, designers have a variety of cues at their disposal to foster the perception of humanness. These cues comprise both the human identity with which a CA is equipped as well as its verbal- and non-verbal communication (Seeger et al. 2018). In this context, Study 6 placed emphasis on the careful selection of cues based on desirable human traits for the CA to provide an appealing, human-like interaction experience without overstating the system's actual capabilities. These capabilities in particular comprise the conversational skills of the CA, i.e. its ability to meaningfully respond to user input (Følstad and Brandtzæg 2017), context-specific fallbacks in case of unanticipated requests (Study 6) as well as dialogue repair approaches (Ashktorab et al. 2019). As shown in Study 2, the conversational capabilities of a CA have a substantial influence on the perception and evaluation of the agent by the user. In addition, data from past interactions can be used to train the capabilities of a CA as demonstrated in Study 6. Thus, not only the design of a CA influences how users interact with the agent, but the interaction in turn impacts the agent's design regarding its conversational capabilities.

The fourth and final component of the framework, *perception and outcome*, describes the perception and results emerging from the interaction with a CA by an individual user in a specific context. This, one the one hand, comprises how users perceive the agent itself, for example with regard to anthropomorphism (humanness, social presence, uncanniness), variables related to technology acceptance (e.g. usefulness) or hedonic aspects of the interaction (e.g. enjoyment). On the other hand, the component encompasses the outcome(s) from the interaction with relevance for the company, such as increases in service satisfaction (e.g. Study 4, Study 5), or an improved perception of the brand (Araujo 2018; Hanus and Fox 2015).

Finally, the *interaction* of a user with a CA in a specific context, manifested in the interplay of these four components, then changes over time as the relationship between a user and the CA as a technological artifact evolves where mental representations of past interactions and outcomes affect future ones (Al-Natour and Benbasat 2009). Due to the social nature of user interactions with CAs, extensive relationships can emerge and continuously change through repeated interaction between a user and a human-like agent (Bickmore and Picard, 2005).

In summary, the framework synthesizes the findings from the studies as well from research in this area area to extend existing conceptual work (e.g. (Seeger et al. 2018) and complement the nascent design theory proposed in Study 6, particularly by highlighting the importance of context and the individual user, and provide practical guidance for crafting CAs by organizing aspects to be considered in the design.

II. Implications

As outlined in the introduction of this dissertation, this research addresses the areas of conversational agents, anthropomorphic design, and human-computer systems design, as well as CA designers in practice. The following chapter discusses the key contributions of this thesis for the three research areas as well as practical implications.

II.1 Implications for Research

This thesis shed light on the design of CAs in an enterprise context by exploring its potential as well as risks associated with increasing the degree of anthropomorphism and coping with limited conversational capabilities. To better understand the interaction of humans with this technology as well as to inform their design, this thesis drew on Social Response Theory and the Theory of Uncanny Valley. The application of these theoretical lenses in the context of CAs as well as the findings from the experimental and design science studies have implications for scholars in the aforementioned areas.

With regard to the first research area, *conversational agents*, the empirical studies placed emphasis on viewing anthropomorphic CAs as social actors in the sense of Nass and Moon (2000). As postulated in Social Response Theory and the CASA paradigm, participants in Studies 2 to 6 showed substantial social responses to the human-like traits and characteristics of the CAs investigated in the articles. These social responses manifested both in the perception of the CA (e.g. reported feelings of humanness and social presence in the interaction) as well as the high expectations participants stated toward CAs with a human-like appearance (e.g. by comparing the CA's behavior to the capabilities of a human service employee instead of a computer system or showing significant negative reactions to modest failure during a conversation). Thus, as long as the CAs fulfilled these expectations concerning social behavior (e.g. offering a polite and personal introduction or maintaining reciprocity in a dialogue with adequate response time) and premature cognitive commitments (e.g. the CA representing a member of the customer service team), they were evaluated positively by the users. In cases, however, were the CA failed to meet these expectations (e.g. by being unable to provide a meaningful reply as in Study 2), the positive judgment of the CA was abruptly attenuated as similarly suggested by Luger and Sellen (2016). Thus, the findings of these studies underline the need to view such artifacts as social actors in order to understand how users perceive anthropomorphic CAs and to guide their design.

Following this understanding of CAs as social actors, the findings of the six studies highlighted the opportunity to adapt existing knowledge and theories from human-human communication in the context of human-CA interaction. For example, Study 5 indicated the potential to use techniques originally from human persuasion (e.g. praising specific behavior or using social facilitation) to increase the persuasiveness of anthropomorphic

CAs. Similarly, Study 4 found that gender-related differences in the perception of human customer service provision to a large extent hold true for service provision with human-like CAs. Further, emerging studies on CA design, such as the work by Gnewuch et al. (2017) where the authors draw on the Gricean's maxims for cooperative conversations (Grice 1975), highlight the opportunity to learn from human-to-human communication and adapt this knowledge when designing anthropomorphic enterprise CAs.

Furthermore, the findings of the studies show that the perception CAs and outcomes fron their use can be better understood by viewing them as socio-technical systems (Goodhue and Thompson 1995; Heinrich et al. 2011) composed of a human user with individual characteristics, the specific context, and the CA as the technology used to complete a task or objective (Zhang and Li 2005). Thus, researchers concerned with understanding user perception of (anthropomorphic) CAs or informing their design can benefit from considering user-related differences (e.g. age, gender, experience) as well as contextual factors (e.g. expected social behavior in customer service settings). Thus, the primary focus of design-related studies on technological properties (e.g. Seeger et al. 2018) in this area can be extended to enable more efficient and effective CA designs by incorporating user characteristics and contextual factors.

For the second research area, *anthropomorphic artifacts*, two major implications arise from the findings of this thesis: First, Study 2 focused on potential detrimental effects of modest response failure of a human-like CA in a professional interaction. In contrast to the strong and abrupt shift in user perception postulated in the Theory of Uncanny Valley (Mori 1970; Mori et al. 2012), the magnitude of the identified negative effect was smaller (though statistically significant). Thus, it indicated that a human-like design with different social cues and modest response failure was still perceived as better than a machine-like design with few social cues and without response failure. These empirical findings could be explained in two different ways: First, the human-like CA design and the resulting degree of human-likeness of the CA was insufficient to reach the tipping point of the Uncanny Valley (Figure 8). Against the background of studies suggesting a differently structured curve for the Uncanny Valley (e.g. MacDorman et al. 2009) or additional aspects besides human-likeness that influence the affective perception of anthropomorphic artifacts (Hanson 2006; Hanson et al. 2005), an alternative explanation could be that the overall appealing design of the CA compensated for the few inhuman qualities, thereby attenuating a strong negative impact of response failure on user perception postulated by the theory. Moreover, the findings of this thesis highlight the need to consider the interplay of anthropomorphic design with given technological limitations of present-day CAs. As the social cues incorporated in the agent's human identity, verbal and non-verbal communication (Seeger et al. 2018) foster expectations towards the social behavior and competencies of the agent, they need to be in line with the system's actual capabilities. A mismatch between the actual conversational capabilities of the agent and the user's expectations represents a key reason for a negative evaluation (Luger and Sellen 2016). In this context, the nascent design theory for anthropomorphic CAs provides specific guidance on how to address the interplay of human-like design with limited conversational capabilities of CAs.

With regard to the third research area addressed by this thesis, *human-computer systems design*, three major implications exist. First, incorporating a suitable set of social cues in the CA's design fosters perception of mindless anthropomorphism which in turn can contribute to further outcomes with relevance for a company, such as service satisfaction as shown Studies 3 and 5, brand perception (Araujo 2018) or trust (Elson et al. 2018; Saffarizadeh et al. 2017). To identify a set of social cues that contributes to the intended user perception (e.g. of a CA as a sympathetic and capable virtual service agent), Study 6 suggested to first reflect on the desired human traits and characteristics and in a second step select the cues drawing on extant studies, such as Feine et al. (2019a). In doing so, the potential negative effects of a "more is more" approach for human-like design (Seeger et al. 2018) can be mitigated and the a match between the anthropomorphic design and system's actual capabilities can be achieved.

Second, the findings of the studies point out the importance of a CA's conversational capabilities (Study 2) in line with the results of further HCI scholars (e.g. Følstad and Brandtzæg 2017; Urban and Mailey 2019). As shown in Study 6, anticipating varying user input in natural language and implementing the required conversational capabilities to provide meaningful replies in an evolving dialogue represents a complex endeavor. To address this challenge, Study 6 applied an iterative approach that combines learning from past conversations, context-specific fallbacks, and preset answer options. In this context, in particular a DSR approach that iterates between design and evaluation (Hevner 2007; Vaishnavi and Kuechler 2015) with a focus on conversational capabilities can be fruitful to understand emerging dialogues with the CA and adjust its capabilities accordingly, thereby treating conversations as the object of design (Følstad and Brandtzæg 2017).

Finally, the presented empirical studies highlight the potential of adaptive CA design in which the agent and its responses are tailored to a specific context (e.g. sentiment-adaptive responses for a frustrated customer in Study 4) or user and its characteristics (e.g. gender as shown in Study 4 or age and experience as indicated in Study 5). Study 4 showed that even subtle changes in a CA design in the form of sentiment-adaptive responses led to a significantly improved perception of the CA as well as overall satisfaction with the service encounter. In this context, studies on anthropomorphic product recommendation agents, such as the work by Qiu and Benbasat (2010), draw on the idea of similarity attraction (Byrne 1971; Byrne et al. 1967) and find that agents that match a user (e.g. regarding demographics and ethnicity) are evaluated more positively by users thant agents without a match. Thus, designing CAs that dynamically adapt to a user and her or his characteristics as well as contextual factors can be beneficial to foster personality- and behavior-related similarity as well as desirable outcomes. Table 51 summarizes the presented implications for scholars in the three areas addressed by this thesis.

Table 51: Major Implications for Research

Research Area	Implication	Explanation
Conversational Agents	(1) Anthropomorphic CAs should be viewed as social actors to understand interaction with these artifacts and guide the design.	Humans show substantial social responses to the human-like traits and characteristics of CAs, influencing individual expectations.
	(2) Existing knowledge and theories from human-to-human interaction can be adapted in the context of human-like CAs.	Users expect CAs to conform with typical human social behavior and often mindlessly interact with CAs as if they were humans.
	(3) Socio-technical systems, including the human user, context, and technology, represent a useful lens to explain how users perceive CAs.	The perception of CAs and outcomes from their use depends not only on technological properties, but also on user characteristics and contextual factors.
Anthropomorphic Artifacts	(1) Human-like design of CAs can yield unintended feelings of uncanniness due to inhuman qualities, however, the effects may not be as strong as posited by the Theory of Uncanny Valley.	Modest response failure of a human-like CA in a professional context is detrimental to user perception of the CA, but does not cause an abrupt shift as hypothesized in the conceptual curve of the Uncanny Valley.
	(2) Interplay between social cues and limited conversational competencies should be considered to avoid a mismatch between user expectations and system capabilities.	Social cues may foster high expectations towards the CA and its competencies, which are difficult to meet with the limited capabilities given in present-day CAs.
Human-Computer Systems Design	(1) Social cues and associated feelings of anthropomorphism contribute to a positive perception, however, the identification of cues should follow careful considerations.	Feelings of humanness in a professional interaction can contribute to company-relevant outcomes, such as service satisfaction, but must not overstate the CA's capabilities.
	(2) Providing CAs with sufficient capabilities represents a complex yet important endeavor and can benefit from an iterative approach in which dialogues are viewed as the object of design.	User input in natural language input varies substantially and is very difficult to (fully) ancitipate beforehand by the designer, thus iterating between design and evaluation and gradually extending the capabilities is helpful.
	(3) Adaptive designs of CAs can further improve the perception of the CA by tailoring responses to the characteristics of the user or conversation context.	Contextual factors, such as emotions during a conversation, and user characteristics, such as demographics or gender, influence individual perception and judgment of the CA.

II.2 Implications for Practice

Complementary to the theoretical contributions, the findings of this thesis and the six included studies have five major implications for designers of anthropomorphic conversational agents in organizational practice.

The first implication refers to the degree of anthropomorphism of a CA and its relation to the agent's actual capabilities. As research on failure of CA pointed out (Luger and Sellen 2016; Ben Mimoun et al. 2012), a gap between user expectations and actual system capabilities represents a frequent reason in practice for user disappointment and even discontinuing of CAs. The findings of this thesis underline this issue by indicating the high expectations that a human-like design fosters (e.g. users expecting the CA to behave like a human member of the customer service team), provide empirical evidence for a negative, abrupt impact when a CA does not meet such expectations (Study 2), as well as provide theoretically-grounded explanations for issues associated with this gap by drawing on Social Response Theory (Nass et al. 1994; Nass and Moon 2000). To address the challenge related to this mismatch, Study 6 showed that actively managing user expectations through the agent's design, such as by indicating exemplary capabilities or politely describing system limitations, and self-identifying the CA as a machine in combination with offering a convenient contact option to a human person represent effective design approaches.

Second, designers can benefit from considering the social responses of users to an agent with a human-like appearance when crafting CAs in practice. As the empirical studies in this thesis showed, the human qualities of CAs trigger substantial social responses, such as related to premature cognitive commitment (e.g. customers using a human customer service employee as a benchmark for the CA) or concerning the social behavior in a conversation (e.g. showing reciprocity). The expectations of users and reactions stemming from these social responses need to be considered when designing CAs. In particular a human-like identity should be constructed carefully as related cues, such as the gender, ethnicity, and avatar substantially influence the perception of the agent and can yield a favourable evaluation, for example through feelings of similarity (Qiu and Benbasat 2010) and trigger cognitive scripts related to social categories (e.g. gender stereotyping (Pfeuffer et al. 2019b).

The third implication relates to the conversational capabilities of a CA. As Studies 2 and 6 have shown, even modest failure to provide a meaningful response in a dialogue can be detrimental to the perception and judgment of a CA by a user. Thus, a small margin for error exists for anthropomorphic CAs in a dialogue as users expect the agent to behave and communicate like an actual human person. In this context, Study 6 outlined a combination of preset answer options (in parts of a conversation is expected to vary substantially or where response failure frequently occurred in the past) with further language-related approaches like closed questions or context-specific fallback replies, to mitigate risks associated with response failure and iteratively improve the conversational capabilities of the agent.

Fourth, the empirical findings of this thesis and the resulting conceptual framework (Figure 40) highlight advantages associated with considering user characteristics, contextual aspects, as well as intended perception and outcomes when designing anthropomorphic CAs in practice. Designers can benefit from reflecting on the individual characteristics of their user base with regard to demographics, experience and disposition and incorporating these in the design of their agent, particularly in the human-like identity (Følstad and Brandtzæg 2017). In case of different user groups (e.g. one with users of higher age and less experience with digital assistants and one with younger users with more technology experience), adaptive designs with multiple representations of a CA as well as interaction styles can be beneficial to dynamically address the individual needs and preferences of each group. Simillarly, the professional context for which the CA is designed (e.g. customer service or marketing and sales) influences user expectations for the agent and should thus be considered by the designer (e.g. by using company guidelines for customer interaction when designing the the agent). Moreover, it is advantegeuous for CA designers to first define the key intended outcomes and perception of the agent (e.g. trustworthiness when sensitive information is exchanged) and then craft the design to match these objectives (e.g. using approaches to build trust known from human-to-human communication).

The fifth and final implication concerns the approach with which a CA is designed. As highlighted by extant research on natural language interaction with software (Følstad and Brandtzæg 2017; McTear et al. 2016), fully anticipating user input remains a challenging endeavor for a designer. Against the background of the identified impact of even modest response failure (Study 2), a need exists to equip CAs with sufficient conversational capabilities. Furthermore, Study 6 and the work by Seeger et al. (2018) emphasize the complex interplay of social cues which makes anticipating user perception of a human-like CA, in particular fostering the perception of anthropomorphism without feelings of uncanniness, challenging. Thus, an iterative design approach comprising design and evaluation phases, as for example used in the DSR project presented in Study 6 based on Kuechler and Vaishnavi (2008), can be very beneficial for a CA design in practice. On the one hand, such an approach can allow to identify previously unanticipated user input and improve the agent's conversational capabilities accordingly. On the other hand, an iterative design can allow to alter the agent's appearance and behavior until a positive user perception is fostered.

An overview of the five major implications for CA designers in company practice is given in Table 52.

Table 52: Major Implications for Practice

Implication	Explanation
(1) The degree of anthropomorphism facilitated by social cues in the design should match agent's capabilities without overstatement while creating transparency for them and existing limitations.	A mismatch between user expectations for a CA fostered by a human-like design and the agent's actual capabilities can abruptly lead to a negative judgment of the agent. Managing user expectations (e.g. by showing exemplary capabilities or highlighting system limitations in a polite way) can prevent such a mismatch.
(2) Designers need to consider the social responses of users to a human-like CA and incorporate such deliberation in their design, particularly when choosing the human-like identity of the agent.	The human-like cues of a CA, such as communication via natural language, trigger social responses, such as premature cognitive commitments when the CA is presented as a member of the customer service team or expectations towards its behavior (e.g. reciprocity) that need to be addressed in the design.
(3) Conversations should be designed carefully to avoid response failure and make selective use of preset answer options as well as structuring elements in an emerging dialogue.	The users' margin for error regarding response failure is very small, thus such failure needs to be avoided by careful conversation design combining preset answer options in situations where user input varies substantially with elements, such as closed questions or context-specific fallback responses.
(4) A CA's design should take into the target users with their characteristics), the professional context, as well as the intended perception of the agent and outcomes from the interaction.	User characteristics (demographics, experience, disposition) influence the perception of a CA. In addition, expectations toward the CA arise from the company context (e.g. regarding the communication style) and the design of a CA influences relevant outcome variables (e.g. satisfaction with the customer service).
(5) Conversational capabilities as well as the incorporated social cues can benefit from iterative design and evaluation to ensure responsiveness and foster an appealing human-like interaction.	User queries in a natural langue are difficult to anticipate for a designer and unexpected input is likely to occur in a conversation. Thus, iteratively extending the agent's conversational capabilities is beneficial. Similarly, an iterative evaluation of the social cues can be fruitful to understand their (complex) interplay.

III. Limitations and Opportunities for Future Research

The findings of this cumulative thesis as well as the implications for research and practice exhibit different limitations and offer potential for further research. The next chapter presents these limitations (III.1) and outlines future research opportunities in the area of anthropomorphic CA design (III.2).

III.1 Limitations

Different limitations should be considered when interpreting the results of this thesis and the included studies. These limitations arise from anthropomorphic enterprise CAs as a rather new research phenomenon in the IS community, the methods and research designs used in studies, as well as the primary focus on quantitative research. First, CAs as a class of technological artifacts started to attract the interest of the IS research community just a few years ago (Diederich et al. 2019a) and terms to describe different types of CAs are often used interchangeably, such as digital assistants (e.g. Wagner and Schramm-Klein 2019), chatbots (e.g. Schuetzler 2019), virtual agents (e.g. Cho (2019)) or smart speakers (e.g. Son and Wonseok 2018). Against this background, it is important to consider that the findings presented in this thesis explicitly address enterprise CAs as described in the research background (Figure 4), i.e. agents with which user interact through written natural language in a company context. While some of the presented results may hold true for different forms of CAs, such as voice-based agents like Alexa or Siri, generalization of the findings with regard to other types of CAs should be treated with caution. Similarly, while the findings of this research can potentially be adapted to other application contexts of CAs outside of organizations, such as education or individual health, they are primarily intended for understanding the design of CAs in a company context.

Furthermore, due to the current strong practical interest in natural language interaction in particular by major technology companies, such as Google and Amazon (Goasduff 2019; Koplowitz and Facemire 2018), CAs represent a fast-paced research phenomenon. In particular the improving design of interactive human-like avatars (Seymour et al. 2018) as well as the emergence of new approaches for building conversational capabilities via supervised machine learning based instead of manual modeling via intents, will give rise to new design-related issues in this research area. While the fundamental findings of this work, such as different social responses to CAs derived from Social Response Theory (Nass and Moon 2000), risks related to the Uncanny Valley (Mori 1970; Mori et al. 2012), as well as the need to balance the degree of anthropomorphism with existing technological limitations and imperfections, are likely to persist, specific characteristics related to CA design can be expected to change over time as CAs as a technological phenomenon continue to evolve.

Additional limitations arise from the selected research methods and designs employed in the six studies. The first study reviewed literature in order to assess the status quo of CA research. While the review (Study 1) provided insights into the current state of design-oriented research on CAs, the actuality of the results is limited as new studies emerge and, in particular, as further aspects of the design and interaction with this technology are studied. The scope of the literature review was deliberately set to IS and HCI research due to the overarching research goal of Study 1, however, potential a from other disciplines, such as cognitive psychology, were thus not included.

Moreover, the experimental studies with 2x1 (Study 3, Study 4) and 2x2 (Study 2, Study 5) designs exhibit strengths regarding precision and control of variables and were purposefully selected to test and extent theory. However, despite the aforementioned strengths, such controlled experiments have weaknesses regarding realism and generalizability of results (Dennis and Valacich 2001). While the lack of realism was partially addressed through applying the experimental results in the final DSR project (Study 5), the experiments can benefit from replication in other contexts or with samples of a different composition (e.g. with regard to the cultural background of the participants). Additionally, the evaluation of user perception after the interaction with the agents by means of surveys with selected constructs limits the richness of insights from these experiments, which represents a key disadvantage of quantitative research (Bryman and Bell 2018). In particular Study 2, in which the empirical results did not fully conform with the propositions of the Theory of Uncanny Valley, highlighted that user affinity towards an anthropomorphic CA may not only be influenced exclusively by its human-likeness, but also by other factors like aesthetics (Hanson 2006; Hanson et al. 2005). However, the quantitative data generated in the experiment did not allow to understand which further factors influenced user perception for the human-like agent.

The DSR project (Study 6) combined both qualitative (semi-structured interview, focus groups) and quantitative (online experiment) approaches to evaluate the artifact throughout the three design cycles. Following the suggestions by Venable et al. (2016), the two qualitative approaches were used during the formative evaluation of the artifact to gain a better understanding of the (partial) design problem and potential solution while the quantitative, experimental approach was used for the summative evaluation of the artifact. While the online experiment demonstrated that the artifact offers the utility to the users it was built for, only single interactions were used to assess the CA. As interaction with and acceptance of technology changes over time (Al-Natour and Benbasat 2009), it can be beneficial to observe how individuals use the CA in multiple interactions and how the perception of the agent evolves (Bickmore and Picard, 2005).

In addition, the DSR project was initiated to address a specific design problem in practice (designing a human-like, responsive CA that allows to simulate a case study-based job interview at the professional services company), which was abstracted in a general DSR problem (designing CAs that offer a human-like interaction while coping with limited conversational capabilities) during the research project. To address this generic problem, a nascent design theory was formulated based on the findings from designing and instantiating a real-life system at the professional services company with a grounding in two kernel theories. Thus, with regard to the two DSR strategies proposed by Iivari (2015), the project followed the second strategy by solving a specific problem through the design of an artifact and, afterwards, compiling the generated, knowledge on a more abstract level to address a class of problems (Iivari 2015). As the resulting design theory was derived from the findings and evaluated in this specific company setting, there is a need to test, validate, and, potentially, extend the theory in other organizational contexts and problem instances (Gregor and Hevner 2013).

Finally, it is important to consider that the DSR project aimed to find a "satisficing" problem solution (Simon, 1996; Gregory and Muntermann, 2014), which in this context in particular meant that it meets the requirement of improving the existing system. Thus, it remains uncertain whether refinements of the design theory can yield even better outcomes, such as a higher degree of anthropomorphism or lower level of uncanniness.

III.2 Opportunities for Future Research

The findings from the studies as well as the presented limitations offer ample opportunities for further studies in the area of anthropomorphic conversational agents. In particular, six major avenues for future research can be outlined.

First, the basic design approaches presented in Studies 4 (empathetic CA) and 5 (persuasive CA) can be further extended and evalauated. The CA in Study 4 used automatic sentiment analysis to adapt responses to negative sentiments in order to emulate empathy. Thus, investigating whether and, if yes, to which extent sentiment-adaptive responses can strengthen positive emotions deserves further investigation. Similarly, Study 5 drew on a subset of the persuasive design elements proposed by Oinas-Kukkonen and Harjumaa (2009) and evaluated their aggregated impact on different types of beliefs (Ajzen 1985, 1991) in the exemplary context of sustainable mobility. Further studies in this area could explore additional persuasive elements, such as rewards or suggestions, assess their isolated impact on users as well as observe how such belief changes induced by persuasive design changes actual behavior, for example in a marketing context where the agent acts as a virtual sales agent.

Second, the design of adaptive CAs represents a promising research opportunity. IS and HCI scholars can draw for example on the user characteristics presented in the conceptual framework proposed in this thesis (Figure 40) to craft CAs that dynamically adapt to the individual user. In particular, adaptive designs can be used to foster the perception of similarity, both with regard to personality as well as behavior of the CA (Al-Natour et al. 2006). For example, researchers could build CAs that try to match the user's personality manifested in the Big Five personality factors (De Raad 2000) or adjust the way they communicate (e.g. more or less emotionally-loaded sentences) to leverage similarity attraction (Byrne 1971; Byrne and Griffitt 1969) and thus improve company-relevant outcomes (e.g. service satisfaction or buying behavior).

Third, the studies in this thesis shed light on the social responses that anthropomorphic CA trigger in humans and indicate that existing theories and knowledge from human-to-human communication can be applied, or at least adapted, to understand human-CA interaction and inform their design. In this context, for example Study 4 showed that gender-related differences regarding affective communication (Chiu 2002; Chiu and Wu 2002) known from human customer service provision hold true for service provision with human-like CAs as well. Further studies find and discuss similar effects. For example, Schuetzler et al. (2018a) demonstrate that an anthropomorphic CA design leads humans to consider the disclosure of sensitive information more carefully in order to hide potentially embarrassing information. However, several studies also report potential differences between human-human and human-CA interaction, such as the work by Pfeuffer et al. (2019b) who discovered that the existence of prevalent gender stereotypes for anthropomorphic CAs significantly depends on further contextual factors. Thus, future research can investigate both the potential as well as the limitations of applying knowledge from human interaction for human-like CAs.

The fourth opportunity for future research is related to the Theory of Uncanny Valley (Mori 1970; Mori et al. 2012). Study 2 identified a significant negative impact of inhuman qualities of anthropomorphic CAs on user perception, however, the discovered effect was not as large as postulated in the Theory of Uncanny Valley. Similarly, empirical evidence for the Uncanny Valley (e.g. Mathur and Reichling 2016) as well as against it (e.g. Hanson 2006) was found for humanoid robots. While several scholars with a focus on CAs emphasize potential negative effects related to the Uncanny Valley (e.g. Rzepka and Berger 2018; Pfeuffer et al. 2019a), we still lack empirically founded knowledge of where the Uncanny Valley comes into play for human-like CAs. Future research could in particular conduct experimental studies where the degree of anthropomorphism is purposefully altered to elicit feelings of uncanniness or eeriness and then, based on empirical observation, theorize on the existence and characteristics of the Uncanny Valley in the context of human-like CAs.

Furthermore, this thesis provided insights on how to design CAs in a company context that offer a human-like interaction yet did not address the question in which contexts (e.g. for which types of tasks or business processes) anthropomorphic design is useful. The work by Seeger et al. (2017) initially explores this question with a focus on trust and proposes that anthropomorphic design of a CA is beneficial in situations where the agent replaces a task carried out by humans whereas a more machine-like design is adequate when a CA replaces a task executed by machines. However, this delineation does not reflect the complexity of the contexts in which such agents are typically introduced. For example, the CA in Study 6 replaced an extant software system, however, a human-like design made sense since the underyling objective was to simulate an interview by an actual human person. In addition, the context (e.g. customer service) may justify a human-like design but some tasks in a specific context could be better provided by a machine-like CA (e.g. when the task at hand is straightforward and the customer just aims to have it completed as fast as possible). Overall, more research is needed that identifies contextual and task characteristics which determine whether a human-like design is beneficial and foster a positive user perception.

Finally, different ethical issues arise when designing human-like CAs that were not in the scope of this research. Study 5 exemplarily demonstrated the potential of human-like CAs to influence individual beliefs, potentially on a large scale. Regardless whether a CA is designed to exert influence on its users or not, the interaction via natural language may impact human communication as well. For example, a report by UNESCO (2019) outlined that CAs can reinforce gender stereotypes as users continuously interact with mostly female voices in a commanding tone. Similarly, Alexa can encourage children by design to say "please" when issuing voice commands (BBC 2019). Furthermore, distinguishing increasingly human-like CAs from actual humans may become difficult for some users, thus giving rise to the issue whether CA has to self-identify as a machine. In short, future research is required that conceptualizes and adapts ethical design principles and frameworks for anthropomorphic CAs.

The six research opportunities are summarized in Table 53 including potential research questions as well suggestions for research methods and theoretical foundations.

Table 53: Opportunities for Future Research on Anthropomorphic CA Design

Research Opportunity	Exemplary Research Question(s)	Research Method	Theoretical Foundation
(1) Advancing the design of empathetic and persuasive CAs	Does a sentiment-adaptive CA design strengthen positive emotions expressed by users? Does persuasive and anthropomorphic CA design influence actual user behavior?	Laboratory or field experiment Field study, potentially long-term	Affective communication in customer service (Chiu and Wu 2002) Persuasive System Design, Theory of Planned Behavior (Ajzen 1985, 1991)
(2) Exploring adaptive CA designs with regard to individual users	Does a CA that dynamically matches a user's personality improve user perception?	Laboratory or field experiment	Similarity-Attraction (Byrne 1971), Big Five Personality Factors (De Raad 2000)
(3) Investigating potential and boundaries of adapting knowledge from human interaction	To which extent can knowledge from human interaction be adapted for the interaction with human-like CAs?	Laboratory or field experiments	Various theories on human interaction, see e.g. Krämer, Pütten and Eimler (2012) for an initial overview
(4) Improving the understanding of the Uncanny Valley in the context of CAs	Which degree of anthropomorphism triggers feelings of uncanniness due to inhuman qualities of human-like CAs?	Laboratory experiment	Theory of Uncanny Valley (Mori 1970; Mori et al. 2012)
(5) Identifying characteristics that determine whether human-like CA is beneficial or not	Which contextual and task-related characteristics determine whether a human-like or machine-like CA is favorable?	Semi- or unstructured interviews	Task-substitution types (Seeger et al. 2017)
(6) Guiding ethical design of increasingly human-like and persuasive CAs	Which ethical issues exist for human-like CAs and how can they be addressed by design?	Literature review, expert interviews	Ethical System Design (Berdichevsky and Neuenschwander 2002)

IV. Concluding Remarks

The contemporary technological phenomenon of human-like CAs attracts increasing interest in IS research as well as in organizational practice where such agents are introduced for innovation and automation. The perception of humanness in the interaction enabled through social cues can have a substantial positive effect on user evaluation of these artifacts and yield further favorable outcomes. At the same time, a higher degree of anthropomorphism can lead to inflated user expectations and poses the risk of feelings of uncanniness. Thus, designing human-like CAs represents a complex endeavor that exhibits both potential for high return and high risk.

The dissertation at hand provided insights on how to address this design challenge and advanced the understanding of human interaction with human-like machines grounded in Social Response Theory and the Theory of Uncanny Valley. Specifically, the studies included in this thesis shed light on the status quo of CA research (Study 1), the detrimental impact of limited conversational capabilities as well its mitigation (Study 2, Study 3), and the potential of anthropomorphic design with a focus on empathy (Study 4) and persuasiveness (Study 5). Furthermore, the results from the experimental studies as well as the existing prescriptive knowledge were brought together in a DSR project in which an anthropomorphic CA was designed and introduced in the field (Study 6). Based on the insights from this research project, a nascent design theory was proposed.

This work makes three major contributions: First, the nascent design theory provides guidance on how to address the overarching design problem of crafting CAs that offer a human-like interaction and at the same time cope with limited conversational capabilities as given in present-day CAs. Second, the conceptual framework presented in the synthesis of the studies' findings offers a systematic and empirically-based structure to understand human interaction with CAs and inform their design in different enterprise contexts. Third, the experimental studies allow to better understand how specific changes in a CA's design yield changes in user perception both with regard to the perception of anthropomorphism as well as further outcome variables, such as service satisfaction or perceived usefulness of the agent.

Based on these contributions as well as the methodological limitations of the studies included in this thesis, six opportunities for future research were outlined that seek to further improve the design of CAs in a company context as well as to foster a better understanding of human interaction with more and more human-like machines. Overall, as this research has shown, thoughtfully designed anthropomorphic CAs hold great potential for companies and are an interesting, multifacted research phenomenon to study due to the social nature of human interaction with such technological artifacts.

References

Abul, M., Siddike, K., Spohrer, J., Demirkan, H., and Kohda, Y. 2018. "People's Interactions with Cognitive Assistants for Enhanced Performances" in *Proceedings of the Hawaii International Conference on System Sciences (HICSS)*, Waikoloa Village, Hawaii, USA, pp. 1640–1648.

Adler, R. F., Iacobelli, F., and Gutstein, Y. 2016. "Are You Convinced? A Wizard of Oz Study to Test Emotional vs. Rational Persuasion Strategies in Dialogues" *Computers in Human Behavior* (57), pp. 75–81.

Ågerfalk, P. J. 2010. "Getting Pragmatic" *European Journal of Information Systems* (19:3), pp. 251–256.

Ajzen, I. 1985. "From Intentions to Actions: A Theory of Planned Behavior" in *Action Control*, J. Kuhl and J. Beckmann (eds.), New York, USA: Springer, pp. 11–39.

Ajzen, I. 1991. "The Theory of Planned Behavior" *Organizational Behavior and Human Decision Processes* (50), pp. 179–211.

Ajzen, I. 2006. "Constructing A Theory of Planned Behavior Questionnaire" Working Paper, Amherst, Massachusetts.

Al-Natour, S., and Benbasat, I. 2009. "The Adoption and Use of IT Artifacts: A New Interaction-Centric Model for the Study of User-Artifact Relationships." *Journal of the Association for Information Systems* (10:9), pp. 661–685.

Al-Natour, S., Benbasat, I., and Cenfetelli, R. T. 2006. "The Role of Design Characteristics in Shaping Perceptions of Similarity: The Case of Online Shopping Assistants" *Journal of the Association for Information Systems* (7:12), pp. 821–861.

Al-Natour, S., Benbasat, I., and Cenfetelli, R. T. 2009. "The Antecedents of Customer Self-Disclosure to Online Virtual Advisors" in *Proceedings of the International Conference on Information Systems (ICIS)*, Phoenix, USA, pp. 1–18.

Allwood, J., Traum, D., and Jokinen, K. 2000. "Cooperation, Dialogue and Ethics" *International Journal of Human Computer Studies* (53:6), pp. 871–914.

Altman, I., Taylor, D. A., and Derlega, V. J. 1997. "Social Penetration: The Development of Interpersonal Relationships" *Contemporary Psychology*.

Appel, J., Von Der Pütten, A., Krämer, N. C., and Gratch, J. 2012. "Does Humanity Matter? Analyzing the Importance of Social Cues and Perceived Agency of a Computer System for the Emergence of Social Reactions during HCI" *Advances in Human-Computer Interaction* (2012), pp. 1–10.

Araujo, T. 2018. "Living up to the Chatbot Hype: The Influence of Anthropomorphic Design Cues and Communicative Agency Framing on Conversational Agent and Company Perceptions" *Computers in Human Behavior* (85), pp. 183–189.

Arnott, D., and Pervan, G. 2012. "Design Science in Decision Support Systems Research: An Assessment Using the Hevner, March, Park, and Ram Guidelines" *Journal of the Association for Information Systems* (13:11), pp. 923–949.

Ashktorab, Z., Jain, M., Liao, V. Q., and Weisz, J. D. 2019. "Resilient Chatbots: Repair Strategy Preferences for Conversational Breakdowns" in *Proceedings of the ACM CHI Conference on Human Factors in Computing Systems*, Glasgow, Scotland, pp. 1–12.

Aylien. 2019. "Aylien." (https://aylien.com, accessed February 5, 2019).

Baeriswyl, M., Staake, T., and Loock, C. 2011. "The Effects of User Identity and Sanctions in Online Communities on Real-World Behavior" in *Proceedings of the International Conference on Information Systems (ICIS)*, Shanghai, China, pp. 1–11.

Baier, D., Rese, A., and Röglinger, M. 2018. "Conversational User Interfaces for Online Shops? A Categorization of Use Cases" in *Proceedings of the International Conference on Information Systems (ICIS)*, San Francisco, USA, pp. 1–17.

Balkanski, C., and Hurault-Plantet, M. 2000. "Cooperative Requests and Replies in a Collaborative Dialogue Model" *International Journal of Human Computer Studies* (53:6), pp. 915–968.

Bandara, W., Gorbacheva, E., Beekhuyzen, J., Furtmueller, E., and Miskon, S. 2015. "Achieving Rigor in Literature Reviews: Insights from Qualitative Data Analysis and Tool-Support" *Communications of the Association for Information Systems* (34:8), pp. 154–204.

Bandura, A. 1977. "Self-Efficacy: Toward a Unifying Theory of Behavioral Change" *Pyschological Review* (84:2), pp. 191–215.

Bandura, A. 1996. *Self-Efficacy: The Exercise of Control*, New York, USA: Freeman.

Banker, R. D., and Kauffman, R. J. 2004. "50th Anniversary Article: The Evolution of Research on Information Systems: A Fiftieth-Year Survey of the Literature in Management Science" *Management Science* (50:3), pp. 281–298.

Bartneck, C., Kulić, D., Croft, E., and Zoghbi, S. 2009. "Measurement Instruments for the Anthropomorphism, Animacy, Likeability, Perceived Intelligence, and Perceived Safety of Robots" *International Journal of Social Robotics* (1:1), pp. 71–81.

Baskerville, R. L. 1999. "Investigating Information Systems with Action Research" *Communications of the Association for Information Systems* (2:October).

Baskerville, R., and Pries-Heje, J. 2010. "Explanatory Design Theory" *Business & Information Systems Engineering* (2:5), pp. 271–282.

Baylor, A. L. 2009. "Promoting Motivation with Virtual Agents and Avatars: Role of Visual Presence and Appearance" *Philosophical Transactions of the Royal Society B: Biological Sciences*.

BBC. 2019. "Amazon Alexa to Reward Kids Who Say: 'Please.'" (https://www.bbc.com/news/technology-43897516, accessed February 23, 2020).

Beale, R., and Creed, C. 2009. "Affective Interaction: How Emotional Agents Affect Users" *International Journal of Human Computer Studies* (67:9), pp. 755–776.

Beer, J. M., Smarr, C. A., Fisk, A. D., and Rogers, W. A. 2015. "Younger and Older Users' Recognition of Virtual Agent Facial Expressions" *International Journal of Human Computer Studies* (75), pp. 1–20.

Berdichevsky, D., and Neuenschwander, E. 2002. "Toward an Ethics of Persuasive Technology" *Communications of the ACM* (42:5), pp. 51–58.

Berg, M. 2014. "Modelling of Natural Dialogues in the Context of Speech-Based Information and Control Systems" Christian-Albrechts-Universität zu Kiel.

Berg, M. 2015. "NADIA: A Simplified Approach Towards the Development of Natural Dialogue Systems" in *Natural Language Processing and Information Systems*, Springer International Publishing, pp. 144–150.

Berry, D. C., Butler, L. T., and De Rosis, F. 2005. "Evaluating a Realistic Agent in an Advice-Giving Task" *International Journal of Human Computer Studies* (63:3), pp. 304–327.

Bertacchini, F., Bilotta, E., and Pantano, P. 2017. "Shopping with a Robotic Companion" *Computers in Human Behavior* (77), pp. 382–395.

Beverungen, D., Breidbach, C. F., and Poeppelbuss, J. 2017. "Smart Service Systems: An Interdisciplinary Perspective" *Information Systems Journal*, pp. 1–4.

Bhattacherjee, A. 2012. "Social Science Research: Principles, Methods, and Practices" *Book 3.*, Tampa, Florida, USA.

Biancardi, B., Cafaro, A., and Pelachaud, C. 2017. "Could a Virtual Agent Be Warm and Competent? Investigating User's Impressions of Agent's Non-Verbal Behaviours" in *Proceedings of the ACM CHI Conference on Human Factors in Computing Systems*, Denver, USA, pp. 22–24.

Bickmore, T. W., Pfeifer, L. M., and Jack, B. W. 2009. "Taking the Time to Care: Empowering Low Health Literacy Hospital Patients with Virtual Nurse Agents" in *Proceedings of the ACM CHI Conference on Human Factors in Computing Systems*, Boston, USA, pp. 1265–1274.

Bickmore, T. W., and Picard, R. W. 2005. "Establishing and Maintaining Long-Term Human-Computer Relationships" *ACM Transactions on Computer-Human Interaction* (12:2), pp. 293–327.

Le Bigot, L., Terrier, P., Amiel, V., Poulain, G., Jamet, E., and Rouet, J. F. 2007. "Effect of Modality on Collaboration with a Dialogue System" *International Journal of Human Computer Studies* (65:12), pp. 983–991.

Bishop, T. 2016. "Coffee from a Chatbot: Starbucks Unveils 'My Starbucks Barista' AI Technology for Mobile Orders." (https://www.geekwire.com/2016/coffee-chatbot-starbucks-unveil-starbucks-barista-ai-technology-placing-mobile-orders/, accessed November 25, 2018).

Bolton, R. N., and Drew, J. H. 2002. "A Multistage Model of Customers' Assessments of Service Quality and Value" *Journal of Consumer Research* (17:4), p. 375.

Boudreau, M.-C., Gefen, D., and Straub, D. 2001. "Validation in Information Systems Research: A State-of-the-Art Assessment" *Management Information Systems Quarterly* (25:1), pp. 1–16.

Brandtzæg, P. B., and Følstad, A. 2018. "Chatbots: Changing User Needs and Motivations" *Interactions* (25:5), pp. 38–43.

Brauer, B., Ebermann, C., and Kolbe, L. M. 2016. "An Acceptance Model for User-Centric Persuasive Environmental Sustainable IS" in *Proceedings of the International Conference on Information Systems (ICIS)*, Dublin, Ireland, pp. 1–22.

Brave, S., Nass, C., and Hutchinson, K. 2005. "Computers That Care: Investigating the Effects of Orientation of Emotion Exhibited by an Embodied Computer Agent" *International Journal of Human Computer Studies* (62:2), pp. 161–178.

Brendel, A. B., Zapadka, P., and Kolbe, L. M. 2017. "Design Science Research in Green IS: Analyzing the Past to Guide Future Research" in *Proceedings of the European Conference on Information Systems (ECIS)*, Guimarães, Portugal, pp. 1–18.

vom Brocke, J., Simons, A., Niehaves, B., Riemer, K., Plattfaut, R., and Cleven, A. 2009. "Reconstructing the Giant: On the Importance of Rigour in Documenting the Literature Search Process" *Proceedings of the European Conference on Information Systems (ECIS)* (9), pp. 2206–2217.

vom Brocke, J., Watson, R. T., Dwyer, C., Elliot, S., and Melville, N. 2013. "Green Information Systems: Directives for the IS Discipline" *Communications of the Association for Information Systems* (33), pp. 509–520.

Bryman, A., and Bell, E. 2018. *Business Research Methods*, (5th editio.), Oxford University Press.

Brynjolfsson, E., and McAfee, A. 2016. *The Second Machine Age: Work, Progress, and Prosperity in a Time of Brilliant Technologies*, New York, USA: Norton & Company.

Burgoon, J. K., Bonito, J. A., Bengtsson, B., Cederberg, C., Lundeberg, M., and Allspach, L. 2000. "Interactivity in Human-Computer Interaction: A Study of Credibility, Understanding, and Influence" *Computers in Human Behavior* (16:6), pp. 553–574.

Burgoon, J. K., Bonito, J. A., Lowry, P. B., Humpherys, S. L., Moody, G. D., Gaskin, J. E., and Giboney, J. S. 2016. "Application of Expectancy Violations Theory to Communication with and Judgments about Embodied Agents during a Decision-Making Task" *International Journal of Human Computer Studies* (91), pp. 24–36.

Burgoon, J. K., and Jones, S. B. 1976. "Toward a Theory of Personal Space Expectations and Their Violations" *Human Communication Research*.

Burmester, M., Schippert, K., Zeiner, K. M., and Platz, A. 2019. "Creating Positive Experiences with Digital Companions" in *Proceedings of the ACM CHI Conference on Human Factors in Computing Systems*, Glasgow, Scotland, pp. 1–6.

Butler, T. 2011. "Compliance with Institutional Imperatives on Environmental Sustainability: Building Theory on the Role of Green IS" *Journal of Strategic Information Systems* (20:1), pp. 6–26.

Byrne, D. 1971. *The Attraction Paradigm*, Michigan, USA: Academic Press.

Byrne, D., and Griffitt, W. 1969. "Similarity and Awareness of Similarity of Personality Characteristics as Determinants of Attraction" *Journal Of Experimental Research In Personality*.

Byrne, D., Griffitt, W., and Stefaniak, D. 1967. "Attraction and Similarity of Personality Characteristics" *Journal of Personality and Social Psychology*.

Cafaro, A., Vilhjalmsson, H. H., and Bickmore, T. 2016. "First Impressions in Human-Agent Virtual Encounters" *ACM Transactions on Computer-Human Interaction* (24:4), pp. 1–40.

Candello, H., Pinhanez, C., and Figueiredo, F. 2017. "Typefaces and the Perception of Humanness in Natural Language Chatbots" in *Proceedings of the ACM CHI Conference on Human Factors in Computing Systems*, Denver, USA, pp. 3476–3487.

Caruana, A., Ewing, M. T., and Ramaseshan, B. 2000. "Assessment of the Three-Column Format SERVQUAL: An Experimental Approach" *Journal of Business Research* (49), pp. 57–65.

Chandra, L., Seidel, S., and Gregor, S. 2015. "Prescriptive Knowledge in IS Research: Conceptualizing Design Principles in Terms of Materiality, Action, and Boundary Conditions" in *Proceedings of the Hawaii International Conference on System Sciences (HICSS)*, pp. 4039–4048.

Chattaraman, V., Kwon, W.-S., Gilbert, J. E., and Ross, K. 2018. "Should AI-Based, Conversational Digital Assistants Employ Social- or Task-Oriented Interaction Style? A Task-Competency and Reciprocity Perspective for Older Adults" *Computers in Human Behavior* (90), pp. 315–330.

Chattaraman, V., Kwon, W. S., and Gilbert, J. E. 2012. "Virtual Agents in Retail Web Sites: Benefits of Simulated Social Interaction for Older Users" *Computers in Human Behavior* (28), pp. 2055–2066.

Chen, A. J. W., Boudreau, M., and Watson, R. T. 2008. "Information Systems and Ecological Sustainability" *Journal of Systems and Information Technology* (10:3), pp. 186–201.

Chiba, Y., and Ito, A. 2012. "Estimating a User's Internal State before the First Input Utterance" *Advances in Human-Computer Interaction*.

Chin, W. W. 1998. "The Partial Least Squares Approach for Structural Equation Modeling" in *Modern Methods for Business Research*, L. Erlbaum (ed.), Hillsdale, New Jersey, pp. 295–336.

Chiu, H. C. 2002. "A Study on the Cognitive and Affective Components of Service Quality" *Total Quality Management* (13:2), pp. 265–274.

Chiu, H. C., and Wu, H. C. 2002. "Exploring the Cognitive and Affective Roles of Service Quality Attitude across Gender" *Service Industries Journal* (22:3), pp. 63–76.

Cho, E. 2019. "Hey Google, Can i Ask You Something in Private? The Effects of Modality and Device in Sensitive Health Information Acquisition from Voice Assistants" in *Proceedings of the ACM CHI Conference on Human Factors in Computing Systems*, Glasgow, Scotland, pp. 1–9.

Clark, L., Pantidi, N., Cooney, O., Doyle, P., Garaialde, D., Edwards, J., Spillane, B., Gilmartin, E., Murad, C., Munteanu, C., Wade, V., and Cowan, B. R. 2019. "What Makes a Good Conversation? Challenges in Designing Truly Conversational Agents" in *Proceedings of the ACM CHI Conference on Human Factors in Computing Systems*, Glasgow, Scotland, pp. 1–12.

"Cleverbot." 2018. (https://www.cleverbot.com, accessed June 6, 2018).

Clickworker. 2018. "Clickworker." (https://www.clickworker.com/, accessed November 26, 2018).

Cohen, J. 1988. *Statistical Power Analysis for the Behavioural Sciences*, (2nd Editio.), Taylor & Francis Inc.

Cooper, H. M. 1988. "Organizing Knowledge Synthesis: A Taxonomy of Literature Reviews" *Knowledge in Society* (1:1), pp. 104–126.

Corbett, J. 2013a. "Using Information Systems to Improve Energy Efficiency: Do Smart Meters Make a Difference?" *Information Systems Frontiers* (15:5), pp. 747–760.

Corbett, J. 2013b. "Designing and Using Carbon Management Systems to Promote Ecologically Responsible Behaviors" *Journal of the Association for Information Systems* (14:7), pp. 339–378.

Corti, K., and Gillespie, A. 2016. "Co-Constructing Intersubjectivity with Artificial Conversational Agents: People Are More Likely to Initiate Repairs of Misunderstandings with Agents Represented as Human" *Computers in Human Behavior* (58), pp. 431–442.

Cowan, B. R., Branigan, H. P., Obregón, M., Bugis, E., and Beale, R. 2015. "Voice Anthropomorphism, Interlocutor Modelling and Alignment Effects on Syntactic Choices in Human-Computer Dialogue" *International Journal of Human Computer Studies* (83), pp. 27–42.

Cowell, A. J., and Stanney, K. M. 2005. "Manipulation of Non-Verbal Interaction Style and Demographic Embodiment to Increase Anthropomorphic Computer Character Credibility" *International Journal of Human Computer Studies* (62:2), pp. 281–306.

Crockett, K., Latham, A., and Whitton, N. 2017. "On Predicting Learning Styles in Conversational Intelligent Tutoring Systems Using Fuzzy Decision Trees" *International Journal of Human Computer Studies* (97), pp. 98–115.

Cyr, D., Head, M., Larios, H., and Pan, B. 2009. "Exploring Human Images in Website Design: A Multi-Method Approach" *Management Information Systems Quarterly* (33:3), p. 539.

Dale, R. 2016. "The Return of the Chatbots" *Natural Language Engineering* (22:5), pp. 811–817.

Danielescu, A., and Christian, G. 2018. "A Bot Is Not a Polyglot" in *Proceedings of the ACM CHI Conference on Human Factors in Computing Systems*, Montréal, Canada, pp. 1–9.

Davenport, T. H., and Kirby, J. 2016. "Just How Smart Are Smart Machines?" *MIT Sloan Management Review* (57:3), pp. 21–25.

Davis, F. D. 1989. "Perceived Usefulness, Perceived Ease of Use, and User Acceptance of Information Technology" *Management Information Systems Quarterly* (13:3), pp. 319–340.

Davis, M. H. 2015. "Empathy and Prosocial Behavior" in *The Oxford Handbook of Prosocial Behavior*, Oxford, England: Oxford University Press.

Dedrick, J. 2010. "Green IS: Concepts and Issues for Information Systems Research" *Communications of the Association for Information Systems* (27:1), pp. 173–184.

Dennis, A. R., Fuller, R. M., and Valacich, J. S. 2014. *Media, Tasks, and Communication A Theory of Media Synchronicity Processes*, (32:3), pp. 575–600.

Dennis, A. R., and Valacich, J. S. 2001. "Conducting Experimental Research in Information Systems" *Communications of the Association for Information Systems* (7:5), pp. 1–41.

Derks, D., Bos, A. E. R., and Von Grumbkow, J. 2008. "Emoticons in Computer-Mediated Communication: Social Motives and Social Context" *Cyberpsychology and Behavior*.

Derrick, D. C., and Ligon, G. S. 2014. "The Affective Outcomes of Using Influence Tactics in Embodied Conversational Agents" *Computers in Human Behavior* (33), pp. 39–48.

Devine, P. G., and Elliot, A. J. 1994. "On the Motivational Nature of Cognitive Dissonance: Dissonance as Psychological Discomfort" *Journal of Personality and Social Psychology* (67:3), pp. 382–394.

Diederich, S., Brendel, A. B., and Kolbe, L. M. 2019a. "On Conversational Agents in Information Systems Research: Analyzing the Past to Guide Future Work" in *Proceedings of the International Conference on Wirtschaftsinformatik*, pp. 1550–1564.

Diederich, S., Brendel, A. B., and Kolbe, L. M. 2019b. "Towards a Taxonomy of Platforms for Conversational Agent Design" in *Proceedings of the International Conference on Wirtschaftsinformatik*, pp. 1100–1114.

Diederich, S., Brendel, A. B., Lichtenberg, S., and Kolbe, L. M. 2019c. "Design for Fast Request Fulfillment or Natural Interaction? Insights from an Online Experiment with a Conversational Agent" in *Proceedings of the European Conference on Information Systems (ECIS)*, Stockholm, Sweden, pp. 1–17.

Diederich, S., Janßen-Müller, M., Brendel, A. B., and Morana, S. 2019d. "Emulating Empathetic Behavior in Online Service Encounters with Sentiment-Adaptive Responses: Insights from an Experiment with a Conversational Agent" in *Proceedings of the International Conference on Information Systems (ICIS)*, Munich, Germany, pp. 1–17.

Diederich, S., Lichtenberg, S., Brendel, A. B., and Trang, S. 2019e. "Promoting Sustainable Mobility Beliefs with Persuasive and Anthropomorphic Design: Insights from an Experiment with a Conversational Agent" in *Proceedings of the International Conference on Information Systems (ICIS)*, Munich, Germany, pp. 1–17.

DiSalvo, C., and Gemperle, F. 2003. *From Seduction to Fulfillment*, p. 67.

Dolata, M., Kilic, M., and Schwabe, G. 2019. "When a Computer Speaks Institutional Talk: Exploring Challenges and Potentials of Virtual Assistants in Face-to-Face Advisory Services" in *Proceedings of the Hawaii International Conference on System Sciences (HICSS)*, Grand Wailea, Maui, pp. 105–114.

Donald, I. J., Cooper, S. R., and Conchie, S. M. 2014. "An Extended Theory of Planned Behaviour Model of the Psychological Factors Affecting Commuters' Transport Mode Use" *Journal of Environmental Psychology* (40), pp. 39–48.

Dreyer, T. 2018. "Lidl UK Launches AI Wine Chatbot to UK Customers with Aspect Software."

Dzindolet, M. T., Peterson, S. A., Pomranky, R. A., Pierce, L. G., and Beck, H. P. 2003. "The Role of Trust in Automation Reliance" *International Journal of Human Computer Studies* (58:6), pp. 697–718.

Ekman, P., and Friesen, W. V. 1969. "The Repertoire of Nonverbal Behavior: Categories, Origins, Usage, and Coding" *Semiotica* (1:1), pp. 49–98.

Elliot, S. 2011. "Transdisciplinary Perspectives on Environmental Sustainability: A Resource Base and Framework for It-Enabled Business Transformation" *Management Information Systems Quarterly* (35:1), pp. 197–236.

Elmorshidy, A. 2013. "Applying the Technology Acceptance and Service Quality Models to Live Customer Support Chat for E-Commerce Websites" *Journal of Applied Business Research* (29:2), pp. 589–596.

Elson, J. S., Derrick, D. C., and Ligon, G. S. 2018. "Examining Trust and Reliance in Collaborations between Humans and Automated Agents" in *Proceedings of the Hawaii International Conference on System Sciences (HICSS)*, Waikoloa Village, Hawaii, USA, pp. 430–439.

Epley, N., Waytz, A., and Cacioppo, J. T. 2007. "On Seeing Human: A Three-Factor Theory of Anthropomorphism" *Psychological Review* (114:4), pp. 864–886.

Fast, E., Chen, B., Mendelsohn, J., Bassen, J., and Bernstein, M. 2017. "Iris: A Conversational Agent for Complex Tasks" in *Proceedings of the ACM CHI Conference on Human Factors in Computing Systems*, Denver, USA, pp. 1–12.

Faul, F., Erdfelder, E., Lang, A.-G., and Buchner, A. 2007. "G*Power 3: A Flexible Statistical Power Analysis Program for the Social, Behavioral, and Biomedical Sciences" *Behavior Research Methods* (39:2), pp. 175–191.

Featherman, M., Thatcher, J., Wright, R. T., and Zimmer, J. C. 2011. "Design Principles for Special Purpose, Embodied, Conversational Intelligence with Environmental Sensors (SPECIES) Agents" *AIS Transactions on Human-Computer Interaction* (3:1), pp. 1–25.

Feine, J., Gnewuch, U., Morana, S., and Maedche, A. 2019a. "A Taxonomy of Social Cues for Conversational Agents" *International Journal of Human-Computer Studies* (132:December), pp. 138–161.

Feine, J., Morana, S., and Gnewuch, U. 2019b. "Measuring Service Encounter Satisfaction with Customer Service Chatbots Using Sentiment Analysis" in *Proceedings of the International Conference on Wirtschaftsinformatik*, pp. 0–11.

Ferrey, A. E., Burleigh, T. J., and Fenske, M. J. 2015. "Stimulus-Category Competition, Inhibition, and Affective Devaluation: A Novel Account of the Uncanny Valley" *Frontiers in Psychology* (6:MAR), pp. 1–16.

Fitzpatrick, G., and Smith, G. 2009. "Technology-Enabled Feedback on Domestic Energy Consumption: Articulating a Set of Design Concerns" *Pervasive Computing* (8:1), pp. 37–44.

Flüchter, K., and Wortmann, F. 2014. "Promoting Sustainable Travel Behavior through IS-Enabled Feedback – Short-Term Success at the Cost of Long-Term Motivation?" in *Proceedings of the International Conference on Information Systems (ICIS)*, Auckland, New Zealand, pp. 1–17.

Fogg, B. J. 2003. "Computers as Persuasive Social Actors" in *Persuasive Technology: Using Computers to Change What We Think and Do*, San Francisco, USA: Morgan Kaufmann Publishers.

Fogg, B. J., and Nass, C. 1997. "How Users Reciprocate to Computers" in *Proceedings of the ACM CHI Conference on Human Factors in Computing Systems*, Atlanta, USA, p. 331.

Følstad, A., and Brandtzæg, P. B. 2017. "Chatbots and the New World of HCI" *Interactions* (24:4), pp. 38–42.

Frey, C. B., and Osborne, M. A. 2017. "The Future of Employment: How Susceptible Are Jobs to Computerisation?" *Technological Forecasting and Social Change* (114), pp. 254–280.

Friestad, M., and Wright, P. 1999. "Everyday Persuasion Knowledge" *Psychology and Marketing*.

Froehlich, J., Dillahunt, T., Klasnja, P., Mankoff, J., Consolvo, S., Harrison, B., and Landay, J. A. 2009. "UbiGreen: Investigating a Mobile Tool for Tracking and Supporting Green Transportation Habits" in *Proceedings of the Conference on Human Factors in Computing Systems*, Boston, USA, pp. 1043–1052.

Fryer, L. K., Nakao, K., and Thompson, A. 2019. "Chatbot Learning Partners: Connecting Learning Experiences, Interest and Competence" *Computers in Human Behavior* (93), pp. 279–289.

Gabbott, M., and Hogg, G. 2004. "The Role of Non-Verbal Communication in Service Encounters: A Conceptual Framework" *Journal of Marketing Management* (17:1–2), pp. 5–26.

Gefen, D., Karahanna, E., and Straub, D. 2003. "Trust and TAM in Online Shopping: An Integrated Model" *Management Information Systems Quarterly* (27:1), pp. 51–90.

Gefen, D., and Straub, D. 1997. "Gender Differences in the Perception and Use of E-Mail: An Extension to the Technology Acceptance Model" *Management Information Systems Quarterly* (21:4), pp. 389–400.

Gefen, D., and Straub, D. 2003. "Managing User Trust in B2C E-Services" *E-Service Journal* (2:2), pp. 7–24.

Gefen, D., and Straub, D. 2004. "Consumer Trust in B2C E-Commerce and the Importance of Social Presence: Experiments in e-Products and e-Services" *Omega* (32:6), pp. 407–424.

Gefen, D., and Straub, D. 2005. "A Practical Guide to Factorial Validity Using PLS-Graph: Tutorial and Annotated Example" *Communications of the Association for Information Systems*, pp. 91–109.

Gholami, R., Watson, R., Hasan, H., Molla, A., and Bjorn-Andersen, N. 2016. "Information Systems Solutions for Environmental Sustainability: How Can We Do More?" *Journal of the Association for Information Systems* (17:8), pp. 521–536.

Gnewuch, U., Adam, M. T. P., Morana, S., and Maedche, A. 2018a. "'The Chatbot Is Typing …' - The Role of Typing Indicators in Human-Chatbot Interaction" *Proceedings of the 17th Annual Pre-ICIS Workshop on HCI Research in MIS*, pp. 0–5.

Gnewuch, U., Morana, S., Adam, M. T. P., and Maedche, A. 2018b. "Faster Is Not Always Better: Understanding the Effect of Dynamic Response Delays in Human-Chatbot Interaction" in *Proceedings of the European Conference on Information Systems (ECIS)*, Portsmouth, United Kingdom, pp. 1–17.

Gnewuch, U., Morana, S., Heckmann, C., and Maedche, A. 2018c. "Designing Conversational Agents for Energy Feedback" in *Proceedings of the International Conference on Design Science Research in Information Systems and Technology (DESRIST)*, Chennai, India, pp. 3–6.

Gnewuch, U., Morana, S., and Maedche, A. 2017. "Towards Designing Cooperative and Social Conversational Agents for Customer Service" in *Proceedings of the International Conference on Information Systems (ICIS)*, Seoul, Korea, pp. 1–13.

Go, E., and Sundar, S. S. 2019. "Humanizing Chatbots: The Effects of Visual, Identity and Conversational Cues on Humanness Perceptions" *Computers in Human Behavior* (97), pp. 304–316.

Goasduff, L. 2019. "Gartner Hype Cycle for Artificial Intelligence." (https://blogs.gartner.com/smarterwithgartner/files/2019/08/CTMKT_736691_Hype_Cycle_for_AI_2019.png, accessed January 28, 2020).

Goldkuhl, G. 2012. "Pragmatism vs Interpretivism in Qualitative Information Systems Research" *European Journal of Information Systems*, pp. 135–146.

Gong, L. 2008. "How Social Is Social Responses to Computers? The Function of the Degree of Anthropomorphism in Computer Representations" *Computers in Human Behavior* (24:4), pp. 1494–1509.

Goodhue, D. L., and Thompson, R. L. 1995. "Task-Technology Fit and Individual Performance" *Management Information Systems Quarterly* (19:2), pp. 213–236.

Google. 2019. "Google Dialogflow." (https://dialogflow.com, accessed March 25, 2019).

Graesser, A. C., Cai, Z., Morgan, B., and Wang, L. 2017. "Assessment with Computer Agents That Engage in Conversational Dialogues and Trialogues with Learners" *Computers in Human Behavior* (76), pp. 607–616.

Gregor, S. 2006. "The Nature of Theory in Information Systems" *Management Information Systems Quarterly* (30:3), pp. 611–642.

Gregor, S., and Hevner, A. R. 2013. "Positioning and Presenting Design Science Research for Maximum Impact" *Management Information Systems Quarterly* (37:2), pp. 337–355.

Gregor, S., and Jones, D. 2007. "The Anatomy of a Design Theory" *Journal of the Association for Information Systems* (8:5), pp. 312–334.

Gregory, R. W., and Muntermann, J. 2014. "Heuristic Theorizing: Proactively Generating Design Theories" *Information Systems Research* (25:3), pp. 639–653.

Grice, H. P. 1975. "Logic and Conversation" *Syntax and Semantics, Vol 3*, pp. 41–58.

Groom, V., Nass, C., Chen, T., Nielsen, A., Scarborough, J. K., and Robles, E. 2009. "Evaluating the Effects of Behavioral Realism in Embodied Agents" *International Journal of Human Computer Studies* (67:10), pp. 842–849.

De Groot, J., and Steg, L. 2007. "General Beliefs and the Theory of Planned Behavior: The Role of Environmental Concerns in the TPB" *Journal of Applied Social Psychology* (37:8), pp. 1817–1836.

Grosz, B. J., and Sidner, C. L. 1986. "Attention, Intentions, and the Structure of Discourse" *Computational Linguistics*.

Grosz, B. J., and Sidner, C. L. 1990. "Plans for Discourse" in *Intentions in Communication*.

Gutierrez, C., and Khizniak, A. 2018. "KLM Handles 2x More Customer Requests with Artificial Intelligence." (https://www.altoros.com/blog/klm-handles-2x-more-customer-requests-with-artificial-intelligence/, accessed January 29, 2020).

Hanson, D. 2006. "Exploring the Aesthetic Range for Humanoid Robots" *Proceedings of the ICCS/CogSci-2006 Long Symposium*, pp. 39–42.

Hanson, D., Olney, A., Pereira, I. A., and Zielke, M. 2005. "Upending the Uncanny Valley" *Proceedings of the AAAI Workshop* (WS05-11:July), pp. 24–31.

Hanus, M. D., and Fox, J. 2015. "Persuasive Avatars: The Effects of Customizing a Virtual Salespersons Appearance on Brand Liking and Purchase Intentions" *International Journal of Human Computer Studies* (84), pp. 33–40.

Harjunen, V. J., Spapé, M., Ahmed, I., Jacucci, G., and Ravaja, N. 2018. "Persuaded by the Machine: The Effect of Virtual Nonverbal Cues and Individual Differences on Compliance in Economic Bargaining" *Computers in Human Behavior* (87), pp. 384–394.

Hasler, B. S., Tuchman, P., and Friedman, D. 2013. "Virtual Research Assistants: Replacing Human Interviewers by Automated Avatars in Virtual Worlds" *Computers in Human Behavior* (29:4), pp. 1608–1616.

Hassanein, K., and Head, M. 2007. "Manipulating Perceived Social Presence through the Web Interface and Its Impact on Attitude towards Online Shopping" *International Journal of Human Computer Studies* (65:8), pp. 689–708.

Heinrich, L. J., Heinzl, A., and Riedl, R. 2011. "Wirtschaftsinformatik: Einführung Und Grundlegung" *Springer*.

Hendriks, B., Meerbeek, B., Boess, S., Pauws, S., and Sonneveld, M. 2011. "Robot Vacuum Cleaner Personality and Behavior" *International Journal of Social Robotics* (3:2), pp. 187–195.

Henkel, C., and Kranz, J. 2018. "Pro-Environmental Behavior and Green Information Systems Research – Review, Synthesis and Directions for Future Research" in *Proceedings of International Conference on Information Systems (ICIS)*, San Francisco, USA, pp. 1–17.

Hevner, A. R. 2007. "A Three Cycle View of Design Science Research" *Scandinavian Journal of Information Systems* (19:192), pp. 87–92.

Hevner, A. R., March, S. T., Park, J., and Ram, S. 2004. "Design Science in Information Systems Research" *Management Information Systems Quarterly* (28:1), pp. 75–105.

Hobert, S. 2019. "Say Hello to ' Coding Tutor '! Design and Evaluation of a Chatbot-Based Learning System Supporting Students to Learn to Program" in *Proceedings of the International Conference on Information Systems*, Munich, Germany, pp. 1–17.

Holtgraves, T., and Han, T. L. 2007. "A Procedure for Studying Online Conversational Processing Using a Chat Bot" *Behavior Research Methods* (39:1), pp. 156–163.

Holtgraves, T. M., Ross, S. J., Weywadt, C. R., and Han, T. L. 2007. "Perceiving Artificial Social Agents" *Computers in Human Behavior* (23:5), pp. 2163–2174.

Hu, T., Xu, A., Liu, Z., You, Q., Guo, Y., Sinha, V., Luo, J., and Akkiraju, R. 2018. "Touch Your Heart: A Tone-Aware Chatbot for Customer Care on Social Media" in *Proceedings of the ACM CHI Conference on Human Factors in Computing Systems*, Montréal, Canada, pp. 1–12.

Huang, T.-H. "Kenneth" Chang, J. C., and Bigham, J. P. 2018. "Evorus: A Crowd-Powered Conversational Assistant Built to Automate Itself Over Time" in *Proceedings of the ACM CHI Conference on Human Factors in Computing Systems*, Montréal, Canada, pp. 1–13.

Iivari, J. 2015. "Distinguishing and Contrasting Two Strategies for Design Science Research" *European Journal of Information Systems* (24:1), pp. 107–115.

Isbister, K., and Nass, C. 2000. "Consistency of Personality in Interactive Characters: Verbal Cues, Non-Verbal Cues, and User Characteristics" *International Journal of Human-Computer Studies* (53), pp. 251–267.

Jacobs, I., Powers, S., Seguin, B., and Lynch, D. 2017. "The Top 10 Chatbots For Enterprise Customer Service" *Forrester Research*. (https://info.247-inc.com/rs/074-HBW-141/images/The-Top-10-Chatbots-For-Enterprise-Customer-Service.pdf).

Johnson, K. 2018. "Facebook Messenger Hits 100,000 Bots." (https://venturebeat.com/2017/04/18/facebook-messenger-hits-100000-bots/, accessed June 5, 2018).

Johnston, R. 1995. "The Determinants of Service Quality: Satisfiers and Dissatisfiers" *International Journal of Service Industry Management* (6:5), pp. 43–51.

Jucks, R., Linnemann, G. A., and Brummernhenrich, B. 2018. "Student Evaluations of a (Rude) Spoken Dialogue System Insights from an Experimental Study" *Advances in Human-Computer Interaction* (2018), pp. 1–10.

Junglas, I., Goel, L., Abraham, C., and Ives, B. 2013. "The Social Component of Information Systems - How Sociability Contributes to Technology Acceptance" *Journal of the Association for Information Systems* (14:10), pp. 585–616.

Kahai, S. S., and Cooper, R. B. 2003. "Exploring the Core Concepts of Media Richness Theory: The Impact of Cue Multiplicity and Feedback Immediacy on Decision Quality" *Journal of Management Information Systems* (20:1), pp. 263–299.

De Keyser, A., Köcher, S., Alkire, L., Verbeeck, C., and Kandampully, J. 2019. "Frontline Service Technology Infusion: Conceptual Archetypes and Future Research Directions" *Journal of Service Management* (30:1), pp. 156–183.

Kim, K. J., Park, E., and Shyam Sundar, S. 2013. "Caregiving Role in Human-Robot Interaction: A Study of the Mediating Effects of Perceived Benefit and Social Presence" *Computers in Human Behavior* (29:4), pp. 1799–1806.

Klopfenstein, L. C., Delpriori, S., Malatini, S., and Bogliolo, A. 2017. "The Rise of Bots: A Survey of Conversational Interfaces, Patterns, and Paradigms" in *Proceedings of the Conference on Designing Interactive Systems*, Edinburgh, United Kingdom, pp. 555–565.

Knijnenburg, B. P., and Willemsen, M. C. 2016. "Inferring Capabilities of Intelligent Agents from Their External Traits" *ACM Transactions on Interactive Intelligent Systems* (6:4), pp. 1–25.

Komiak, S. Y. X., and Benbasat, I. 2006. "The Effects of Personalization and Familiarity on Trust and Adoption of Recommendation Agents" *Management Information Systems Quarterly* (30:4), pp. 941–960.

Koo, C., and Chung, N. 2014. "Examining the Eco-Technological Knowledge of Smart Green IT Adoption Behavior: A Self-Determination Perspective" in *Technological Forecasting and Social Change* (Vol. 88), Ho Chi Minh City, Vietnam, pp. 140–155.

Koplowitz, R., and Facemire, M. 2018. "The Forrester New Wave: Conversational Computing Platforms." (https://www.forrester.com/report/The+Forrester+New+Wave+Conversational+Computing+Platforms+Q2+2018/-/E-RES137816, accessed January 28, 2020).

Koufaris, M. 2002. "Applying the Technology Acceptance Model and Flow Theory to Online Consumer Behavior" *Journal of the Association for Information Systems* (13:2), pp. 205–223.

Krämer, N. 2010. "Psychological Research on Embodied Conversational Agents: The Case of Pedagogical Agents" *Journal of Media Psychology*.

Krämer, N. C., Lucas, G., Schmitt, L., and Gratch, J. 2018. "Social Snacking with a Virtual Agent – On the Interrelation of Need to Belong and Effects of Social Responsiveness When Interacting with Artificial Entities" *International Journal of Human Computer Studies* (109), pp. 112–121.

Krämer, N. C., Pütten, A. M. Von Der, and Eimler, C. 2012. "Human-Agent and Human-Robot Interaction THeory: Similarities to and Differences from Human-Human Interaction" *Studies in Computational Intelligence* (396:January), pp. 263–285.

Krämer, N., Kopp, S., Becker-Asano, C., and Sommer, N. 2013. "Smile and the World Will Smile with You - The Effects of a Virtual Agent's Smile on Users' Evaluation and Behavior" *International Journal of Human Computer Studies* (71:3), pp. 335–349.

Kuechler, W., and Vaishnavi, V. 2008. "Theory Development in Design Science Research: Anatomy of a Research Project" *Proceedings of the Third International Conference on Design Science Research in Information Systems and Technology* (May 7-9), pp. 1–15.

Lampe, C. A. C., Ellison, N., and Steinfield, C. 2007. "A Familiar Face(Book): Profile Elements as Signals in an Online Social Network" *Proceedings of the Conference on Human Factors in Computing Systems* (January), pp. 435–444.

Langer, E. J. 1992. "Matters of Mind: Mindfulness/Mindlessness in Perspective" *Consciousness and Cognition* (1), pp. 289–305.

Langrial, S., Lehto, T., and Oinas-Kukkonen, H. 2012. "Native Mobile Applications For Personal Wellbeing: A Persuasive Systems Design Evaluation" in *Proceedings of the Pacific Asia Conference on Information Systems (PACIS)*, Ho Chi Minh City, Vietnam, pp. 1–16.

Lankton, N., McKnight, D. H., and Tripp, J. 2015. "Technology, Humanness, and Trust: Rethinking Trust in Technology" *Journal of the Association for Information Systems* (16:10), pp. 880–918.

Larivière, B., Bowen, D., Andreassen, T. W., Kunz, W., Sirianni, N. J., Voss, C., Wünderlich, N. V., and De Keyser, A. 2017. "'Service Encounter 2.0': An Investigation into the Roles of Technology, Employees and Customers" *Journal of Business Research* (79), pp. 238–246.

Le, N. T., and Wartschinski, L. 2018. "A Cognitive Assistant for Improving Human Reasoning Skills" *International Journal of Human Computer Studies* (117), pp. 45–54.

Lee, C., Jung, S., Kim, S., and Lee, G. G. 2009. "Example-Based Dialog Modeling for Practical Multi-Domain Dialog System" *Speech Communication* (51:5), pp. 466–484.

Lee, K. M., Jung, Y., Kim, J., and Kim, S. R. 2006. "Are Physically Embodied Social Agents Better than Disembodied Social Agents? The Effects of Physical Embodiment, Tactile Interaction, and People's Loneliness in Human-Robot Interaction" *International Journal of Human Computer Studies* (64:10), pp. 962–973.

Lee, K., Park, J., and Suh, J. 2018. "Investigating Knowledge Flows Between Information Systems and Other Disciplines: Seeking Greater Research Opportunities" *The DATA BASE for Advances in Information Systems* (49:2), pp. 14–34.

Lee, S. Y., and Choi, J. 2017. "Enhancing User Experience with Conversational Agent for Movie Recommendation: Effects of Self-Disclosure and Reciprocity" *International Journal of Human Computer Studies* (103), pp. 95–105.

Lehto, T., Oinas-Kukkonen, H., and Drozd, F. 2012. "Factors Affecting Perceived Persuasiveness of a Behavior Change Support System" in *Proceedings of the International Conference on Information Systems (ICIS)*, Orlando, Florida, pp. 1–15.

Leidner, D. 2018. "Review and Theory Symbiosis: An Introspective Retrospective" *Journal of the Association for Information Systems* (19:06), pp. 552–567.

Leite, I., Pereira, A., Mascarenhas, S., Martinho, C., Prada, R., and Paiva, A. 2013. "The Influence of Empathy in Human-Robot Relations" *International Journal of Human Computer Studies* (71:3), pp. 250–260.

Lemon, K. N., and Verhoef, P. C. 2016. "Understanding Customer Experience Throughout the Customer Journey" *Journal of Marketing* (80:6), pp. 69–96.

Liao, Q. V., Hussain, M. M., Chandar, P., Davis, M., Crasso, M., Wang, D., Muller, M., Shami, N. S., and Geyer, W. 2018. "All Work and No Play? Conversations with a Question-and-Answer Chatbot in the Wild" in *Proceedings of the ACM CHI Conference on Human Factors in Computing Systems*, Montréal, Canada, pp. 1–13.

Lindenberg, S., and Steg, L. 2013. "Goal-Framing Theory and Norm-Guided Environmental Behavior" in *Encouraging Sustainable Behavior: Psychology and the Environment*, H. van Trijp (ed.), New York, USA: Psychology Press, pp. 37–54.

Liu, B. 2010. "Sentiment Analysis and Subjectivity in: Handbook of Natural Language Processing, Second Edition" in *Handbook of Natural Language Processing, Second Edition*, Taylor & Francis, p. 568.

Liu, B. 2012. *Sentiment Analysis and Opinion Mining*, Morgan & Claypool Publishers.

Liu, K. K., and Picard, R. W. 2004. "Embedded Empathy in Continuous, Interactive Health Assessment" in *Proceedings of the Workshop on Computer-Human Interaction Challenges in Health Assessment*, pp. 1–4.

Lo, S. H., Peters, G. J. Y., and Kok, G. 2012. "A Review of Determinants of and Interventions for Proenvironmental Behaviors in Organizations" *Journal of Applied Social Psychology* (42:12), pp. 2933–2967.

Loock, C.-M., Staake, T., and Thiesse, F. 2013. "Motivating Energy-Efficient Behavior with Green IS: An Investigation of Goal Setting and the Role of Defaults" *Management Information Systems Quarterly* (37:4), pp. 1313–1332.

Luger, E., and Sellen, A. 2016. "'Like Having a Really Bad PA': The Gulf between User Expectation and Experience of Conversational Agents" in *Proceedings of the ACM CHI Conference on Human Factors in Computing Systems*, San José, USA, pp. 5286–5297.

MacDorman, K. F. 2006. "Subjective Ratings of Robot Video Clips for Human Likeness, Familiarity, and Eeriness: An Exploration of the Uncanny Valley" in *Proceedings of the ICCS/CogSci-2006 Long Symposium: Toward Social Mechanisms of Android Science*, Canada, pp. 1–4.

MacDorman, K. F., Green, R. D., Ho, C. C., and Koch, C. T. 2009. "Too Real for Comfort? Uncanny Responses to Computer Generated Faces" *Computers in Human Behavior* (25:3), pp. 695–710.

MacDorman, K. F., and Ishiguro, H. 2006. "The Uncanny Advantage of Using Androids in Cognitive and Social Science Research" *Interaction Studies* (7:3), pp. 297–337.

Maedche, A., Legner, C., Benlian, A., Berger, B., Gimpel, H., Hess, T., Hinz, O., Morana, S., and Söllner, M. 2019. "AI-Based Digital Assistants" *Business & Information Systems Engineering* (4), pp. 1–28.

Maedche, A., Morana, S., Schacht, S., Werth, D., and Krumeich, J. 2016. "Advanced User Assistance Systems" *Business & Information Systems Engineering* (58:5), pp. 367–370.

Maglio, P. P., Vargo, S. L., Caswell, N., and Spohrer, J. 2009. "The Service System Is the Basic Abstraction of Service Science" *Information Systems and E-Business Management* (7), pp. 395–406.

Malhotra, A., Melville, N. P., and Watson, R. T. 2013. "Spurring Impactful Research on Information Systems for Envionmental Sustainability" *Management Information Systems Quarterly* (37:4), pp. 1265–1274.

Manyika, J., Chui, M., Lund, S., and Ramaswamy, S. 2017. "What's Now and next in Analytics, AI and Automation" *McKinsey Global Institute Briefing Note* (May), pp. 1–12.

Marett, K., Otondo, R. F., and Taylor, S. G. 2012. "Assessing the Effects of Benefits and Institutional Influences on the Continued Use of Environmentally Munificent Bypass Systems in Long-Haul Trucking" *Management Information Systems Quarterly* (I:4), pp. 1–9.

Marinova, D., de Ruyter, K., Huang, M. H., Meuter, M. L., and Challagalla, G. 2017. "Getting Smart: Learning From Technology-Empowered Frontline Interactions" *Journal of Service Research* (20:1), pp. 29–42.

Markus, M. L., Majchrzak, A., and Gasser, L. 2002. "A Design Theory for Systems That Support Emergent Knowledge Processes" *Management Information Systems Quarterly* (26:3), pp. 179–212.

Mathur, M. B., and Reichling, D. B. 2016. "Navigating a Social World with Robot Partners: A Quantitative Cartography of the Uncanny Valley" *Cognition* (146), pp. 22–32.

Matsushita, M., Maeda, E., and Kato, T. 2004. "An Interactive Visualization Method of Numerical Data Based on Natural Language Requirements" *International Journal of Human Computer Studies* (60:4), pp. 469–488.

Mayer, R. E., Johnson, W. L., Shaw, E., and Sandhu, S. 2006. "Constructing Computer-Based Tutors That Are Socially Sensitive: Politeness in Educational Software" *International Journal of Human Computer Studies* (64:1), pp. 36–42.

McKevitt, P., Partridge, D., and Wilks, Y. 1999. "Why Machines Should Analyse Intention in Natural Language Dialogue" *International Journal of Human-Computer Studies* (51:5), pp. 947–989.

McAfee, A., and Brynjolfsson, E. 2017. *Machine, Platform, Crowd: Harnessing Our Digital Future*, Norton & Company.

McQuiggan, S. W., and Lester, J. C. 2007. "Modeling and Evaluating Empathy in Embodied Companion Agents" *International Journal of Human Computer Studies* (65:4), pp. 348–360.

McTear, M. 2017. "The Rise of the Conversational Interface: A New Kid on the Block?" *Lecture Notes in Computer Science*.

McTear, M., Callejas, Z., and Griol, D. 2016. *The Conversational Interface: Talking to Smart Devices*, Basel, Switzerland: Springer Publishing Company.

Meier, P., Beinke, J. H., Fitte, C., Behne, A., and Teuteberg, F. 2019. "FeelFit – Design and Evaluation of a Conversational Agent to Enhance Health Awareness" in *Proceedings of the International Conference on Information Systems*, Munich, Germany, pp. 1–17.

Melville, N. P. 2010. "Information Systems Innovation for Environmental Sustainability" *Management Information Systems Quarterly* (34:1), pp. 1–21.

Meuter, M. L., Ostrom, A. L., Roundtree, R. I., and Bitner, M. J. 2000. "Self-Service Technologies:Understanding Customer Satisfaction with Technology-Based Service Encounters" *Journal of Marketing* (64:July), pp. 50–64.

Ben Mimoun, M. S., Poncin, I., and Garnier, M. 2012. "Case Study-Embodied Virtual Agents: An Analysis on Reasons for Failure" *Journal of Retailing and Consumer Services* (19:6), pp. 605–612.

Ben Mimoun, M. S., Poncin, I., and Garnier, M. 2017. "Animated Conversational Agents and E-Consumer Productivity: The Roles of Agents and Individual Characteristics" *Information and Management* (54:5), pp. 545–559.

Mohr, L., and Bitner, M. J. 1991. "Mutual Understanding Between Customers and Employees In Service Encounters." *Advances in Consumer Research* (18), pp. 611–617.

Moon, Y. 2003. "Don't Blame the Computer: When Self-Disclosure Moderates the Self-Serving Bias" *Journal of Consumer Psychology*.

Moosa, M. M., and Ud-Dean, S. M. M. 2010. "Danger Avoidance: An Evolutionary Explanation of Uncanny Valley" *Biological Theory* (5:1), pp. 12–14.

Morana, S., Friemel, C., Gnewuch, U., Maedche, A., and Pfeiffer, J. 2017. "Interaktion Mit Smarten Systemen – Aktueller Stand Und Zukünftige Entwicklungen Im Bereich Der Nutzerassistenz" *Wirtschaftsinformatik & Management* (5), pp. 42–51.

Mori, M. 1970. "The Uncanny Valley" *Energy*.

Mori, M., MacDorman, K. F., and Kageki, N. 2012. "The Uncanny Valley" *IEEE Robotics and Automation Magazine* (19:2), pp. 98–100.

Mosier, K. L., and Skitka, L. J. 1996. "Human Decision Makers and Automated Decision Aids: Made for Each Other?" in *Automation and Human Performance: Theory and Applications*, pp. 201–220.

Mou, Y., Xu, K., and Xia, K. 2018. "Unpacking the Black Box: Examining the (de)Gender Categorization Effect in Human-Machine Communication" *Computers in Human Behavior*.

Mueller, M., Leukel, J., and Sugumaran, V. 2014. "The State of Design Science Research within the BISE Community: An Empirical Investigation" *Proceedings of the International Conference on Information Systems (ICIS)*, pp. 1–15.

Nass, C., and Moon, Y. 2000. "Machines and Mindlessness: Social Responses to Computers" *Journal of Social Issues* (56:1), pp. 81–103.

Nass, C., Moon, Y., and Carney, P. 1999. "Are Respondents Polite to Computers? Social Desirability and Direct Responses to Computers" *Journal of Applied Social Psychology*.

Nass, C., Steuer, J., and Tauber, E. R. 1994. "Computers Are Social Actors" in *Proceedings of the ACM CHI Conference on Human Factors in Computing Systems*, Boston, USA, p. 204.

NextIT. 2018. "Helping a Railroad Service Conduct Business." (http://nextit.com/case-studies/amtrak, accessed November 1, 2018).

Nguyen, Q. N., and Sidorova, A. 2017. "AI Capabilities and User Experiences: A Comparative Study of User Reviews for Assistant and Non-Assistant Mobile Apps" in *Proceedings of the Americas Conference on Information Systems (AMCIS)*, Boston, USA, pp. 1–10.

Niewiadomski, R., and Pelachaud, C. 2010. "Affect Expression in ECAs: Application to Politeness Displays" *International Journal of Human Computer Studies* (68:11), pp. 851–871.

Nunamaker, J. F., Briggs, R. O., Derrick, D. C., and Schwabe, G. 2015. "The Last Research Mile: Achieving Both Rigor and Relevance in Information Systems Research" *Journal of Management Information Systems* (32:3), pp. 10–47.

Nunamaker, J. F., Derrick, D. C., Elkins, A. C., Burgoon, J. K., and Patton, M. W. 2011. "Embodied Conversational Agent-Based Kiosk for Automated Interviewing" *Journal of Management Information Systems* (28:1), pp. 17–48.

Oinas-Kukkonen, H., and Harjumaa, M. 2009. "Persuasive Systems Design: Key Issues, Process Model, and System Features" *Communications of the Association for Information Systems* (24:1), p. 96.

Oracle. 2016. *Can Virtual Experiences Replace Reality? The Future Role for Humans in Delivering Customer Experience*, p. 19.

Orlikowski, W. J., and Baroudi, J. J. 1991. "Studying Information Technology in Organizations: Research Approaches and Assumptions" *Information Systems Research* (2:1), pp. 1–28.

Otoo, B. A., and Salam, A. F. 2018. "Mediating Effect of Intelligent Voice Assistant (IVA), User Experience and Effective Use on Service Quality and Service Satisfaction and Loyalty" in *Proceedings of the International Conference on Information Systems (ICIS)*, San Francisco, USA, pp. 1–9.

Palvia, P., Leary, D., Mao, E., Midha, V., Pinjani, P., and Salam, A. F. 2004. "Research Methodologies in MIS: An Update" *Communications of the Association for Information Systems* (14:1), pp. 526–542.

Parasuraman, A., Zeithaml, V. A., and Berry, L. L. 1985. "A Conceptual Model of Service Quality and Its Implications for Future Research" *Journal of Marketing* (49:4), pp. 41–50.

Parasuraman, A., Zeithaml, V. A., and Berry, L. L. 1988. "SERVQUAL: A Multiple-Item Scale for Measuring Consumer Perceptions of Service Quality" *Journal of Retailing* (64:1), pp. 12–40.

Paredes, D. 2019. "Boston Consulting Group's New Advisor Is a Digital Human." (https://www.cio.com/article/3509747/boston-consulting-group-s-new-advisor-is-a-digital-human.html, accessed January 24, 2020).

Park, E. K., and Sundar, S. S. 2015. "Can Synchronicity and Visual Modality Enhance Social Presence in Mobile Messaging?" *Computers in Human Behavior* (45), pp. 121–128.

Peffers, K., Tuunanen, T., and Niehaves, B. 2018. "Design Science Research Genres: Introduction to the Special Issue on Exemplars and Criteria for Applicable Design Science Research" *European Journal of Information Systems* (27:2), Taylor & Francis, pp. 129–139.

Pereira, A. T., Prada, R., and Paiva, A. 2014. "Improving Social Presence in Human-Agent Interaction" in *Proceedings of the ACM CHI Conference on Human Factors in Computing Systems*, Toronto, Canada, pp. 1449–1458.

Pereira, R., and Baranauskas, M. C. C. 2015. "A Value-Oriented and Culturally Informed Approach to the Design of Interactive Systems" *International Journal of Human Computer Studies* (80), pp. 66–82.

Perez, S. 2016. "Starbucks Unveils a Virtual Assistant That Takes Your Order via Messaging or Voice." (https://techcrunch.com/2017/01/30/starbucks-unveils-a-virtual-assistant-that-takes-your-order-via-messaging-or-voice/?guccounter=1, accessed November 23, 2018).

Pfeuffer, N., Benlian, A., Gimpel, H., and Hinz, O. 2019a. "Anthropomorphic Information Systems" *Business & Information Systems Engineering*, pp. 1–16.

Pfeuffer, N., Toutaoui, J., Adam, M., Hinz, O., and Benlian, A. 2019b. "Mr. and Mrs. Conversational Agent - Gender Stereotyping in Judge-Advisor Systems and the Role of Egocentric Bias" in *Proceedings of the International Conference on Information Systems*, Munich, Germany, pp. 1–17.

Pickard, M. D., Roster, C. A., and Chen, Y. 2016. "Revealing Sensitive Information in Personal Interviews: Is Self-Disclosure Easier with Humans or Avatars and under What Conditions?" *Computers in Human Behavior* (65), pp. 23–30.

Pitt, L. F., Parent, M., Junglas, I., Chan, A., and Spyropoulou, S. 2011. "Integrating the Smartphone into a Sound Environmental Information Systems Strategy: Principles, Practices and a Research Agenda" *Journal of Strategic Information Systems* (20:1), pp. 27–37.

Powers, A., and Kiesler, S. 2006. "The Advisor Robot: Tracing People's Mental Model from a Robot's Physical Attributes" in *Proceedings of the 2006 ACM Conference on Human-Robot Interaction*, Salt Lake City, USA, pp. 1–8.

Price, L., Arnould, E., and Deibler, S. 1995. "Consumers' Emotional Responses to Service Encounters: The Influence of the Service Provider" *International Journal of Service Industry Management* (6:3), pp. 34–63.

Purington, A., Taft, J. G., Sannon, S., Bazarova, N. N., and Taylor, S. H. 2017. "'Alexa Is My New BFF': Social Roles, User Satisfaction, and Personification of the Amazon Echo" in *Proceedings of the ACM CHI Conference on Human Factors in Computing Systems* (Vol. Part F1276), Denver, USA, pp. 2853–2859.

Von Der Pütten, A. M., Krämer, N. C., Gratch, J., and Kang, S. H. 2010. "'It Doesn't Matter What You Are!' Explaining Social Effects of Agents and Avatars" *Computers in Human Behavior* (26:6), pp. 1641–1650.

Qiu, L., and Benbasat, I. 2009. "Evaluating Anthropomorphic Product Recommendation Agents: A Social Relationship Perspective to Designing Information Systems" *Journal of Management Information Systems* (25:4), pp. 145–182.

Qiu, L., and Benbasat, I. 2010. "A Study of Demographic Embodiments of Product Recommendation Agents in Electronic Commerce" *International Journal of Human Computer Studies* (68:10), pp. 669–688.

Quynh, N., and Sidorova, A. 2018. "Understanding User Interactions with a Chatbot: A Self-Determination Theory Approach" in *Proceedings of the Americas Conference on Information Systems (AMCIS)*, New Orleans, USA, pp. 1–5.

De Raad, B. 2000. *The Big Five Personality Factors: The Psycholexical Approach to Personality*, Hogrefe & Huber Publishers.

Reeves, B., and Nass, C. 1996. *The Media Equation: How People Treat Computers, Television and New Media Like Real People and Places*, The Center for the Study of Language and Information Publications.

Rezvani, M. 2020. "Why Your Chatbot Needs a Vertical Focus." (https://venturebeat.com/2016/11/06/why-your-chatbot-needs-a-vertical-focus/, accessed January 23, 2020).

Riek, L. D., Rabinowitch, T. C., Chakrabartiz, B., and Robinson, P. 2009. "Empathizing with Robots: Fellow Feeling along the Anthropomorphic Spectrum" *Proceedings of the 3rd International Conference on Affective Computing and Intelligent Interaction*.

Ringle, C. M., Sarstedt, M., and Straub, D. W. 2012. "A Critical Look at the USE of PLS-SEM in MIS Quarterly" *Management Information Systems Quarterly* (36:1), pp. 1–8.

Roca, J. C., and Gagné, M. 2008. "Understanding E-Learning Continuance Intention in the Workplace: A Self-Determination Theory Perspective" *Computers in Human Behavior*.

Rodrigue, J. P., Comtois, C., and Slack, B. 2013. *The Geography of Transport Systems*, (4th editio.), London, United Kingdom: Taylor & Francis.

Römer, B., Reichhart, P., and Picot, A. 2015. "Smart Energy for Robinson Crusoe: An Empirical Analysis of the Adoption of IS-Enhanced Electricity Storage Systems" *Electronic Markets* (25:1), pp. 47–60.

Rosenthal-Von Der Pütten, A. M., and Krämer, N. C. 2014. "How Design Characteristics of Robots Determine Evaluation and Uncanny Valley Related Responses" *Computers in Human Behavior* (36), pp. 422–439.

De Rosis, F., Pelachaud, C., Poggi, I., Carofiglio, V., and De Carolis, B. 2003. "From Greta's Mind to Her Face: Modelling the Dynamics of Affective States in a Conversational Embodied Agent" *International Journal of Human Computer Studies* (59:1–2), pp. 81–118.

Ryan, R. M., and Deci, E. L. 2000. "Self-Determination Theory and the Facilitation of Intrinsic Motivation, Social Development, and Well-Being." *The Psychologist*.

Rzepka, C., and Berger, B. 2018. "User Interaction with AI-Enabled Systems: A Systematic Review of IS Research" in *Proceedings of the International Conference on Information Systems (ICIS)*, San Francisco, USA, pp. 1–16.

Saffarizadeh, K., Boodraj, M., and Alashoor, T. M. 2017. "Conversational Assistants: Investigating Privacy Concerns, Trust, and Self-Disclosure" in *Proceedings of the International Conference on Information Systems (ICIS)*, Seoul, Korea, pp. 0–12.

Sah, Y. J., and Peng, W. 2015. "Effects of Visual and Linguistic Anthropomorphic Cues on Social Perception, Self-Awareness, and Information Disclosure in a Health Website" *Computers in Human Behavior* (45), pp. 392–401.

Sakamoto, D., Kanda, T., Ono, T., Kamashima, M., Imai, M., and Ishiguro, H. 2005. "Cooperative Embodied Communication Emerged by Interactive Humanoid Robots" *International Journal of Human Computer Studies* (62:2), pp. 247–265.

Sarikaya, R. 2017. "The Technology behind Personal Digital Assistants: An Overview of the System Architecture and Key Components" *IEEE Signal Processing Magazine* (34:1), pp. 67–81.

Scherer, A., Wünderlich, N. V., and von Wangenheim, F. 2015. "The Value of Self-Service: Long-Term Effects of Technology-Based Self-Service Usage on Customer Retention" *Management Information Systems Quarterly* (39:1), pp. 177–200.

Schroeder, J., and Schroeder, M. 2018. "Trusting in Machines: How Mode of Interaction Affects Willingness to Share Personal Information with Machines" in *Proceedings of the Hawaii International Conference on System Sciences (HICSS)* (Vol. 9), Waikoloa Village, Hawaii, USA, pp. 472–480.

Schuetzler, Ryan M., Giboney, J. S., Grimes, G. M., and Nunamaker, J. F. 2018a. "The Influence of Conversational Agents on Socially Desirable Responding" in *Proceedings of the Hawaii International Conference on System Sciences (HICSS)* (Vol. 9), Waikoloa Village, Hawaii, USA, pp. 283–292.

Schuetzler, Ryan M, Grimes, G. M., and Giboney, J. S. 2018b. "An Investigation of Conversational Agent Relevance, Presence, and Engagement" in *Proceedings of the Americas Conference on Inf. Systems (AMCIS)*, New Orleans, USA, pp. 1–10.

Schuetzler, R. M., Grimes, G. M., and Giboney, J. S. 2019. "The Effect of Conversational Agent Skill on User Behavior during Deception" *Computers in Human Behavior* (97), pp. 250–259.

Schuetzler, R. M., Grimes, G. M., Giboney, J. S., and Buckman, J. 2014. "Facilitating Natural Conversational Agent Interactions: Lessons from a Deception Experiment" in *Proceedings of the International Conference on Information Systems (ICIS)*, Auckland, New Zealand, pp. 1–16.

Sebastian, J., and Richards, D. 2017. "Changing Stigmatizing Attitudes to Mental Health via Education and Contact with Embodied Conversational Agents" *Computers in Human Behavior* (73), pp. 479–488.

Seeber, I., Bittner, E., Briggs, R. O., de Vreede, T., de Vreede, G.-J., Elkins, A., Maier, R., Merz, A., Oeste-Reiß, S., Randrup, N., Schwabe, G., and Söllner, M. 2019. "Machines as Teammates: A Research Agenda on AI in Team Collaboration" *Information & Management*, p. 103174.

Seeger, A.-M., Pfeiffer, J., and Heinzl, A. 2017. "When Do We Need a Human? Anthropomorphic Design and Trustworthiness of Conversational Agents" in *Special Interest Group on Human-Computer Interaction* (Vol. 15), pp. 1–6.

Seeger, A.-M., Pfeiffer, J., and Heinzl, A. 2018. "Designing Anthropomorphic Conversational Agents: Development and Empirical Evaluation of a Design Framework" in *Proceedings of the International Conference on Information Systems (ICIS)*, San Francisco, USA, pp. 1–17.

Seidel, S., Chandra Kruse, L., Székely, N., Gau, M., and Stieger, D. 2017. "Design Principles for Sensemaking Support Systems in Environmental Sustainability Transformations" *European Journal of Information Systems* (27:2), pp. 221–247.

Sen, C. 2016. "Mastercard Makes Commerce More Conversational With Launch of Chatbots for Banks and Merchants." (https://newsroom.mastercard.com/press-releases/mastercard-makes-commerce-more-conversational-with-launch-of-chatbots-for-banks-and-merchants/, accessed January 29, 2020).

Setia, P., Venkatesh, V., and Jogleklar, S. 2013. "Leveraging Digital Technologies: How Information Quality Leads to Localized Capabilities and Customer Service Performance" *Management Information Systems Quarterly* (37:2), pp. 565–590.

Seymour, M., Riemer, K., and Kay, J. 2017. "Interactive Realistic Digital Avatars - Revisiting the Uncanny Valley" in *Proceedings of the Hawaii International Conference on System Sciences (HICSS)*, Waikoloa Vil., Hawaii, USA, pp. 547–556.

Seymour, M., Riemer, K., and Kay, J. 2018. "Actors, Avatars and Agents: Potentials and Implications of Natural Face Technology for the Creation of Realistic Visual Presence" *Journal of the Association for Information Systems* (19), pp. 953–981.

Shamekhi, A., Liao, Q. V., Wang, D., Bellamy, R. K. E., and Erickson, T. 2018. "Face Value? Exploring the Effects of Embodiment for a Group Facilitation Agent" in *Proceedings of the ACM CHI Conference on Human Factors in Computing Systems*, Montréal, Canada, pp. 1–13.

Shawar, B. E., and Atwell, E. 2007. "Chatbots: Are They Really Useful?" in *LDV-Forum* (Vol. 22), pp. 29–49.

Shevchuk, N., and Oinas-Kukkonen, H. 2016. "Exploring Green Information Systems and Technologies as Persuasive Systems: A Systematic Review of Applications in Published Research" in *Proceedings of the International Conference on Information Systems (ICIS)*, Dublin, Ireland, pp. 1–11.

Shi, Y., Yan, X., Ma, X., Lou, Y., and Cao, N. 2018. "Designing Emotional Expressions of Conversational States for Voice Assistants" in *Proceedings of the ACM CHI Conference on Human Factors in Computing Systems*, Montréal, Canada, pp. 1–6.

Short, J., Williams, E., and Christie, B. 1976. *The Social Psychology of Telecommunications*, London, United Kingdom.

Simon, H. A. 1996. *The Sciences of the Artificial*, (Third.), Cambridge: MIT Press.

SoftBank. 2020. "Product Information for Humanoid Robot Pepper." (https://www.softbankrobotics.com/emea/en/pepper, accessed January 31, 2020).

Sohn, S. 2019. "Can Conversational User Interfaces Be Harmful? The Undesirable Effects on Privacy Concern" in *Proceedings of the International Conference on Information Systems*, Munich, Germany, pp. 1–9.

Son, Y., and Wonseok, O. 2018. "' Alexa, Buy Me a Movie!': How AI Speakers Reshape Digital Content Consumption and Preference" in *Proceedings of the International Conference on Information Systems (ICIS)*, San Francisco, USA, pp. 1–17.

Steg, L., Dreijerink, L., and Abrahamse, W. 2005. "Factors Influencing the Acceptability of Energy Policies: A Test of VBN Theory" *Journal of Environmental Psychology* (25:4), pp. 415–425.

Stock, R. M. 2018. "Can Service Robots Hamper Customer Anger and Aggression After a Service Failure?" in *Proceedings of the International Conference on Information Systems (ICIS)*, San Francisco, USA, pp. 1–15.

Stock, R. M., and Merkle, M. 2018. "Customer Responses to Robotic Innovative Behavior Cues During the Service Encounter" in *Proceedings of the International Conference on Information Systems (ICIS)*, San Francisco, USA, pp. 1–17.

Stock, R., Merkle, M., Eidens, D., Hannig, M., Heineck, P., Nguyen, M. A., and Völker, J. 2019. "Understanding Employee Trust in Assistive Robots When Robots Enter Our Workplace: Understanding Employee Trust in Assistive Robots" in *Proceedings of the International Conference on Information Systems*, Munich, Germany, pp. 1–9.

Strait, M., Vujovic, L., Floerke, V., Scheutz, M., and Urry, H. 2015. "Too Much Humanness for Human-Robot Interaction" in *Proceedings of the ACM CHI Conference on Human Factors in Computing Systems*, Seoul, Korea, pp. 3593–3602.

Strohmann, T., Fischer, S., Siemon, D., Brachten, F., Lattemann, C., Robra-Bissantz, S., and Stieglitz, S. 2018. "Virtual Moderation Assistance: Creating Design Guidelines for Virtual Assistants Supporting Creative Workshops" in *Proceedings of the Pacific Asia Conference on Information Systems (PACIS)*, Yokohama, Japan, pp. 3580–3594.

Sugumaran, V., and Davis, K. 2001. "A Natural Language-Based Multi-Agent System for Legal Research" in *Proceedings of the Americas Conference on Information Systems (AMCIS)*, Boston, USA.

Tavanapour, N., and Bittner, E. A. C. 2018. "Automated Facilitation for Idea Platforms: Design and Evaluation of a Chatbot Prototype" in *Proceedings of the International Conference on Information Systems (ICIS)*, San Francisco, USA, pp. 1–9.

Taylor, S. 1994. "Waiting for Service: The Relationship between Delays and Evaluations of Service" *Journal of Marketing* (58:2), pp. 56–69.

Tinwell, A., Grimshaw, M., Nabi, D. A., and Williams, A. 2011. "Facial Expression of Emotion and Perception of the Uncanny Valley in Virtual Characters" *Computers in Human Behavior* (27:2), pp. 741–749.

Tinwell, A., and Sloan, R. J. S. 2014. "Children's Perception of Uncanny Human-like Virtual Characters" *Computers in Human Behavior* (36), pp. 286–296.

Topbots. 2016. "Staples' 'That Was Easy.'" (Staples' "That Was Easy" accessed November 25, 2018).

Toxtli, C., Monroy-Hernández, A., and Cranshaw, J. 2018. "Understanding Chatbot-Mediated Task Management" in *Proceedings of the ACM CHI Conference on Human Factors in Computing Systems*, Montréal, Canada, pp. 1–6.

UNESCO. 2019. "I'd Blush If I Could - Closing Gender Divides in Digital Skills through Education" (Vol. 306).

Urbach, N., and Ahlemann, F. 2010. "Structural Equation Modeling in Information Systems Research Using Partial Least Squares" *Journal of Information Technology Theory and Application (JITTA)* (11:2), pp. 5–40.

Urban, M., and Mailey, S. 2019. "Conversation Design: Principles, Strategies, and Practical Application" in *Proceedings of the ACM CHI Conference on Human Factors in Computing Systems*, Glasgow, Scotland, pp. 1–3.

Vaccaro, K., Agarwalla, T., Shivakumar, S., and Kumar, R. 2018. "Designing the Future of Personal Fashion Experiences Online" in *Proceedings of the ACM CHI Conference on Human Factors in Computing Systems*, Montréal, Canada, pp. 1–11.

Vaishnavi, V., and Kuechler, W. 2015. *Design Science Research in Information Systems*, (1), pp. 1–62.

Venable, J., Pries-Heje, J., and Baskerville, R. 2016. "FEDS: A Framework for Evaluation in Design Science Research" *European Journal of Information Systems* (25:1), pp. 77–89.

Vergragt, P. J., and Brown, H. S. 2007. "Sustainable Mobility: From Technological Innovation to Societal Learning" *Journal of Cleaner Production* (15:11–12), pp. 1104–1115.

Verhagen, T., van Nes, J., Feldberg, F., and van Dolen, W. 2014. "Virtual Customer Service Agents: Using Social Presence and Personalization to Shape Online Service Encounters" *Journal of Computer-Mediated Communication* (19:3), pp. 529–545.

de Visser, E. J., Monfort, S. S., McKendrick, R., Smith, M. A. B., McKnight, P. E., Krueger, F., and Parasuraman, R. 2016. "Almost Human: Anthropomorphism Increases Trust Resilience in Cognitive Agents" *Journal of Experimental Psychology: Applied* (22:3), pp. 331–349.

Vogel-Meijer, K. 2018. "KLM: Making Airline Customer Service Soar with Messenger." (https://www.facebook.com/business/success/klm-messenger, accessed November 1, 2018).

Vugt, H. C. Van, Bailenson, J. N., Hoorn, J. F., and Konijn, E. A. 2010. "Effects of Facial Similarity on User Responses to Embodied Agents" *ACM Transactions on Computer-Human Interaction* (17:2), pp. 1–27.

Wagner, K., and Schramm-Klein, H. 2019. "Alexa, Are You Human? Investigating the Anthropomorphism of Digital Voice Assistants – A Qualitative Approach" in *Proceedings of the International Conference on Information Systems*, Munich, Germany, pp. 1–17.

Wakefield, J. 2016. "Would You Want to Talk to a Machine?" (https://www.bbc.com/news/technology-36225980, accessed July 9, 2017).

Wakefield, R. L. 2015. "The Acceptance and Use of Innovative Technology" *The DATA BASE for Advances in Information Systems* (46:4), pp. 48–67.

Walls, J. G., Widmeyer, G. R., and El Sawy, O. A. 1992. "Building an Information System Design Theory for Vigilant EIS" *Information Systems Research*.

Wang, N., Johnson, W. L., Mayer, R. E., Rizzo, P., Shaw, E., and Collins, H. 2008. "The Politeness Effect: Pedagogical Agents and Learning Outcomes" *International Journal of Human Computer Studies* (66:2), pp. 98–112.

Wang, W., and Benbasat, I. 2005. "Trust in and Adoption of Online Recommendation Agents" *Journal of the Association for Information Systems* (6:3), pp. 72–101.

Watanabe, M., Ogawa, K., and Ishiguro, H. 2015. "Can Androids Be Salespeople in the Real World?" in *Proceedings of the ACM CHI Conference on Human Factors in Computing Systems*, Seoul, Korea, pp. 781–788.

Waytz, A., and Norton, M. I. 2014. "Botsourcing and Outsourcing: Robot, British, Chinese, and German Workers Are for Thinking-Not Feeling-Jobs" *Emotion* (14), pp. 434–444.

Webster, J., and Watson, R. 2002. "Analyzing the Past to Prepare for the Future: Writing a Literature Review" *Management Information Systems Quarterly* (26:2), xiii–xxiii.

Weizenbaum, J. 1966. "ELIZA—a Computer Program for the Study of Natural Language Communication between Man and Machine" *Communications of the ACM* (9:1), pp. 36–45.

Weizenbaum, J. 1976. *Computer Power and Human Reason: From Judgment to Calculation*, New York, USA: W.H. Freeman and Company.

Welch, C. 2018. "Google Just Gave a Stunning Demo of Assistant Making an Actual Phone Call." (https://www.theverge.com/2018/5/8/17332070/google-assistant-makes-phone-call-demo-duplex-io-2018, accessed May 18, 2018).

Wels-Lips, I., van der Ven, M., and Pieters, R. 1998. "Critical Services Dimensions: An Empirical Investigation across Six Industries" *International Journal of Service Industry Management* (9:3), pp. 286–309.

Wiese, E., and Weis, P. P. 2019. "It Matters to Me If You Are Human - Examining Categorical Perception in Human and Nonhuman Agents" *International Journal of Human Computer Studies*.

Willing, C., Brandt, T., and Neumann, D. 2017. "Intermodal Mobility" *Business & Information Systems Engineering* (59:3), pp. 173–179.

Wilson, K. 2002. "Evaluating Images of Virtual Agents" in *Proceedings of the ACM CHI Conference on Human Factors in Computing Systems*, Minneapolis, USA, p. 856.

Windhager, S., Slice, D. E., Schaefer, K., Oberzaucher, E., Thorstensen, T., and Grammer, K. 2008. "Face to Face: The Perception of Automotive Designs" *Human Nature* (19:4), pp. 331–346.

Winkler, R., Söllner, M., Neuweiler, M. L., Conti Rossini, F., and Leimeister, J. M. 2019. "Alexa, Can You Help Us Solve This Problem?" in *Proceedings of the ACM CHI Conference on Human Factors in Computing Systems*, Glasgow, Scotland, pp. 1–6.

References

Wünderlich, N. V., and Paluch, S. 2017. "A Nice and Friendly Chat With a Bot: User Perceptions of AI-Based Service Agents" in *Proceedings of the International Conference on Information Systems (ICIS)*, Seoul, Korea, pp. 1–11.

Wynn, D., and Williams, C. K. 2012. "Principles for Conducting Critical Realist Case Study Research in Information Systems" *Management Information Systems Quarterly* (36:3), pp. 787–810.

Xu, A., Liu, Z., Guo, Y., Sinha, V., and Akkiraju, R. 2017. "A New Chatbot for Customer Service on Social Media" in *Proceedings of the ACM CHI Conference on Human Factors in Computing Systems*, Denver, USA, pp. 3506–3510.

Yan, A., Solomon, S., Mirchandani, D., Lacity, M., and Porra, J. 2013. "The Role Of Service Agent, Service Quality , And User Satisfaction In Self -Service" in *Proceedings of the International Conference on Information Systems (ICIS)*, Milan, Italy, pp. 1–21.

Yim, D. 2011. "Tale of Two Green Communities: Energy Informatics and Social Competition on Energy Conservation Behavior" in *Proceedings of Americas Conference on Information Systems (AMCIS)*, Detroit, USA, pp. 1–13.

Yu, T. K., Lin, M. L., and Liao, Y. K. 2017. "Understanding Factors Influencing Information Communication Technology Adoption Behavior: The Moderators of Information Literacy and Digital Skills" *Computers in Human Behavior* (71), pp. 196–208.

Yuan, L. (Ivy), and Dennis, A. R. 2019. "Acting Like Humans? Anthropomorphism and Consumer's Willingness to Pay in Electronic Commerce" *Journal of Management Information Systems* (36:2), Routledge, pp. 450–477.

Zadrozny, W., Budzikowska, M., Chai, J., Kambhatla, N., Levesque, S., and Nicolov, N. 2000. "Natural Language Dialogue for Personalized Interaction" *Communications of the ACM* (43:8), pp. 116–120.

Zajonc, R. B., and Markus, H. 2002. "Affective and Cognitive Factors in Preferences" *Journal of Consumer Research* (9:2), p. 123.

Zanna, M. P., and Rempel, J. K. 1988. "Attitudes: A New Look at an Old Concept" in *The Social Psychology of Knowledge*, New York, USA: Cambridge University Press, pp. 315–334.

Zhang, P., and Li, N. 2005. "The Intellectual Development of Human-Computer Interaction Research: A Critical Assessment of the MIS Literature (1990-2002)" *Journal of the Association for Information Systems* (6:11), pp. 227–292.

Appendix

Appendix A. Overview of the Author's Individual Contribution to the Studies Included in this Thesis

No.	Section	Title	Authors	Contribution [%]
1	B.I.	On the Design of Conversational Agents: A Synthesis of IS and HCI Research	Diederich Brendel Morana Kolbe	80 7.5 7.5 5
2	B.II.	Not Human After All: Exploring the Impact of Response Failure on User Perception of Anthropomorphic Conversational Service Agents	Diederich Lembcke Brendel Kolbe	75 20 2.5 2.5
3	B.II.	Design for Fast Request Fulfillment or Natural Interaction? Insights from an Online Experiment with a Conversational Agent	Diederich Brendel Lichtenberg Kolbe	80 7.5 7.5 5
4	B.III.	Emulating Empathetic Behavior in Online Service Encounters with Sentiment-Adaptive Responses: Insights from an Experiment with a Conversational Agent	Diederich Janßen-Müller Brendel Morana	80 10 5 5
5	B.III.	Promoting Sustainable Mobility Beliefs with Persuasive and Anthropomorphic Design: Insights from an Experiment with a Conversational Agent	Diederich Lichtenberg Brendel Trang	75 20 2.5 2.5
6	B.IV.	Designing Anthropomorphic Enterprise Conversational Agents	Diederich Brendel Kolbe	85 10 5

Appendix B. Overview of the Author's Further Studies on Conversational Agents as of March 2020

Title (Year)	Authors	Outlet	Ranking[1]	Status
Supporting Design Thinking and Inclusive Education with Innovative Tutoring Technologies: The Case of Anthropomorphic Conversational Agents for Persona Building (2020)	Lembcke Diederich Brendel	Proceedings of the European Conference on Information Systems	B	Accepted (conditionally)
On Conversational Agents in Information Systems Research: Analyzing the Past to Guide Future Work (2019)	Diederich Brendel Kolbe	Proceedings of Internationale Tagung Wirtschaftsinformatik	C	Published
Towards a Taxonomy of Platforms for Conversational Agent Design (2019)	Diederich Brendel Kolbe	Proceedings of Internationale Tagung Wirtschaftsinformatik	C	Published
Towards Designing an Anthropomorphic Conversational Agent for Assisting Job Interview Preparation (2019)	Diederich Brendel Kolbe	Proceedings of the Workshop on Designing User Assistance in Interactive Intelligent Systems	n.a.	Published
Zum Design von Chatbots zur Förderung nachhaltigen Mobilitätsverhaltens: Eine literaturbasierte Ableitung von Designprinzipien (book section in: Neue Dimensionen der Mobilität) (2019)	Diederich Lichtenberg Brendel Kolbe	Book section	n.a.	Published

1) According to VHB-JOURQUAL 3

Appendix C. Overview of the Author's Further Studies in Other Research Areas as of March 2020

Title (Year)	Authors	Outlet	Ranking[1]	Status
Where Are We Now and Where Should We Be? – Reflections on the Current Status of Replication Research in IS	Brendel **Diederich** Niederman	European Journal of Information Systems	A	Revision (2nd round)
Supporting Non-Communicable Disease Prevention through a mHealth Application in Decentralized Healthcare Systems: Action Design Research in Eswatini	Greve Lichtenberg **Diederich** Brendel	Proceedings of the European Conference on Information Systems	B	Accepted (conditionally)
Short Message Discussions: On the Conversational Nature of Microblogging in a Large Consultancy Organisation (2011)	Riemer **Diederich** Richter Scifleet	Proceedings of the 15th Pacific Asia Conference on Information Systems	C	Published
Let's Travel the World Together: Toward an Understanding of Motivational Antecedents in Business Trip Ridesharing Services (2020)	Herrenkind Lembcke **Diederich** Trang Kolbe	Proceedings of Internationale Tagung Wirtschaftsinformatik	C	Forthcoming
Managerial Challenges in IT Programmes: Evidence from Multiple Case Study Research	Teubner **Diederich**	Working Papers ERCIS — European Research Center for Information Systems	n.a.	Published
User Acceptance of Mobile Business Intelligence Services	Brockmann Stieglitz Kmieciak **Diederich**	Proceedings of the First International Workshop on Web Services and Social Media	n.a.	Published
Tweet Talking — Exploring The Nature Of Microblogging at Capgemini Yammer (2011)	Riemer **Diederich** Richter Scifleet	Business Information Systems Working Paper, University of Sydney	n.a.	Published
Capgemini: Microblogging als Konversationsmedium (book section in: Wettbewerbsfaktor Business Software: Prozesse erfolgreich mit Software optimieren) (2011)	Richter Schäfer Riemer **Diederich**	Book section	n.a.	Published

1) According to VHB-JOURQUAL 3

Appendix D. Curriculum Vitae

Personal Information

Name:	Stephan Diederich
Date of birth:	17.04.1987
Place of birth:	Dortmund, Germany
Nationality:	German

Academic Career

03/2018 – 03/2020	**University of Göttingen** (Göttingen, Germany) PhD Candidate at the Chair of Information Management
05/2013 – 12/2014	**University of Münster** (Münster, Germany) Research Assistant at the Interorganisational Systems Group
04/2011 – 03/2013	**University of Münster** (Münster, Germany) M.Sc. Information Systems
09/2010 – 01/2011	**University of Sydney** (Sydney, Australia) Term abroad
10/2007 – 01/2011	**University of Münster** (Münster, Germany) B.Sc. Information Systems
08/1997 – 06/2007	**Phoenix-Gymnasium Dortmund** (Dortmund, Germany) Abitur

Working Experience (Selection)

03/2015 – today	**Roland Berger GmbH** (Hamburg, Germany) Management Consultant
08/2012 – 09/2012	**Deloitte Consulting GmbH** (Düsseldorf, Germany) Summer Associate
07/2012 – 08/2012	**Microsoft Deutschland GmbH** (Münster, Germany) Independent Contractor
03/2010 – 04/2010	**City University of London** (London, United Kingdom) Intern at the Center for Human Computer Interaction Design

Awards and Scholarships

06/2013	**MeisterSinger-AlumniUM-Master-Award** (University of Münster)
10/2011 – 03/2013	**Deutschlandstipendium** (Federal Ministry of Education and Research)

Göttinger Wirtschaftsinformatik

Herausgeber: Prof. Dr. J. Biethahn • Prof. Dr. L. M. Kolbe • Prof. Dr. M. Schumann

Band 31: Christian Stummeyer
Integration von Simulationsmethoden und hochintegrierter betriebswirtschaftlicher PPS-Standardsoftware im Rahmen eines ganzheitlichen Entwicklungsansatzes
ISBN 3-89712-874-8

Band 32: Stefan Wegert
Gestaltungsansätze zur IV-Integration von elektronischen und konventionellen Vertriebsstrukturen bei Kreditinstituten
ISBN 3-89712-924-8

Band 33: Ernst von Stegmann und Stein
Ansätze zur Risikosteuerung einer Kreditversicherung unter Berücksichtigung von Unternehmensverflechtungen
ISBN 3-89873-003-4

Band 34: Gerald Wissel
Konzeption eines Managementsystems für die Nutzung von internen sowie externen Wissen zur Generierung von Innovationen
ISBN 3-89873-194-4

Band 35: Wolfgang Greve-Kramer
Konzeption internetbasierter Informationssysteme in Konzernen
Inhaltliche, organisatorische und technische Überlegungen zur internetbasierten Informationsverarbeitung in Konzernen
ISBN 3-89873-207-X

Band 36: Tim Veil
Internes Rechnungswesen zur Unterstützung der Führung in Unternehmensnetzwerken
ISBN 3-89873-237-1

Band 37: Mark Althans
Konzeption eines Vertriebscontrolling-Informationssystems für Unternehmen der liberalisierten Elektrizitätswirtschaft
ISBN 3-89873-326-2

Band 38: Jörn Propach
Methoden zur Spielplangestaltung öffentlicher Theater
Konzeption eines Entscheidungsunterstützungssystems auf der Basis Evolutionärer Algorithmen
ISBN 3-89873-496-X

Cuvillier Verlag Göttingen
Nonnenstieg 8 • 37075 Göttingen

Göttinger Wirtschaftsinformatik
Herausgeber: Prof. Dr. J. Biethahn • Prof. Dr. L. M. Kolbe • Prof. Dr. M. Schumann

Band 39: Jochen Heimann
DV-gestützte Jahresabschlußanalyse
Möglichkeiten und Grenzen beim Einsatz computergeschützter Verfahren zur Analyse und Bewertung von Jahresabschlüssen
ISBN 3-89873-499-4

Band 40: Patricia Böning Spohr
Controlling für Medienunternehmen im Online-Markt
Gestaltung ausgewählter Controllinginstrumente
ISBN 3-89873-677-6

Band 41: Jörg Koschate
Methoden und Vorgehensmodelle zur strategischen Planung von Electronic-Business-Anwendungen
ISBN 3-89873-808-6

Band 42: Yang Liu
A theoretical and empirical study on the data mining process for credit scoring
ISBN 3-89873-823-X

Band 43: Antonios Tzouvaras
Referenzmodellierung für Buchverlage
Prozess- und Klassenmodelle für den Leistungsprozess
ISBN 3-89873-844-2

Band 44: Marina Nomikos
Hemmnisse der Nutzung Elektronischer Marktplätze aus der Sicht von kleinen und mittleren Unternehmen eine theoriegeleitete Untersuchung
ISBN 3-89873-847-7

Band 45: Boris Fredrich
Wissensmanagement und Weiterbildungsmanagement
Gestaltungs- und Kombinationsansätze im Rahmen einer lernenden Organisation
ISBN 3-89873-870-1

Band 46: Thomas Arens
Methodische Auswahl von CRM Software
Ein Referenz-Vorgehensmodell zur methodengestützten Beurteilung und Auswahl von Customer Relationship Management Informationssystemen
ISBN 3-86537-054-3

Cuvillier Verlag Göttingen
Nonnenstieg 8 • 37075 Göttingen

Göttinger Wirtschaftsinformatik

Herausgeber: Prof. Dr. J. Biethahn • Prof. Dr. L. M. Kolbe • Prof. Dr. M. Schumann

Band 47: Andreas Lackner
Dynamische Tourenplanung mit ausgewählten Mataheuristiken
Eine Untersuchung am Beispiel des kapazitätsrestriktiven dynamischen
Tourenplanungsproblems mit Zeitfenstern
ISBN 3-86537-084-5

Band 48: Tobias Behrensdorf
Service Engineering in Versicherungsunternehmen
unter besonderer Berücksichtigung eines Vorgehensmodells zur Unterstützung durch
Informations- und Kommunikationstechnologien
ISBN 3-86537-110-8

Band 49: Michael Range
Aufbau und Betrieb konsumentenorientierter Websites im Internet
Vorgehen und Methoden unter besonderer Berücksichtigung der Anforderungen von kleinen
und mittleren Online-Angeboten
ISBN 3-86537-490-5

Band 50: Gerit Grübler
Ganzheitliches Multiprojektmanagement
Mit einer Fallstudie in einem Konzern der Automobilzulieferindustrie
ISBN 3-86537-544-8

Band 51: Birte Pochert
Konzeption einer unscharfen Balanced Scorecard
Möglichkeiten der Fuzzyfizierung einer Balanced Scorecard zur Unterstützung
des Strategischen Managements
ISBN 3-86537-671-1

Band 52: Manfred Peter Zilling
Effizienztreiber innovativer Prozesse für den Automotive Aftermarket
Implikationen aus der Anwendung von kollaborativen und integrativen
Methoden des Supply Chain Managements
ISBN 3-86537-790-4

Band 53: Mike Hieronimus
Strategisches Controlling von Supply Chains
Entwicklung eines ganzheitlichen Ansatzes unter Einbeziehung der Wertschöpfungspartner
ISBN 3-86537-799-8

Band 54: Dijana Bergmann
Datenschutz und Datensicherheit unter besonderer Berücksichtigung des elektronischen
Geschäftsverkehrs zwischen öffentlicher Verwaltung und privaten Unternehmen
ISBN 3-86537-894-3

Cuvillier Verlag Göttingen
Nonnenstieg 8 • 37075 Göttingen

Göttinger Wirtschaftsinformatik
Herausgeber: Prof. Dr. J. Biethahn • Prof. Dr. L. M. Kolbe • Prof. Dr. M. Schumann

Band 55: Jan Eric Borchert
Operatives Innovationsmanagement in Unternehmensnetzwerken
Gestaltung von Instrumenten für Innovationsprojekte
ISBN 3-86537-984-2

Band 56: Andre Daldrup
Konzeption eines integrierten IV-Systems zur ratingbasierten Quantifizierung des regulatorischen und ökonomischen Eigenkapitals im Unternehmenskreditgeschäft unter Berücksichtigung von Basel II
ISBN 978-3-86727-189-9

Band 57: Thomas Diekmann
Ubiquitous Computing-Technologien im betrieblichen Umfeld
Technische Überlegungen, Einsatzmöglichkeiten und Bewertungsansätze
ISBN 978-3-86727-194-3

Band 58: Lutz Seidenfaden
Ein Peer-to-Peer-basierter Ansatz zur digitalen Distribution wissenschaftlicher Informationen
ISBN 978-3-86727-321-3

Band 59: Sebastian Rieger
Einheitliche Authentifizierung in heterogenen IT-Strukturen für ein sicheres e-Science-Umfeld
ISBN 978-3-86727-329-9

Band 60: Ole Björn Brodersen
Eignung schwarmintelligenter Verfahren für die betriebliche Entscheidungsunterstützung
Untersuchungen der Particle Swarm Optimization und Ant Colony Optimization anhand eines stochastischen Lagerhaltungs- und eines universitären Stundenplanungsproblems
ISBN 978-3-86727-777-5

Band 61: Jan Sauer
Konzeption eines wertorientierten Managementsystems unter besonderer Berücksichtigung des versicherungstechnischen Risikos
ISBN 978-3-86727-858-4

Band 62: Adam Melski
Datenmanagement in RFID-gestützten Logistiknetzwerken
RFID-induzierte Veränderungen, Gestaltungsmöglichkeiten und Handlungsempfehlungen
ISBN 978-3-86955-041-1

Cuvillier Verlag Göttingen
Nonnenstieg 8 • 37075 Göttingen

Göttinger Wirtschaftsinformatik

Herausgeber: Prof. Dr. J. Biethahn • Prof. Dr. L. M. Kolbe • Prof. Dr. M. Schumann

Band 63: Thorsten Caus
Anwendungen im mobilen Internet
Herausforderungen und Lösungsansätze für die Entwicklung und Gestaltung mobiler Anwendungen
ISBN 978-3-86955-399-3

Band 64: Nils-Holger-Schmidt
Environmentally Sustainable Information Management
Theories and concepts for Sustainability, Green IS, and Green IT
ISBN 978-3-86955-825-7

Band 65: Lars Thoroe
RFID in Reverse-Logistics-Systemen
ISBN 978-3-86955-902-5

Band 66: Stefan Bitzer
Integration von Web 2.0-Technologien in das betriebliche Wissensmanagement
ISBN 978-3-86955-918-6

Band 67: Matthias Kießling
IT-Innovationsmanagement
Gestaltungs- und Steuerungsmöglichkeiten
ISBN 978-3-95404-104-6

Band 68: Marco Klein
HR Social Software
Unternehmensinterne Weblogs, Wikis und Social Networking Services für Prozesse des Personalmanagements
ISBN 978-3-95404-247-0

Band 69: Malte Schmidt
Migration vom Barcode zur passiven RFID-Technologie in der automobilen Logistik
Exemplarische Untersuchung am Beispiel eines Automobilherstellers
ISBN 978-3-95404-441-2

Band 70: Janis Kossahl
Konzeptuelle Grundlagen zur Etablierung einer Informationsplattform in der Energiewirtschaft
Ein Beitrag zur Energiewende aus der Perspektive der Wirtschaftsinformatik
ISBN 978-3-95404-524-2

Cuvillier Verlag Göttingen
Nonnenstieg 8 • 37075 Göttingen

Göttinger Wirtschaftsinformatik

Herausgeber: Prof. Dr. J. Biethahn • Prof. Dr. L. M. Kolbe • Prof. Dr. M. Schumann

Band 71: Stefan Friedemann
IT-gestützte Produktionsplanung mit nachwachsenden Rohstoffen
unter Berücksichtigung von Unsicherheiten
ISBN 978-3-95404-606-5

Band 72: Arne Frerichs
Unternehmensfinanzierung mit Peer-to-Peer-gestützter Mittelvergabe
ISBN 978-3-95404-624-9

Band 73: Ullrich C. C. Jagstaidt
Smart Metering Information Management
Gestaltungsansätze für das Informationsmanagement und für
Geschäftsmodelle der Marktakteure in der Energiewirtschaft
ISBN 978-3-95404-696-6

Band 74: Sebastian Busse
Exploring the Role of Information Systems in the Development of Electric Mobility
Understanding the Domain and Designing the Path
ISBN 978-3-95404-727-7

Band 75: Christoph Beckers
Management von Wasserinformationen in der Fleischindustrie
Analyse von Sytemanforderungen zur produktspezifischen Ausweisung
von Water Footprints
ISBN 978-3-95404-809-0

Band 76: Hendrik Hilpert
Informationssysteme für die Nachhaltigkeitsberichterstattung in Unternehmen
Empirische Erkenntnisse und Gestaltungsansätze zur Datengrundlage, Erfassung
und Berichterstattung von Treibhausgasemissionen
ISBN 978-3-95404-908-0

Band 77: Simon Thanh-Nam Trang
Adoption, Value Co-Creation, and Governance of Inter-Organizational Information
Technology in Wood Networks
ISBN 978-3-7369-9031-9

Band 78: Stefan Gröger
IT-Unterstützung zur Verbesserung der Drittmittel-Projekt-Bewirtschaftung an
Hochschulen - Referenzprozessgestaltung, Artefakt-Design und Nutzenpotenziale
ISBN 978-3-7369-9077-7

Cuvillier Verlag Göttingen
Nonnenstieg 8 • 37075 Göttingen

Göttinger Wirtschaftsinformatik
Herausgeber: Prof. Dr. J. Biethahn • Prof. Dr. L. M. Kolbe • Prof. Dr. M. Schumann

Band 79: Johannes Schmidt
Demand-Side Integration Programs for Electric Transport Vehicles
unter Berücksichtigung von Unsicherheiten
ISBN 978-3-7369-9123-1

Band 80: Christian Tornack
IT-gestütztes Nachfolgemanagement in Großunternehmen
ISBN 978-3-7369-9161-3

Band 81: Shanna Appelhanz
Tracking & Tracing-Systeme in Wertschöpfungsnetzwerken für die
industrielle stoffliche Nutzung nachwachsender Rohstoffe
ISBN 978-3-7369-9207-8

Band 82: Henning Krüp
IT Corporate Entrepreneurship – Identifying Factors for IT Innovations
in Non-IT Companies
ISBN 978-3-7369-9253-5

Band 83: Andre Hanelt
Managing the Digital Transformation of Business Models –
An Incumbent Firm Perspective
ISBN 978-3-7369-9254-2

Band 84: Björn Pilarski
Mobile Personalinformationssysteme
Empirische Erkenntnisse und Gestaltungsansätze zum
Einsatz mobiler Anwendungen im Personalmanagement
ISBN 978-3-7369-9291-7

Band 85: Everlin Piccinini
Digital Transformation of Business - Understanding this Phenomenon in
the Context of the Automotive Industry
ISBN 978-3-7369-9323-5

Band 86: Matthias Eisel
Analyzing the Range Barrier to Electric Vehicle Adoption -
The Case of Range Anxiety
ISBN 978-3-7369-9379-2

Cuvillier Verlag Göttingen
Nonnenstieg 8 • 37075 Göttingen

Göttinger Wirtschaftsinformatik

Herausgeber: Prof. Dr. J. Biethahn • Prof. Dr. L. M. Kolbe • Prof. Dr. M. Schumann

Band 87: Gerrit Remané
Digital Business Models in the Mobility Sector: Using Components and Types to Understand Existing and Design New Business Models
ISBN 978-3-7369-9544-4

Band 88: Thierry Jean Ruch
Consumerization of IT –
Studies to Explore the Phenomenon and Implications for IT Management, Information Security, and Organizational Security
ISBN 978-3-7369-9558-1

Band 89: Carolin Ebermann
Die Förderung von nachhaltigem Mobilitätsverhalten durch erhöhte User-Experience und den Einsatz von Informationssystemen
ISBN 978-3-7369-9568-0

Band 90: Sebastian Zander
Interorganizational Information Systems for the Efficient Utilization of Renewable Resources - Insights from Networks in the Wood Industry
ISBN 978-3-7369-9584-0

Band 91: Ilja Nastjuk
The Dark and the Bright Side of Digitalization -
The Case of Sustainable Mobility
ISBN 978-3-7369-9586-4

Band 92: Aaron Mengelkamp
Informationen zur Bonitätsprüfung auf Basis von Daten aus sozialen Medien
ISBN 978-3-7369-9628-1

Band 93: Alfred Benedikt Brendel
Applied Design Science Research in the Context of Smart and Sustainable Mobility
The Case of Vehicle Supply and Demand Management in Shared Vehicle Services
ISBN 978-3-7369-9685-4

Band 94: Markus Mandrella
IT-Based Value Co-Creation in Inter-Organizational Networks
Theory Integration, Extension, and Adaptation to the Wood Industry
ISBN 978-3-7369-9695-3

Cuvillier Verlag Göttingen
Nonnenstieg 8 • 37075 Göttingen

Göttinger Wirtschaftsinformatik
Herausgeber: Prof. Dr. J. Biethahn • Prof. Dr. L. M. Kolbe • Prof. Dr. M. Schumann

Band 95: Benjamin Brauer
Persuasive User-Centric Green IS
Exploring the Role and Paving the Way of Information Systems to Induce Pro-Environmental Behavior Change
ISBN 978-3-7369-9764-6

Band 96: Sebastian Hobert
Empirische Erkenntnisse und Gestaltungsansätze zum Einsatz von Wearable Computern im Industriesektor
ISBN 978-3-7369-9794-3

Band 97: Björn Hildebrandt
Digitalization of Mobility - Understanding the Transformational Impacts of Pervasive Digital Technologies on Business Models in the Mobility Sector
ISBN 978-3-7369-9827-8

Band 98: Jasmin Decker
Micro Learning und Mobile Learning in Unternehmen – Empirische Erkenntnisse und Gestaltungsempfehlungen zum Einsatz mobiler Lernanwendungen
ISBN 978-3-7369-9835-3

Band 99: Jan Moritz Anke
IT-gestützte Lern- und Assessmentmodule für nachhaltiges Wirtschaften
Empirische Erkenntnisse und Gestaltungsansätze zum Einsatz IT-gestützter Lern- und Assessmentmodule
ISBN 978-3-7369-9986-2

Band 100: Daniel Leonhardt
Organizing for Digital Innovation – The Role of the IT Function
ISBN 978-3-7369-7060-1

Band 101: Shahin Tofangshi
Towards a Theory for Designing Machine Learning Systems for Complex Decision Making Problems
ISBN 978-3-7369-7200-1

Cuvillier Verlag Göttingen
Nonnenstieg 8 • 37075 Göttingen